Language
in Thought
and Action

FIFTH EDITION

Language in Thought and Action

Fifth Edition

S. I. HAYAKAWA

and

Alan R. Hayakawa

HARCOURT BRACE JOVANOVICH COLLEGE PUBLISHERS

Fort Worth   Philadelphia   San Diego   New York   Orlando   Austin
San Antonio   Toronto   Montreal   London   Sydney   Tokyo

To Margedant Peters Hayakawa

Preface

THIS BOOK began in the winter of 1938–39, when I was an instructor in the English department at the University of Wisconsin at Madison. It was decided that the freshman English course, taken by about 2,200 students, would be divided into three groups—one based on the "great books," a second applying the study of current events, the third using the new approach of general semantics. These pedagogical approaches arose from the interests of instructors and teaching assistants. Professor Wright Thomas, the head of freshman English instruction, knew of my fascination with the work of Alfred Korzybski and the emerging field of general semantics, and asked me to write a text for use the following fall.

So the first edition of this book, titled *Language in Action*, was typed, mimeographed and spiral-bound for distribution to about 700 freshmen The response was gratifying. Interest from other campuses was almost immediate, and more copies were bound and distributed. The following year, ten publishers expressed interest in signing the book. I selected the firm then known as Harcourt Brace & Company because they had published the works of T. S. Eliot and e. e. cummings, two of the poets I most admired.

The mimeographed edition survived into a second year, however, as publication of the first hardcover edition of *Language in Action* was delayed because the Book-of-the-Month Club chose it as the nonfiction selection for December, 1941. Later, the book was updated and expanded, appearing in 1949 under the title *Language in Thought and Action*. The work has been translated into eight languages: Chinese, Finnish, French, German, Japanese, Portuguese, Spanish, and Swedish. This fifth edition marks the fiftieth anniversary of the book's inception.

To learn to think more clearly, to speak and write more effectively, and to listen and read with greater understanding—these have been the goals of language study from the medieval trivium to the present-day English class. This book views those traditional goals through the lens of modern semantics—that is, through an understanding of the roles and the different uses of language: language to persuade and control, language to transmit information, language to foster social cohesion, and language as artistic expression. Words that convey no information may nevertheless move carloads of shaving cream or cake mix. Words can start marches in the streets—and can stir others to stone marchers. Words that make little conventional sense as prose can make a great deal of sense as poetry. Words that seem clear to some may puzzle others. With words we sugarcoat our nastiest motives and worst behavior, but with words we also formulate

our highest ideals and aspirations. (Do the words we utter arise as a result
of our thoughts, or are our thoughts determined by the linguistic systems
we happen to have been taught? To what extent does our language make,
as well as shape, our meanings?)

To perceive how language works, what pitfalls it conceals, what its
possibilities are, is to comprehend a crucial aspect of the complicated business of living the life of a human being. To be concerned with the relation
between language and reality, between words and what they stand for in
the speaker's or listener's thoughts and emotions, is to approach the study
of language as both an intellectual and a moral discipline.

Perhaps an illustration will clarify my position. What is the teacher's
duty when a child says in class, "Taters ain't doin' good this year"? Traditionally, teachers of English and speech will correct the child's grammar, pronunciation, and diction. Teachers with a semantic orientation
will give priority to a different task. They will question the student: "What
potatoes do you mean? Those on your parents' farm, or those throughout
the county? How do you know? From personal observation? From reports
from credible sources?" In short, teachers of semantics primarily will concern themselves—and teach their students primarily to concern themselves—with the truth, the adequacy, and the degree of trustworthiness
of statements. Often when students bored with studying grammar and
diagramming sentences become intrigued by the content and purposes of
communication, their hostility to linguistic instruction vanishes, and problems of grammatical and syntactical propriety are solved in passing.

Today the public is aware, perhaps to an unprecedented degree, of the
role of communication in human affairs. This awareness arises in large
part out of the urgency of the tensions existing everywhere between nations, classes, and individuals, in a world that is undergoing rapid change
and reorganization. It arises, too, out of the enormous powers for good
and evil—powers apparent to even the least reflective members of society—that lie in the media of mass communication: the press, the movie
industry, radio, and television.

The vacuum tube and transistor produced a twentieth-century revolution in communication, a revolution probably more far-reaching in its
effects than the invention of printing that ushered in the Renaissance. The
rising aspirations of the peoples of Asia, Africa, and Latin America are
due to the combined advances in transportation and communication: air-
planes, jeeps, and helicopters bring newspapers, magazines, movies, and
especially radio and television. In thousands of remote villages, my African students used to tell me, people who formerly had no cultural contacts
beyond the next village gather today around transistor radios to hear the
news from London, New York, Tokyo, and Moscow—and begin the process of becoming citizens of a larger semantic world.

Television, too, is changing the world. American commercial television invites all viewers to participate fully in the benefits of an industrial and democratic culture by buying toothpastes and detergents and automobiles, by taking an interest in national and international affairs, by sharing the emotions, dreams, aspirations, and values that are depicted in the entertainment. Television offers its rewards indiscriminately—not only to people at all economic levels in this country but, through the rebroadcasting of American programs to people throughout the world. What kinds of forces it is unleashing—in terms of knowledge of a wider world and demands for participation in the material wealth of that world—we have not yet begun to fathom. A revolution in the patterns and techniques of communication always has more consequences than are dreamed of at the time the innovations are introduced. The increased density of the world communication network, resulting from technological advances, means an increased tempo of social change—and therefore an increased need for semantic sophistication.

The original version of this book, *Language in Action*, was in many respects a response to the dangers of propaganda, especially as exemplified by Adolf Hitler's success in persuading millions to share his maniacal and destructive views. It was my conviction then, as it remains now, that we need to have a habitually critical attitude toward language—our own as well as that of others—both to provide for our personal well-being and to ensure that we will function adequately as world citizens. Hitler is gone, but if the majority of our fellow citizens are more susceptible to the slogans of fear and race hatred than to those of peaceful accommodation and mutual respect, our political liberties remain at the mercy of any eloquent and unscrupulous demagogue.

Semanticists study interaction through communication. Communication leads sometimes to cooperation, sometimes to conflict. The basic ethical assumption of semantics is that cooperation is preferable to conflict. This assumption, implicit in *Language in Action*, was made explicit as a central theme in *Language in Thought and Action*. It remains the theme of the Fifth Edition.

In recognition of the increasing influence of television, the Fifth Edition includes a new chapter on the medium and its effects. Some minor reorganization has occurred: the chapter titled "Art as Order" has been moved to Book Two, where it leads more naturally into the following chapter on "Poetry and Advertising." Much of the Fourth Edition chapter on "The Society Behind Our Symbols" has been deleted.

The "Applications," which until this edition followed each chapter, have been gathered together in an appendix at the end of the book in the interest of textual continuity and for reader convenience. A book on semantics is not something simply to be read and put aside. Its principles, to be meaningful, must be implemented in one's own thinking, speaking, writing, and behavior; they must be tested against one's own observations and experience. The "Applications" therefore have a double purpose; they offer a means whereby the reader may, in addition to reading about semantics, take on the semanticist's point of view by undertaking actual semantic investigations and exercises. They are also a way of urging the reader not to take my word alone for anything herein. (I further hope the reader will find the "Applications" amusing. The world is, fortunately, filled with people who say and write wonderfully preposterous things for the semanticist's notebook.) The "Applications" have been shortened somewhat. Some are new to this edition, and some that had been deleted from earlier editions have been revived.

Once again, examples and references throughout the text have been updated, and recent titles have been added to the reference lists found in several of the "Applications" and to the bibliography. Additionally, the book is still enlivened by my friend William H. Schneider's semantic cartoons, reprinted from his book, *Danger: Men Talking*.

Insight into human symbolic behavior and into human interaction through symbolic mechanisms comes from all sorts of disciplines: not only from linguistics, philosophy, psychology, and cultural anthropology, but from attitude research and public opinion study, from new techniques in psychotherapy, from physiology and neurology, from mathematical biology and cybernetics. How are all these separate insights to be brought together and synthesized? This is a task which I cannot claim to have performed here, but I have examined the problem long enough to believe that it cannot be done without some set of broad and informing principles such as that found in Alfred Korzybski's body of work. My deepest debt, therefore, is to the general semantics ("non-Aristotelian system") of Alfred Korzybski. I have also drawn heavily upon the works of other contributors to semantic thought, especially C. K. Ogden and I. A. Richards, Thorstein Veblen, Edward Sapir, Susanne Langer, Leonard Bloomfield, Karl R. Popper, Thurman Arnold, Jerome Frank, Jean Piaget, Charles Morris, Wendell Johnson, Irving J. Lee, Ernst Cassirer, Anatol Rapoport, and Stuart Chase. I am also deeply indebted to the writings of numerous psychologists and psychiatrists who hold one or another of the dynamic points of view inspired by Sigmund Freud, including Karl Menninger, Carl Rogers, Kurt Lewin, Abraham Maslow, Prescott Lecky, Rudolph Dreikurs, and Milton Rokeach. I have also found extremely helpful the writings of cultural anthropologists, especially those of Benjamin Lee Whorf, Ruth Benedict, Clyde Kluckhohn, Leslie A. White, Margaret Mead, Dorothy Lee, and Weston La Barre.

In preparation for this Fifth Edition, Michael Vivion and Sarah Morgan of the University of Missouri at Kansas City carefully read the text and suggested alterations and shifts of emphasis. Some of their ideas, especially in updating references to current events and popular culture, are incorporated here. In revising, expanding, updating, and editing the text and "Applications," I have been assisted by my son, Alan R. Hayakawa, who works for Newhouse News Service as Washington correspondent for the Portland *Oregonian*.

Since anything approaching a full citation of sources would have made these pages appear unduly formidable, I have appended, in lieu of detailed documentation, a list of books I have found especially useful. However, none of the authors whose works I have profited by is to be held accountable for the errors or shortcomings of this book or for the liberties I have taken in the restatement, application, and modification of existing theories.

Finally, this Fifth Edition would not have come into being without the continuing enthusiasm and support of Marlane Miriello, acquisitions editor; Paula Bryant, production editor; Mandy Van Dusen, production manager; Don Fujimoto, designer; and Rebecca Lytle, art editor.

I am likewise indebted to many students; to innumerable colleagues in the teaching profession, including those who have sent in comments and those who proposed specific "Applications" and provided help with earlier editions; to business executives, training directors, and advertising people; to friends in medicine, law, labor relations, and government, especially my former colleagues in the United States Senate. Their criticisms and discussions have helped me clarify and enlarge my views.

S. I. Hayakawa
Mill Valley, California
May 1989

Contents

_____ BOOK TWO _____
Language and Thought

BOOK ONE

The Functions of Language

CHAPTER 1

Language and Survival

One cannot but wonder at this constantly recurring phrase "getting something for nothing," as if it were the peculiar and perverse ambition of disturbers of society. Except for our animal outfit, practically all we have is handed to us gratis. Can the most complacent reactionary flatter himself that he invented the art of writing or the printing press, or discovered his religious, economic and moral convictions, or any of the devices which supply him with meat and raiment or any of the sources of such pleasure as he may derive from literature or the fine arts? In short, civilization is little else than getting something for nothing.

JAMES HARVEY ROBINSON

What Animals Shall We Imitate?

People who think of themselves as tough-minded and realistic tend to take it for granted that human nature is selfish and that life is a struggle in which only the fittest may survive. According to this philosophy, the basic law by which people must live, in spite of their surface veneer of civilization, is the struggle of the jungle. The "fittest" are those who can bring to the struggle superior force, superior cunning, and superior ruthlessness.

The wide currency of this philosophy of the "survival of the fittest" enables people who act ruthlessly and selfishly, whether in personal rivalries, business competition, or international relations, to assuage their consciences by telling themselves that they are only obeying a law of nature. But a disinterested observer is entitled to ask whether the ruthlessness of the tiger, the cunning of the fox, and obedience to the law of the jungle are, in their *human* applications, actually evidence of *human* fitness to survive. If human beings are to pick up pointers on behavior from the lower animals, are there not animals other than beasts of prey from which we might learn lessons in survival?

We might, for example, look to the rabbit or the deer and define fitness to survive as superior speed in running away from our enemies. We might point to the earthworm or the mole and attribute their fitness to survive to the ability to keep out of sight and out of the way. We might examine the oyster or the housefly and define fitness as the ability to propagate our kind faster than our enemies can eat us up. In *Brave New World*, Aldous Huxley described a world designed by those who would model human beings after the social ants. The world, under the management of a super-brain trust, might be made as well integrated, smooth, and efficient as an ant colony and, as Huxley shows, just about as meaningless. If we simply look to animals in order to define what we mean by "fitness to survive," there is no limit to the subhuman systems of behavior that can be devised: we may emulate lobsters, dogs, sparrows, parakeets, giraffes, skunks, or the parasitical worms because they have all obviously survived in one way or another. We are still entitled to ask, however, if *human* survival does not revolve around a different kind of fitness from that of the lower animals.

Because of the wide acceptance of competition as the force which drives our world, it is worthwhile to look into the present scientific standing of the phrase "survival of the fittest." Biologists distinguish between two kinds of struggle for survival. First, there is the *interspecific* struggle, warfare between different species of animals, as between wolves and deer, or men and bacteria. Second, there is the *intraspecific* struggle, warfare among members of a single species, as when rats fight other rats or human beings fight each other. A great deal of evidence in modern biology indicates that those species that have developed elaborate means of intraspecific competition often make themselves unfit for interspecific competition, so that such species are either already extinct or are threatened with extinction at any time. The peacock's tail, although useful in sexual competition against other peacocks, is only a hindrance in coping with the environment or competing against other species. The peacock could therefore be wiped out overnight by a sudden change in ecological balance. There is evidence, too, that strength and fierceness in fighting and killing other animals, whether in interspecific or intraspecific competition, have never been enough in themselves to guarantee the survival of a species. Many mammoth reptiles, equipped with magnificent offensive and defensive armaments, ceased millions of years ago to walk the earth.[1]

If we are going to talk about human survival, one of the first things to do, even if we grant that people must fight to live, is to distinguish between those qualities that are useful in fighting the environment and other species (for example, floods, storms, wild animals, insects, or bacteria) and those qualities (such as aggressiveness) that are useful in fighting other people. There are also characteristics important to human survival that do not involve fighting.

The principle that if we don't hang together we shall all hang separately was discovered by nature long before it was put into words by Benjamin Franklin. Cooperation within a species (and sometimes with other species) is essential to the survival of most living creatures.

Human beings are the *talking* animals. Any theory of human survival that leaves this fact out of account is no more scientific than would be a theory of beaver survival that failed to consider the interesting uses a beaver makes of its teeth and flat tail. Let us see what talking—human communication—means.

Cooperation

If someone shouts at you, "Look out!" and you jump just in time to avoid being struck by a car, you owe your escape from injury to the fundamental cooperative act by which most of the higher animals survive: namely, communication by means of noises. You did not see the car coming; nevertheless, someone did see it and made certain *noises* to *communicate* the alarm to you. In other words, *although your nervous system* did not record the danger, you were unharmed because another's nervous system did. You had, for the time being, the advantage of an extra nervous system in addition to your own.

---

[1]For example, "the brain of the massive (about two tons) stegosaur weighed only about 70 grams, or 2 ½ ounces. . . . By contrast, even the brain of the sheep—which is not a particularly brilliant animal—weighs about 130 grams, greater both in absolute size and even more so relatively to body size. . . . So far as strength is concerned, nothing could stop one of the great dinosaurs when it was on its way; but while it is all very well to be able to go where you are going, the reasons for going and what is seen and understood on the way are even more important." Weston La Barre, *The Human Animal* (1954), pp. 24–25.

Indeed, most of the time when we are listening to the noises people make, or looking at the black marks on paper that stand for such noises, we are drawing upon the experiences of others in order to make up for what we ourselves have missed. Now, obviously, the more we can make use of the nervous systems of others to supplement our own, the easier it is for us to survive. And, of course, the more individuals there are in a group accustomed to cooperating by making helpful noises at each other, the better it is for all—within the limits, naturally, of the group's talents for organization. Birds and animals congregate with their own kind and make noises when they find food or become alarmed. In fact, gregarious-ness as an aid to self-defense and survival is forced upon animals as well as upon human beings by the necessity of uniting nervous systems even more than by the necessity of uniting physical strength. Societies, both animal and human, might almost be regarded as huge cooperative nervous systems.

While animals use only a few limited cries, however, human beings use extremely complicated systems of sputtering, hissing, gurgling, clucking, and cooing noises called *language*, with which they express and report what goes on in their nervous systems. Language is, in addition to being more complicated, immeasurably more flexible than the animal cries from which it was developed—so flexible indeed that it can be used not only to report the tremendous variety of things that go on in the human nervous system, but to report those reports. That is, when an animal yelps, it may cause a second animal to yelp in imitation or in alarm, but the second yelp is not *about* the first yelp. But when someone says, "I see a river," a second person can say, "He says he sees a river"—which is a statement about a statement. About this statement-about-a-statement further statements can be made—and about those, still more. *Language, in short, can be about language.* This is a fundamental way in which human noise-making systems differ from the cries of animals.

The Pooling of Knowledge

In addition to having developed language, human beings have also developed means of making, on clay tablets, bits of wood or stone, skins of animals, paper and microchips, more or less permanent marks and scratches that *stand for* language. These marks enable us to communicate with people who are beyond the reach of our voices, both in space and in time. There is a long course of evolution from the marked trees that indicated Indian trails to the metropolitan daily newspaper, but they have this in common: they pass on what one individual has known to other individuals for their convenience or, in the broadest sense, instruction. Many of the lobstick trails in the Canadian woods, marked by Indians long since dead, can be followed to this day. Archimedes is dead, but we still have his reports about what he observed in his experiments in physics. Keats is dead, but his poetry can still tell us how he felt on first reading Chapman's Homer. Elizabeth Barrett is dead, but we can know how she felt about Robert Browning. From books and magazines, we learn how hundreds of people whom we shall never be able to see have felt and thought. Satellites transmit facts about the world we live in to our newspapers, radios, and televisions. All this information is useful to us at one time or another in solving our own problems.

Human beings, then, are never dependent for information on direct experience alone. Even those in a primitive culture can make use of the experience of neighbors, friends, relatives, and ancestors, communicated by means of language. Therefore, instead of remaining helpless because of the limitations of their own experience and knowledge, instead of having to rediscover what others have already discovered, instead of exploring the false trails others have explored and repeating their errors, they can *go on from where others left off*. Language, that is to say, makes progress possible.

Indeed, most of what we call the human characteristics of our species is expressed and developed through our ability to cooperate by means of our systems of making meaningful noises and meaningful scratches on paper. Even people who belong to cultures in which writing has not been invented are able to exchange information and to hand down from generation to generation considerable stores of traditional knowledge. There seems, however, to be a limit both to the trustworthiness and to the amount of knowledge that can be transmitted orally. This is so despite the fact that preliterate people often exhibit remarkable feats of memory, such as the ability to remember every landmark and detail of a journey of hundreds of miles or the ability to recall verbatim folktales and sagas that may take days to recite. Literate people, who rely on notebooks and reference books, have relatively poor memories. Still, when writing is invented, a tremendous step forward is taken. The accuracy of reports can be checked and rechecked by successive generations of observers. The amount of knowledge accumulated ceases to be limited by people's ability to remember what has been told them.

The result is that in any literate culture of a few centuries' standing, human beings accumulate vast stores of knowledge—far more than any individual in that culture can read in his lifetime, let alone remember. These stores of knowledge, which are being added to constantly, are made widely available to all who want them through such mechanical processes as printing and computer data banks and through such distributive agencies as the book trade, the newspaper and magazine trade, library systems, and computer networks. All of us who can read any of the major European or Asian languages are potentially in touch with the intellectual resources of centuries of human endeavor in all parts of the civilized world.

A physician, for example, who does not know how to treat a patient suffering from a rare disease can look up the disease in the *Index Medicus*, which may send him or her in turn to medical journals, or to a computer data service like Medline to find articles and abstracts indexed by the National Medical Library. In so doing, the physician may find records of similar cases as reported and described by a physician in Rotterdam in 1873, by another physician in Bangkok in 1909, and by still other physicians in Kansas City in 1974. Such records may shed light on the case at hand. Again, a person worried about ethics is not dependent merely upon the pastor of the Elm Street Baptist Church, but may consult Confucius, Aristotle, Jesus, Spinoza, and many others whose reflections on ethical problems are on record. If one is worried about love, one can get advice not only from one's parents or friends, but from the works of Sappho, Ovid, Propertius, Shakespeare, John Donne, Erich Fromm, or any of a thousand others who knew something about it and wrote down what they knew.

Language is the indispensable mechanism of human life—of life such as ours that is molded, guided, enriched, and made possible by the accumulation of the *past* experience of members of our species. Dogs, cats, or chimpanzees do not, so far as we can tell, increase their wisdom, their information, or their control over their environment from one generation to the next. Human beings do. The cultural accomplishments of the ages, the invention of cooking, of weapons, of writing, of printing, of methods of building, of games and amusements, of means of transportation, and the discoveries of all the arts and sciences come to us as *free gifts from the dead*. These gifts, which none of us has done anything to earn, offer us not only the opportunity for a richer life than any of our forebears enjoyed but also the opportunity to add to the sum total of human achievement by our own contributions, however small.

To be able to read and write, therefore, is to learn to profit by and to take part in the greatest of human achievements—that which makes all other human achievements possible—namely, the pooling of our experience in great cooperative stores of knowledge, available (except where special privilege, censorship, or suppression stand in the way) to all. From the warning cry of the savage to the latest scientific monograph or news bulletin, language is social. Cultural and intellectual cooperation is, or should be, the great principle of human life.

This is by no means an easy principle to accept or to understand—except as a kind of pious truism that we, as well-meaning people, would like to believe. We live in a highly competitive society, each of us trying to outdo the other in wealth, in popularity or social prestige, in dress, in scholastic grades, or in golf scores. As we read our daily papers, there is always news of conflict rather than of cooperation—between labor and management, between rival corporations or movie stars, between political parties and nations. Over us all hangs the perpetual fear of another war even more unthinkably horrible than the last. One is often tempted to say that conflict, rather than cooperation, is the great governing principle of human life.

But what such a philosophy overlooks is that despite all the competition at the surface, there is a huge substratum of cooperation *taken for granted* that keeps the world going. The coordination of the efforts of actors, writers, engineers, musicians, photographers, utility companies, typists, program directors, advertising agencies, and hundreds of others is required to create a single television program. Tens of thousands of persons cooperate in the production of automobiles, including suppliers and shippers of raw materials from different parts of the earth. Any organized business activity is an elaborate act of cooperation in which every individual worker contributes a share. A lockout or strike is a *withdrawal of cooperation:* things are regarded as "back to normal" when cooperation is restored. As individuals we may compete for jobs, but our function in the job, once we get it, is to contribute, at the right time and place, to that innumerable series of cooperative acts that eventually results in cars being manufactured, in cakes appearing in pastry shops, in department stores serving their customers, in trains and airlines running on schedule.

This network of cooperation is intricate and complex, and it has been relatively effective. But because it rests so profoundly upon human agreement, it is also fragile.

Small groups of dissidents using such tactics as intimidation and violence can disrupt society and create chaos, breaking down the network of cooperation. What is important for our purposes here is that all this coordination for the functioning of society is *of necessity achieved by language, or else it is not achieved at all.*

The Niagara of Words

And how does all this affect you and me—and the celebrated "Man in the Street"—or "T. C. Mits," as he was christened by Lillian and Hugh Lieber of Long Island University in their book *The Education of T. C. Mits.* From the moment he switches on a morning news broadcast until he falls asleep at night over a novel or in front of the television, Mits is, like all other people living in the modern world, immersed in words. Newspaper editors, politicians, salesmen, disc jockeys, columnists, luncheon speakers and clergymen; colleagues, friends, relatives, wife and children; market reports, direct-mail advertising, books, billboards, talk shows—all assail him with words, all day long. And Mits himself is constantly contributing to that Niagara every time he puts on an advertising campaign, delivers a speech, writes a letter, or chats with friends.

When things go wrong in Mits's life—when he is worried, perplexed, or nervous; or when family, business, or national affairs are not going as he thinks they should—he blames a number of things: the weather, his health, the state of his nerves, or his colleagues at work. If the problem is larger, he may blame his environment, the economic system, a foreign nation, or the cultural patterns of society. The difficulties of other people he may attribute to these causes or to "human nature." It rarely occurs to him to investigate the nature of that daily verbal Niagara as a possible source of trouble.

Indeed, there are few occasions on which Mits thinks about language as such. He pauses from time to time over a grammatical point. Occasionally he runs into advertisements on "how to increase your word power" and wonders if he shouldn't try to become a more effective speaker. Confronted by the Niagara of words—the magazines he hasn't time to keep up with and the books he knows he should read—he wonders if a course in speed-reading wouldn't help.

Once in a while he is struck by the fact that some people—always other people—twist the meanings of words, especially during the course of an argument, so that words are often very tricky. Sometimes he notices with irritation that words can mean different things. This condition, he feels, could be corrected if people would only consult dictionaries to learn the "true meanings" of words. He knows, however, that they will not—at least no more often than he does—so he puts this down as another instance of the weakness of human nature.

This is unfortunately about the limit of Mits's linguistic speculation. And here Mits is typical not only of the general public but also of many scientists, publicists, and writers. Like most people, he takes words as much for granted as the air he breathes, and he gives them about as much thought.

Nevertheless, Mits is profoundly involved in the words he absorbs and uses daily. Words in the newspaper make him pound his fist on the breakfast table. Words spoken to him by his superiors puff him up with pride or send him scurrying to work harder. Words that he has overheard being spoken about him behind his back worry him sick. Words that he spoke before a clergyman some years ago have committed him to one woman for life. Words written on pieces of paper keep him at his job and bring bills in the mail every month that keep him paying and paying. With words woven into almost every detail of his life, it seems amazing that Mits's thinking about language should be so limited.

Mits may have noticed that when large masses of people, for example those under totalitarian regimes, are permitted to hear and read only carefully selected words, their conduct becomes so strange that he can only regard it as mad. Yet he regards some individuals who have the same education and the same access to varied sources of information as being nevertheless just as mad. He listens to the views of some of his neighbors and cannot help wondering, "How can they think such things? Don't they see the same things happening that I see? They must be crazy!" "Does such madness," he asks, "illustrate again the 'inevitable frailty of human nature'?" Mits, who as an American likes to regard all things as possible, does not like the conclusion that "nothing can be done about it," but often he can hardly see how to escape it.

One reason for Mits's failure to get any further in thinking about language is the belief that words are not really important: what is important is the "ideas" they stand for. But what is an idea if it is not the *verbalization* of a cerebral itch? This has seldom occurred to Mits. The fact that the implications of one set of terms may lead inevitably into blind alleys, while the implications of another set of terms may not; the fact that the historical or sentimental associations of some words make calm discussion impossible; the fact that language has a multitude of different kinds of use and that great confusion arises from mistaking one kind of use for another; the fact that a person speaking a language of a structure entirely different from that of English, such as Japanese, Chinese, or Turkish, may not even think the same thoughts as an English-speaking person—these are unfamiliar notions to Mits, who has always assumed that the important thing is to get one's ideas straight first, after which the words take care of themselves.

Whether he realizes it or not, however, Mits is affected every hour of his life not only by the words he hears and uses *but also by his unconscious assumptions about language.* If, for example, he likes the name Albert and would like to christen his child by that name but avoids doing so because he once knew an Albert who committed suicide, he is operating, whether he realizes it or not, under certain assumptions about the relationship of language to reality. Such unconscious assumptions determine the way he acts, whether wisely or foolishly. Words—the way he uses them and the way he takes them when spoken by others—largely shape his beliefs, his prejudices, his ideals, his aspirations. They constitute the moral and intellectual atmosphere in which he lives—in short, his *semantic environment.*

This book is devoted, then, to the study of relationships among language, thought, and behavior. We shall examine language and people's linguistic habits as they reveal themselves in thinking (at least nine-tenths of which is talking to one's self), speaking, listening, reading, and writing.

Disarmament conference

The Symbolic Process

Animals struggle with each other for food or for leadership, but they do not, like human beings, struggle with each other for things that *stand for* food or leadership, such things as our paper symbols of wealth (money, bonds, titles), badges of rank to wear on our clothes, or low-number license plates. For animals, the relationship in which one thing *stands for* something else does not appear to exist except in very rudimentary form. A chimpanzee is said to be capable of being taught to drive a car, but there would be one thing wrong with its driving: its reactions are such that if a red light shows when it is halfway across a street, it will stop in the middle of the crossing, while if a green light shows while another car is stalled in its path, it will go ahead regardless of consequences. In other words, so far as a chimpanzee is concerned, the red light can hardly be said to *stand for* stop; it *is* stop.

Let us then introduce two terms to represent this distinction between the "red light *is* stop" relationship, which the chimpanzee understands, and the "red light *stands for* stop" relationship, which only the human being understands. To the chimpanzee, the red light is, we shall say, a *signal*, and we shall term its reaction a *signal reaction: that is, a complete and invariable reaction that occurs whether or not the conditions warrant.* To the human being, on the other hand, the red light is, in our terminology, a *symbol*, and we shall term the human reaction a *symbol reaction; that is, a delayed reaction, conditional upon the circumstances.* In other words, the nervous system capable only of signal reactions *identifies the signal with the thing for which the signal stands;* the human nervous system, however, working under normal conditions, understands *no necessary connection* between the symbol and that for which the symbol stands. Human beings do not automatically jump up in the expectation of being fed whenever they hear a refrigerator door slam.

Human beings, because they can understand certain things to *stand for* other things, have developed what we shall term the *symbolic process.* Whenever two or more human beings can communicate with each other, they can, by agreement, make anything stand for anything. Feathers worn on the head can be made to stand for tribal chieftainship; cowrie shells or rings of brass or pieces of paper can stand for wealth; crossed sticks can stand for a set of religious beliefs; buttons, elks' teeth, ribbons, special styles of ornamental haircutting, or tattooing can stand for social affiliations. The symbolic process permeates human life at the most savage as well as at the most civilized levels. Warriors, medicine men, police officers, nurses, cardinals, and queens wear costumes that symbolize their occupations. Athletes collect trophies and college students collect membership keys in honorary societies to symbolize victories in their respective fields. There are very few things that people do or want to do, possess or want to possess that have not, in addition to their mechanical or biological value, a symbolic value.

Fashionable clothes, as Thorstein Veblen pointed out in his *Theory of the Leisure Class* (1899), are highly symbolic: material, cut, and ornament are dictated only partly by considerations of warmth, comfort, or practicability. The more we dress up in fine clothes, the more we restrict our freedom of action. But by means of delicate embroideries, easily soiled fabrics, starched shirts, high heels, long fingernails, and other such sacrifices of comfort, the wealthy classes manage to symbolize the fact that they don't have to work for a living. The not so wealthy, on the other hand, by imitating these symbols of wealth, symbolize their conviction that, even if they do work for a living, they are just as good as anybody else.

Again, we select our furniture to serve as visible symbols of our taste, wealth, and social position. We may choose a house on the basis of a feeling that it "looks well" to have a "good address." We trade in perfectly good cars for later models, not always to get better transportation, but to give evidence to the community that we can afford such luxuries. (I once had an eight-year-old car in good running condition. A friend of mine, a repairman who knew the car, kept urging me to trade it in for a new model. "But why?" I asked. "The old car's in fine shape still." "Yeah, but what the hell," the mechanic said, "all you've got is transportation.")

With the changes in American life since Veblen's time, many changes have taken place in our ways of symbolizing social status. Once, a deeply tanned skin indicated a life spent in farming and other outdoor labor, and women in those days went to a great deal of trouble shielding themselves from the sun with parasols, wide hats, and long sleeves. More recently, a pale skin has indicated confinement in offices and factories, while a deeply tanned skin suggests a life of leisure—of trips to Florida, Sun Valley, and Hawaii. Hence, a sun-darkened skin, once considered ugly because it symbolized work, came to be considered beautiful because it symbolizes leisure. And pallid people in New York, Chicago, and Toronto who cannot afford midwinter trips to the West Indies find comfort in browning themselves during visits to tanning salons. Recently, concern over the health hazards of too much sun has affected the symbolism of suntans yet again.

Food, too, is highly symbolic. Religious dietary regulations such as those of the Catholics, Jews, Moslems and Hindus are observed in order to symbolize adherence to one's religion. Specific foods symbolize specific festivals and observances in almost every country—for example, cherry pie on George Washington's birthday and haggis on Burns' Nicht. Eating together has been a highly symbolic act throughout all of human history. "Companion" means one with whom you share your bread. Such complicated and apparently unnecessary behavior leads philosophers, both amateur and professional, to ask over and over again, "Why can't human beings live simply and naturally?"

The trouble is that, as Susanne K. Langer has said, "The symbol-making function is one of man's primary activities. . . . It is the fundamental process of the mind, and goes on all the time." One may try to live a simple life with little concern for symbols of affluence, social status, and the like, but one soon discovers that the rejection of symbolism is itself symbolic. Wearing a necktie is symbolic, but not wearing a necktie is equally symbolic. Parents and children have had bitter quarrels in recent years over hair styles—long, short, spiked, shaved. Such quarrels are not really about hair but about the symbolic meanings involved in how hair is worn.

Perhaps some of us would like to escape the complexity of human life for the relative simplicity of such lives as dogs and cats lead. But the symbolic process, which makes possible the absurdities of human conduct, also makes possible language and therefore all the human achievements dependent upon language. The fact that more things can go wrong with motorcars than with wheelbarrows is no reason for going back to wheelbarrows. Similarly, the fact that the symbolic process makes complicated follies possible is no reason to return to a cat-and-dog existence. To understand the symbolic process is to be able to use it to advantage; not to understand it is to remain forever its victim.

Language as Symbolism

Of all forms of symbolism, language is the most highly developed, most subtle, and most complicated. Human beings have agreed, in the course of centuries of mutual dependency, to let the various noises that they can produce with their lungs, throats, tongues, teeth, and lips systematically stand for specified happenings in their nervous systems. We call that system of agreements *language*. For example, we who speak English have been so trained that when our nervous systems register the presence of a certain kind of animal, we may make the following noise: "There's a cat." Anyone hearing us expects, on looking in the same direction, to experience a similar event in his or her nervous system—one that would have led to an identical verbal response. Similarly, we have been so trained that when we are conscious of wanting food, we make the noise, "I'm hungry."

There is *no necessary connection between the symbol and that which is symbolized.* Just as one can wear a Los Angeles Dodgers baseball cap without being a Dodger fan, so can one make the noise "I'm hungry" without being hungry. Furthermore, just as social rank can be symbolized by diamonds in the ears, by tattooing on the breast, by gold ornaments on the watch chain, by a thousand different devices according to the culture we live in, so the fact of being hungry can be symbolized by a thousand different noises according to the culture we live in: "*J'ai faim*," or "*Es hungert mich*," or "*Ho appetito*," or "*Hara ga hetta*," and so on.

However obvious these facts may appear at first glance, they are actually not so obvious as they seem except when we take special pains to think about the subject. Symbols and things symbolized are independent of each other; nevertheless, all of us have a way of feeling as if, and sometimes acting as if, there were necessary connections. For example, there is the vague sense that we all have that foreign languages are inherently absurd: "Foreigners have funny names for things; why don't they call things by their right names?" This feeling exhibits itself most strongly in those American and English tourists who seem to believe that they can make the people of any country understand English if they shout it loud enough. Like the little boy who is reported to have said, "Pigs are called pigs because they are such dirty animals," they feel that the symbol is inherently connected in some way with the thing symbolized. Then there are the people who feel that since snakes are "nasty, slimy creatures" the word "snake" is a *nasty, slimy word*. (Incidentally, snakes are not slimy.)

The Pitfalls of Drama

Naiveté regarding the symbolic process extends to symbols other than words, of course. In the case of drama (stage, movies, television), there appear to be people in almost every audience who never quite fully realize that a film or television show is a set of fictional, symbolic representations. An actor is one who symbolizes other people, real or imagined. But Larry Hagman, who plays the wicked, cunning J. R. Ewing on television's *Dallas*, reports that fans sometimes denounce *him* for J. R.'s ruthless behavior. Robert Young, the actor who played the title role in *Marcus Welby, M.D.*, has often been asked for medical advice. During Congressional hearings in the 1980s, actresses Sissy Spacek, Jessica Lange, and Sally Field testified before Congress on the farm crisis, not because of their farm experience but because they had *acted in films* depicting the difficulties of farm life. In perhaps the most famous example, scores of astonished patriots rushed to recruiting offices to help defend the nation, when, on October 30, 1938, the United States was "invaded" by an "army from Mars" in a radio dramatization of H. G. Wells's *The War of the Worlds*.

The Word Is Not the Thing

The above examples illustrate some confusion toward words and what, if anything, they stand for. There would be little point in mentioning these incidents if we were *all uniformly and permanently aware* that symbols are independent of what is symbolized. But we are not. Most of us have, in some area or other of our thinking, improper habits of evaluation. For this, society itself is to blame: most societies systematically encourage, concerning certain topics, the habitual confusion of symbols with things symbolized. For example, if a Japanese schoolhouse caught fire, it used to be obligatory in the days of emperor worship to try to rescue the emperor's *picture* (there was one in every schoolhouse), even at the risk of one's life. (If you got burned to death, you were posthumously ennobled.) In our society, we are encouraged to go into debt in order that we may display, as symbols of prosperity, shiny new automobiles. Strangely enough, the possession of new automobiles even under these conditions makes their "owners" *feel* prosperous. In all societies, the symbols of piety, of civic virtue, or of patriotism are often prized above actual piety, civic virtue, or patriotism. During the 1988 election campaign, George Bush visited a flag-making factory to show that he was a patriot. In one way or another, we are all like the student who cheats on exams in order to make Phi Beta Kappa: it is often more important to have the symbol than what it stands for.

The habitual confusion of symbols with things symbolized, whether on the part of individuals or societies, is serious enough at all levels of culture to provide a perennial human problem. The charge against the Pharisees, it will be remembered, was that they were obsessively concerned with the symbols of piety at the expense of an adequate concern with its spirit. But with the pervasiveness of modern communication systems, the problem of confusing verbal symbols with realities assumes peculiar urgency. We are constantly being talked at, by teachers, preachers, salespeople, public-relations counsels, governmental agencies, and movie sound tracks. The cries of the hawkers of soft drinks, detergents, and perfumes pursue us into our homes, thanks to radio and television—and in some households the sets are never turned off from morning to night. Our mailboxes are stuffed with advertising. Billboards confront us on the highway, and we even take portable televisions and radios with us to the seashore.

We live in an environment shaped and largely created by hitherto un-paralleled semantic influences: mass-circulation newspapers and maga-zines which are given to reflecting, in many cases, the prejudices and obses-sions of their reporters and editors; radio and television programs, both local and network, almost completely dominated by commercial motives; public-relations counsels who are simply well-paid craftsmen in the art of manipulating and reshaping our semantic environment in ways favorable to their clients. It is an exciting environment, but fraught with danger: it is only a slight exaggeration to say that Hitler conquered Austria by radio. Today, the full resources of advertising agencies, public-relations experts, radio, television, and slanted news stories are brought to bear in order to influence our decisions in election campaigns, especially in presidential election years.

Citizens of a modern society need, therefore, more than that ordinary "common sense" which was defined by Stuart Chase as that which tells you that the world is flat. They need to be systematically aware of the powers and limitations of symbols, especially words, if they are to guard against being driven into complete bewilderment by the complexity of their semantic environment.

The first of the principles governing symbols is this: The symbol is *not* the thing symbolized; the word is *not* the thing; the map is *not* the territory it stands for.

The symbol —— ┐
The map ———— ┤ ——————**IS NOT**——————— ├—— the thing symbolized
The word —— ┘   ├—— the territory
                                                              └—— the thing

Maps and Territories

There is a sense in which we all live in two worlds. First, we live in the world of happenings that we know at first hand. This is an extremely small world, consisting only of that continuum of things that we have actually seen, felt, or heard—the flow of events constantly passing before our senses. So far as this world of personal experience is concerned, Africa, South America, Asia, Washington, New York, or Los Angeles do not exist if we have never been to these places. Desmond Tutu is only a name if we have never seen him. When we ask ourselves how much we know at first hand, we discover that we know very little indeed.

Most of our knowledge, acquired from parents, friends, school, newspapers, books, conversation, speeches, and television, is received *verbally*—that is, in words. Most of our knowledge of history, for example, comes to us only in words. The only proof that we have that the Battle of Waterloo ever took place is that we have had reports to that effect. These reports are not provided by people who saw it happen, but are based on other reports: reports of reports of reports, which go back ultimately to the firsthand accounts of people who did see it happening. It is through reports, then, and through reports of reports, that we receive most knowledge: about government, about what is happening in the Middle East, about what movie is showing at the nearest theater—about everything, in fact, that we do not know through direct experience.

Let us call the world that comes to us through words the *verbal world*, as opposed to the world we know or are capable of knowing through our own experience, which we shall call the *extensional world*. Human beings, like any other creatures, begin to make their acquaintance with the extensional world from infancy. Unlike other creatures, however, human beings begin to receive, as soon as they can learn to understand, reports, reports of reports, reports of reports of reports. In addition, they derive or receive inferences—conclusions drawn from some sort of evidence. These inferences may be made from reports or from other inferences. By the time a child is a few years old, has gone to school and to Sunday school, has made

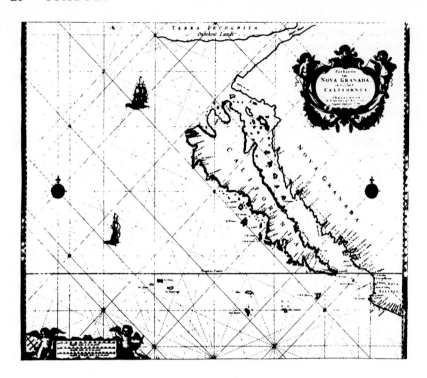

a few friends, has spent some hours watching television, he or she has accumulated a considerable amount of second- and third-hand information about morals, language, history, nature, people, games—all of which information constitutes one's verbal world.

Now, to use the famous metaphor introduced by Alfred Korzybski in *Science and Sanity*, this verbal world ought to stand in relation to the extensional world as a *map* does to the *territory* it is supposed to represent. If a child grows to adulthood with a verbal world in his head that corresponds fairly closely to the extensional world that he finds around him in his widening experience, he is in relatively small danger of being shocked or hurt by what he finds, because his verbal world has told him what, more or less, to expect. He is prepared for life. If, however, he grows up with a false map in his head—that is, with a head crammed with error and superstition—he will constantly be running into trouble, wasting his efforts and acting like a fool. He will not be adjusted to the world as it is; this lack of adjustment may have all manner of serious consequences.

| Verbal (Intensional World) | Reports | Map |
| Extensional World | Experience | Territory |

Some of the follies we commit because of false maps in our heads are so commonplace that we do not even think of them as remarkable. There are those who try to protect themselves from harm by carrying a rabbit's foot. Some refuse to sleep on the thirteenth floor of hotels—a situation so common that many hotels, even in our scientific culture, skip "13" in numbering their floors and rooms. Some hope to make their teeth whiter by changing their brand of toothpaste. Some plan their lives on the basis of astrological predictions. All such people are living in verbal worlds that bear little, if any, resemblance to the extensional world.

No matter how beautiful a map may be, it is useless to a traveler unless it accurately shows the relationship of places to each other, the structure of the territory. If we draw, for example, a big dent in the outline of a lake for artistic reasons, the map is worthless. If we are just drawing maps for fun, without paying any attention to the structure of the region, there is nothing in the world to prevent us from putting in all the extra curlicues and twists we want in the lakes, rivers, and roads. No harm will be done *unless someone tries to plan a trip by such a map.*

Similarly, by means of imaginary or false reports or by false inferences from good reports or by mere rhetorical exercises, we can manufacture at will, with language, "maps" that have no reference to the extensional world. Here again no harm will be done unless someone makes the mistake of regarding such "maps" as representing real territories.

We all inherit a great deal of useless knowledge, and a great deal of misinformation and error, so that there is always a portion of what we have been told that must be discarded. It should be noticed that there are three ways of getting false maps of the world into our heads: first, by having them given to us; second, by making them up for ourselves by misreading true maps; third, by constructing them ourselves by misreading territories. But the cultural heritage that is transmitted to us—our socially pooled knowledge, both scientific and humane, has been valued principally because we believe that it gives us accurate maps of experience. The analogy of verbal worlds to maps is an important one which will be referred to frequently throughout this book.

CHAPTER 3

Reports, Inferences, Judgments

To put it briefly, in human speech, different sounds have different meanings. To study this coordination of certain sounds with certain meanings is to study language. This coordination makes it possible for man to interact with great precision. When we tell someone, for instance, the address of a house he has never seen, we are doing something which no animal can do.

LEONARD BLOOMFIELD

Vague and insignificant forms of speech, and abuse of language, have so long passed for mysteries of science; and hard or misapplied words with little or no meaning have, by prescription, such a right to be mistaken for deep learning and height of speculation, that it will not be easy to persuade either those who speak or those who hear them, they are but the covers of ignorance and hindrance of true knowledge.

JOHN LOCKE

To EXCHANGE information, the basic symbolic act is the *report* of what we have seen, heard, or felt: "It is raining." "You can get those at the hardware store for $2.75." "The solution contains .02% iodine." "The gross profits for December were $253,876.98." We also frequently rely on reports of reports: "The National Weather Service says a tropical storm is developing in the Gulf of Mexico." "According to the Timberlake report, the company lost 23% of its sales in the first quarter of this year." "The papers say there was a four-car accident on Highway 41 near Evansville." Reports adhere to the following rules: first, they are *verifiable*; second, they exclude, as far as possible, *inferences*, *judgements*, and the use of *"loaded"* words. (These terms will be discussed later.)

Verifiability

Reports are verifiable. For example, the price of the item at the hardware store may have increased; we could verify the price by calling the store. We can analyze the solution ourselves to verify the percentage of iodine. We could audit the company's books. Sometimes, of course, we may not be able to verify the report's content ourselves. We may not be able to drive to Evansville to see the physical evidence of the crash; we may not have access to the Timberlake report. Nevertheless, the nature of the report is such that, given the proper resources, it can be verified—or, if inaccurate, it can be invalidated.

Even in a world like today's, in which everybody seems to be fighting everyone else, *we still, to a surprising degree, trust each other's reports.* We have agreed to agree, even if roughly, on the names of many things: on what constitutes a "meter," "yard," "bushel," and so on, and on how to measure time. As a result, much of daily life proceeds with little danger of our misunderstanding each other. To a surprising degree, we trust each other's reports. We ask directions of total strangers when we are traveling. We follow directions on road signs without being suspicious of the people who put the signs up. We read books of information about science, mathematics, automotive engineering, travel, geography, the history of costume, and other such factual matters, and we usually assume that the author is doing her best to tell us as truly as she can what she knows. And we are safe in so assuming most of the time. With the interest given today to the discussion of biased reporting and propaganda, and the general mistrust of many of the communications we receive, we are likely to forget that we still have an enormous amount of reliable information available and that deliberate misinformation, except in warfare, still is more the exception than the rule. The desire for self-preservation that compelled people to evolve means for the exchange of information also compels them to regard the giving of false information as profoundly reprehensible.

At its highest development, the language of reports is known as science. By "highest development" we mean greatest general usefulness. Presbyterian and Catholic, worker and capitalist, German and Englishman, *agree* on the meanings of such symbols as *2 X 2 = 4, 100°C, HNO₃, Quercus agrifolia,* and so on. But how, it may be asked, can there be agreement even about this much among people who are at each other's throats about practically everything else?

The answer is that circumstances *compel them to agree,* whether they wish to or not. If, for example, there were a dozen different religious sects in the United States, each insisting on its own way of naming the time of the day and the days of the year, the necessity of having a dozen different calendars, a dozen different kinds of watches, and a dozen sets of schedules for business hours, trains, and television programs, to say nothing of the effort that would be required for translating terms from one nomenclature to another, would make life as we know it impossible.

The language of reports, then, including the more precise reports of science, is "map" language, and because it gives us reasonably accurate representations of the "territory," it enables us to get work done. Such language may often be what is commonly termed dull or uninteresting reading; one does not usually read logarithmic tables or telephone directories for entertainment. But we could not get along without them. There are numberless occasions in the talking and writing we do in everyday life that require that we state things *in such a way that everybody will agree with our formulation.*

Inferences

Writing reports is an effective means of increasing linguistic awareness. Practice in writing reports, as suggested in the exercises at the end of the book, will constantly provide examples of the principles of language and interpretation under discussion. The reports should be about firsthand experience—scenes the reader has witnessed, meetings and social events he has taken part in, people he knows well. The reports should be of such a nature that they can be verified and agreed upon. For the purposes of the exercise, inferences are to be excluded.

Not that inferences are not important. In everyday life and in science, we rely as much on inferences as on reports. Nevertheless, it is important to be able to distinguish between them.

An inference, as we shall use the term, is *a statement about the unknown based on the known.* On an elementary level, the difference between a report and an inference is demonstrated in the following statement: "He's afraid of women." This statement does not report; it draws an inference from some set of observable data: "He blushes and stammers whenever a woman speaks to him. He never speaks to women at parties."

In some areas of thought, such as geology, paleontology and nuclear

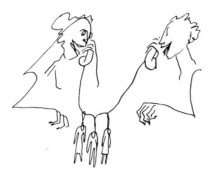

Fun with inferences

physics, reports are the foundations, but inferences—and inferences upon inferences—form the main body of the science. For example, a geologist may use the facts from a report to advise an oil company whether or not to drill in a particular place. The geologist infers from the report that there is oil. A physician making an initial diagnosis examines a patient's symptoms, then makes an inference about an intestinal condition that cannot be seen.

In short, inferences are extremely important. We may infer from the material and cut of a woman's clothes the nature of her wealth or social position; we may infer from the character of the ruins the origin of the fire that destroyed the building; we may infer the nature of the Soviet Union's geopolitical strategy from its actions across the globe; we may infer from the shape of land the path of a prehistoric glacier; we may infer from a halo on an unexposed photographic plate that it has been in the vicinity of radioactive materials.

Inferences may be carefully or carelessly made. They may be made on the basis of a broad background of previous experience with the subject matter or with no experience at all. For example, the inferences a good mechanic can make about the condition of an engine by listening to it are often startlingly accurate, while the inferences made by an amateur may be entirely wrong.

In any case, the common characteristic of inferences is that they are statements about matters that are not directly known, made on the basis of what has been observed. Generally speaking, the quality of inference is directly related to the quality of the report or observations from which it stems and to the abilities of the one making the inference.

Judgments

Another barrier to clear thinking is the confusion of reports and judgments. By judgments we shall mean expressions of the speaker's approval or disapproval of the occurrences, persons, or objects he is describing. To say, "It is a wonderful car" is not a report; to say, "It has been driven 50,000 miles without requiring repairs" is a report. "Jack lied to us" is a judgment, while "Jack said he didn't have the car keys, but later, when he pulled a handkerchief out of his pocket, the keys fell out" is a report. Similarly, when a newspaper says, "The senator has been stubborn, uncooperative, and defiant," or "The senator courageously stood by his principles," the paper is judging and evaluating rather than reporting.

Many people would regard statements like the following as statements of "fact": "Mary lied to us," "Jerry is a thief," "Robin is clever." As ordinarily employed, however, the word "lied" involves first an inference (that Mary knew otherwise and deliberately misstated the facts) and second a judgment (that the speaker disapproves of what he infers that Mary did). To say, "Jerry was convicted of theft and served two years in San Quentin" is a verifiable report—we could look up the court and prison records. To say a man is a "thief" is to say in effect, "He has stolen *and will steal again*"—which is more a prediction than a report. Even to say, "He has stolen" is to make an inference and simultaneously to pass a judgment on an act about which there may have been a difference of opinion based on the evidence at the time.

Verifiability rests upon the external observation of facts, not upon the heaping up of judgments. If one person says, "Peter is a deadbeat," and another says, "I think so, too," the statement has not been verified. In court cases, considerable trouble is sometimes caused by witnesses who cannot distinguish their judgments from the facts on which those judgments are based. Cross-examinations under these circumstances go something like this:

> Witness: That scumbag ripped me off.
> Defense attorney: Your honor, I object.
> Judge: Objection sustained. (Witness's remark is stricken from the record.) Now, try to tell the court exactly what happened.
> Witness: He ripped me off, the dirty scum.
> Defense attorney: Your honor, I object. (The remark is again stricken.)
> Judge: Sustained. Will the witness try to stick to the facts?
> Witness: But I'm telling you the facts, your honor. He did rip me off.

This can continue indefinitely unless the cross-examiner exercises some ingenuity in order to get at the facts behind the judgment. To the witness it is a "fact" that he was "ripped off." Often, long, patient questioning is required before the factual bases of the judgment are revealed.

Of course, many words simultaneously report and judge. For the kind of strict reporting discussed here, these should be avoided. Instead of "sneaked in," one might say "entered quietly"; instead of "politicians," "candidates"; instead of "bureaucrat," "public official"; instead of "bum," "homeless person"; instead of "crackpots," "holders of unconventional views." A newspaper reporter may not write, "A crowd of suckers came to listen to Senator Smith last evening in that rickety firetrap and ex-dive that disfigures the south side of town," but rather, "Between 75 and 100 people heard an address last evening by Senator Smith at the Evergreen Gardens near the southern city limits."

How Judgments Stop Thought

A judgment ("He is a fine boy," "It was a beautiful service," "Baseball is a healthful sport," "She is an awful bore") is a *conclusion*, evaluating a number of previously observed facts. The reader is probably familiar with the fact that many students, when called upon to write "themes," have difficulty in writing papers of the required length because their ideas give out after a paragraph or two. Often, the reason is that those early paragraphs contain so many such judgments that there is little left to be said. When the conclusions are carefully excluded, however, and observed facts are given instead, there is never any trouble about the length of papers; in fact, they tend to become too long, since inexperienced writers, when told to give facts, often give more than are necessary.

Still another consequence of judgments early in the course of a written exercise—and this applies also to hasty judgments in everyday thought—is the temporary blindness they induce. When, for example, a discussion starts with the words, "He was a real Wall Street executive," "She was a typical yuppie," or "Ernest Hemingway was a sexist who had little idea how to portray women in his fiction," the writer must make all later statements consistent with those judgments. The result is that all the individual characteristics of this particular "executive," "yuppie," or even Hemingway as a unique writer with a unique stance toward women are lost entirely; and the rest of the essay is likely to deal not with observed facts, but with the writer's *private notion* (based on previously read stories, movies, pictures, etc.) of what "Wall Street executives" or "yuppies" are like. Premature judgment often prevents us from seeing what is directly in front of us. Even a writer sure at the beginning of a written exercise that the man being described is a "redneck" or that the scene is a "beautiful residential suburb" will conscientiously keep such notions out of his head, lest his vision be obstructed.

Snarl-Words and Purr-Words

Language is not an isolated phenomenon. Our concern is with language in action—in the full context of nonlinguistic events which are its setting. The making of noises, like other muscle activities, is sometimes involuntary. Our responses to powerful stimuli, such as to things that make us very angry, are a complex of muscular and physiological events: the contracting

The compliment

of fighting muscles, the increase of blood pressure, a change in body chemistry, *and* the making of noises such as growls and snarls. We are a little too dignified, perhaps, to growl like dogs, but we do the next best thing and substitute series of words such as "You dirty sneak!" "The filthy scum!" Similarly, if we are pleasurably agitated, we may, instead of purring or wagging the tail, say things like "She's the sweetest little girl in all the world!"

Such statements have less to do with reporting the outside world than they do with our inadvertently reporting the state of our internal world; they are the human equivalents of snarling and purring. On hearing "She's the sweetest girl in the whole world," the listener would be wise to allocate the meaning correctly—as a revelation of the speaker's state of mind and not as a revelation about the girl.

Although this observation may seem obvious, it is surprising how often, when such a statement is made, both the speaker and the hearer feel that something has been said about the girl. This error is especially common in the interpretation of utterances of orators and editorialists in some of their more excited denunciations of "leftists," "fascists," "Wall Street," "right-wingers," and in their glowing support of "our way of life." Constantly, because of the impressive sound of the words, the elaborate structure of the sentences, and the appearance of intellectual progression, we get the feeling that something is being said about something. On closer examination, however, we discover that these utterances really say "What I hate ('liberals,' 'Wall Street,') I hate very, very much," and "What I like ('our way of life') I like very, very much." We may call such utterances *snarl-words* and *purr-words*.

On the other hand, if the snarl-words and purr-words are accompanied by verifiable reports (which would also mean that we have previously agreed as to what specifically is meant by the terms used), we might find reason to accept the emotional position of the speaker or writer. But snarl-words and purr-words as such, unaccompanied by verifiable reports, offer nothing further to discuss, except possibly the question "Why do you feel as you do?"

Issues like gun control, abortion, capital punishment, and elections often lead us to resort to the equivalent of snarl-words and purr-words. It is usually fruitless to argue such statements as "Reagan was the great Teflon president—nothing stuck," "She is anti-life," "Wagner's music is just a cacophony of hysterical screeching," "People who don't want to control the purchase of handguns are nuts." To take sides on such issues phrased in such judgmental ways is to reduce communication to a level of stubborn imbecility. But to ask questions relating to the statements (Why do you like or dislike President Reagan? Why are you for or against gun control?) is to learn something about the beliefs of others. After listening to their opinions and the reasons for them, we may leave the discussion slightly wiser, slightly better informed, and perhaps less one-sided than we were before the discussion began.

Slanting

Not all forms of judgments are as direct as the ones discussed above. In the course of writing reports, despite all efforts to keep judgments out, some will creep in. An account of a man, for example, may read like this:

"He had apparently not shaved for several days, and his face and hands were covered with grime. His shoes were torn, and his coat, which was several sizes too small for him, was spotted with dried clay."

Though no judgment has been directly stated, one is obviously implied. Let us contrast this with another description of the same man:

"Although his face was bearded and neglected, his eyes were clear, and he looked straight ahead as he walked rapidly down the road. He seemed very tall; perhaps the fact that his coat was too small for him emphasized that impression. He was carrying a book under his left arm, and a small terrier ran at his heels."

In this example, the impression about the man is considerably changed, simply by the inclusion of new details and the subordination of unfavorable ones. Even if explicit judgments are kept out of one's writing, implied judgments will get in.

How, then, can we ever give an impartial report? The answer is, of course, that we cannot attain complete impartiality while we use the language of everyday life. Even with the very impersonal language of science, the task is sometimes difficult. Nevertheless, we can, by being aware of the favorable or unfavorable feelings that certain words and facts can arouse, attain enough impartiality for practical purposes. Such awareness enables us *to balance implied favorable and unfavorable judgments against each other.* To learn to do this, it is a good idea to write *two* essays at a time on the same subject, both strict reports, to be read side by side: the first to contain facts and details likely to prejudice the reader in favor of the subject, the second to contain those likely to prejudice the reader against it. For example:

FOR	AGAINST
He had white teeth.	His teeth were uneven.
His eyes were blue, his hair blond and abundant.	He rarely looked people straight in the eye.
He had on a clean blue shirt.	His shirt was frayed at the cuffs.
He often helped his wife with the dishes.	He rarely got through drying the dishes without breaking a few.
His pastor spoke very highly of him.	His grocer said he was always slow about paying his bills.
He liked dogs.	He disliked children.

This process of selecting details that are favorable or unfavorable to the subject being described may be termed *slanting*. Slanting gives no explicit judgments, but it differs from reporting in that it deliberately or inadvertently makes certain judgments inescapable. One-sided or biased slanting, not uncommon in private gossip and backbiting and all too common in the "interpretive reporting" of newspapers and magazines, can be described as a technique of lying without actually telling any lies.

Discovering One's Bias

When a news account tells a story in a way we dislike, leaving out facts we think important and playing up others in a way we think unfair, we are tempted to say, "Look how unfairly they've slanted the story!" Such a statement, of course, is an inference about the story's reporters and editors. We are assuming that what seems important or unimportant to us is equally weighty or trivial to them, and on the basis of that assumption we infer that the writers and editors "deliberately" gave the story a misleading emphasis. Is this necessarily the case? Can the reader, as an outsider, determine whether a story assumes a given form because the editors "deliberately slanted it that way" or because that was the way the events appeared to them?

The point is that, by the process of selection and abstraction imposed on us by our own interests and background, experience comes to all of us—including editors—already "slanted." What is important to a 50-year-old suburban lawyer will likely be different from what is important to a 20-year-old, unemployed, inner-city parent.

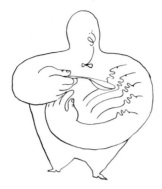

Press secretary spoon-feeding the press

The writer who is neither an advocate nor an opponent avoids slanting, except in search of special literary effects. The avoidance of slanting is not only a matter of being impartial; it is even more importantly a matter of making good maps of the territory of experience. The profoundly biased individual cannot make good maps because she can see an enemy *only* as an enemy and a friend *only* as a friend. The individual with genuine skill in writing—and in thinking—can with imagination and insight look at the same subject from many points of view. The following examples may illustrate the fullness and solidity of descriptions thus written:

Adam turned to look at him. It was, in a way, as though this were the first time he had laid eyes on him. He saw the strong, black shoulders under the red-check calico, the long arms lying loose, forward over the knees, the strong hands, seamed and calloused, holding the reins. He looked at the face. The thrust of the jawbone was strong, but the lips were heavy and low, with a piece of chewed straw hanging out one side of the mouth. The eyelids were pendulous, slightly swollen-looking, and the eyes bloodshot. Those eyes, Adam knew, could sharpen to a quick, penetrating, assessing glance. But now, looking at that slack, somnolent face, he could scarcely believe that. ROBERT PENN WARREN, *Wilderness*

Soon after the little princess, there walked in a massively built, stout young man in spectacles, with a cropped head, light breeches in the mode of the day, with a high lace ruffle and a ginger-coloured coat. This stout young man [Pierre] was the illegitimate son of a celebrated dandy of the days of Catherine, Count Bezuhov, who was now dying in Moscow. He had not yet entered any branch of the service; he had only just returned from abroad, where he had been educated, and this was his first appearance in society. Anna Pavlovna greeted him with a nod reserved for persons of the very lowest hierarchy in her drawing-room. . . .

Pierre was clumsy, stout and uncommonly tall, with huge, red hands; he did not, as they say, know how to come into a drawing-room and still less how to get out of one, that is, how to say something particularly agreeable on going away.

Moreover, he was dreamy. He stood up, and picking up a three-cornered hat with the plume of a general in it instead of his own, he kept hold of it, pulling the feathers until the general asked him to restore it. But all his dreaminess and his inability to enter a drawing-room or talk properly in it were atoned for by his expression of good-nature, simplicity and modesty.

COUNT LEO TOLSTOY, *War and Peace*
(Translated by Constance Garnett)

CHAPTER 4

Contexts

[On being asked to define New Orleans jazz]: Man, when you got to ask what it is, you'll never get to know.   LOUIS ARMSTRONG

Dictionary definitions frequently offer verbal substitutes for an unknown term which only conceal a lack of real understanding. Thus a person might look up a foreign word and be quite satisfied with the meaning "bullfinch" without the slightest ability to identify or describe this bird. Understanding does not come through dealings with words alone, but rather with the things for which they stand. Dictionary definitions permit us to hide from ourselves and others the extent of our ignorance.   H. R. HUSE

How Words Mean

I ONCE GOT INTO a dispute with an Englishwoman over the pronunciation of a word and offered to look it up in the dictionary. The Englishwoman said firmly, "What for? I am English. I was born and brought up in England. The way I speak *is* English." Such self-assurance about one's own language is not uncommon among the English. In the United States, however, anyone who is willing to quarrel with the dictionary is regarded as either eccentric or mad.

It is widely believed that every word has a correct indisputable meaning and that teachers and books are the supreme authority in matters of meaning and usage. Few people ask by what authority the writers of dictionaries and grammars say what they say.

The task of writing a dictionary begins with reading vast amounts of the literature of the period or subject that the dictionary is to cover. As the editors read, they copy on cards every interesting or rare word, every unusual or peculiar occurrence of a common word, a large number of common words in their ordinary uses, and also the sentences in which each of these words appears, thus:

> pail
> The dairy *pails* bring home increase of milk
> KEATS, *Endymion*
> I, 44–45

That is to say, the context of each word is collected, along with the word itself. For a really big job of dictionary-writing, such as the *Oxford English Dictionary* (usually bound in about twenty-five volumes), millions of such cards are collected, and the task of editing occupies decades. As the cards are collected, they are alphabetized and sorted. When the sorting is completed, there will be anywhere from two or three to several hundred illustrative quotations for each word, each on its card.

To define a word, then, the dictionary editor uses the cards illustrating the word, each representing an actual use of the word by a writer of some literary or historical importance. The editor reads the cards carefully, discards some, rereads the rest, and divides the stack according to what seem to be the several senses of the word. The editor cannot be influenced by an idea of what a given word *ought* to mean, but must work according to what the collected quotations reveal about the word.

The writing of a dictionary, therefore, is not a task of setting up authoritative statements about the "true meanings" of words, but a task of *recording*, to the best of one's ability, what various words *have meant* to authors in the distant or immediate past. The *writer of a dictionary is a historian, not a lawgiver*. If, for example, we had been writing a dictionary in 1890, or even as late as 1919, we would have said that the word "broadcast" meant "to scatter" (seed, for example); but we could not have decreed that from 1921 on, the most common meaning of the word should become "to disseminate audible messages, etc., by radio or television transmission." To regard the dictionary as an "authority," therefore, is to credit dictionary writers with gifts of prophecy which they do not possess. In choosing our words when we speak or write, we can be *guided* by the historical record afforded us by the dictionary, but we cannot be *bound* by it, because new situations, new experiences, new inventions, new feelings, are always compelling us to give new uses to old words. Looking under a "hood," we should ordinarily have found, five hundred years ago, a monk; today, we find an automobile engine.

Verbal and Physical Contexts

The way dictionary writers arrive at definitions is merely the systematization of the way we all learn the meanings of words, beginning at infancy and continuing for the rest of our lives. Let us say that we have never heard the word "oboe" before, and we overhear a conversation in which the following sentences occur:

He used to be the best *oboe* player in town. . . . Whenever they came to that *oboe* part in the third movement, he used to get very excited. . . . I saw him one day at the music shop, buying a new reed for his *oboe*. . . . He never liked to play the clarinet after he started playing the *oboe*. He said it wasn't as much fun, because it was too easy.

Although the word may be unfamiliar, its meaning becomes clear to us as we listen. After hearing the first sentence, we know that an "oboe" is "played," so that it must be either a game or a musical instrument. With the second sentence, the possibility of its being a game is eliminated. With each succeeding sentence, the possibilities as to what an "oboe" may be are narrowed down until we get a fairly clear idea of what is meant. This is how we learn from *verbal context*, arriving at a workable definition by understanding one word in relation to the others with which it appears.

But even independently of this, we learn by *physical and social context*. Let us say that we are playing golf and that we have hit the ball in a certain way with certain unfortunate results, so that our companion says to us, "That's a bad *slice*." He repeats this remark every time our ball fails to go straight. If we are reasonably bright, we learn in a very short time to say, when it happens again, "That's a bad *slice*." On one occasion, however, our friend says to us, "That's not a *slice* this time; that's a *hook*."

In this case we consider what has happened, and we wonder what is different about the last stroke from those previous. As soon as we make the distinction, we have added still another word to our vocabulary. The result is that after nine holes of golf, we can use both these words accurately—and perhaps several others as well, such as "divot," "number-five iron," "approach shot," *without ever having been told what they mean.* Indeed, we may play golf for years without ever being able to give a dictionary definition of "to slice": "To strike (the ball) so that the face of the club draws inward across the face of the ball, causing it to curve toward the right in flight (with a right-handed player)" (*Webster's New International Dictionary*). But even without being able to give such a definition, we would still be able to use the word accurately whenever the occasion arose.

We learn the meanings of practically all our words (which are, it will be remembered, merely complicated noises), not from dictionaries, not from definitions, but from hearing these noises as they accompany actual situations in life and learning to associate certain noises with certain situations. Even as dogs learn to recognize "words," as for example by hearing "biscuit" at the same time as an actual biscuit is held before their noses, so do we all learn to interpret language by being aware of the happenings that accompany the noises people make at us—by being aware, in short, of contexts.

The "definitions" given by little children in school show clearly how they associate words with situations. They almost always define in terms of physical and social contexts: "Punishment is when you have been bad and you have to sit on the stairs for time out." "Newspapers are what the paperboy brings." These are good definitions. The main reason that they cannot be used in dictionaries is that they are *too* specific; it would be impossible to list the myriads of situations in which every word has been used. For this reason, dictionaries give definitions on a high level of abstraction, that is, with particular references left out for the sake of conciseness. This is another reason why it is a great mistake to regard a dictionary definition as telling us all about a word.

Extensional and Intensional Meaning

In talking about meaning, it is helpful to employ some special terms. The first of these is *extensional meaning. The extensional meaning of an utterance is that to which it points in the extensional (physical) world.* An extensional meaning is something that cannot be expressed in words because it *is* that which the word stands for—it is the territory rather than the map. An easy way to remember this is to *put your hand over your mouth and point* whenever you are asked to give an extensional meaning.

Of course, we cannot always point to the extensional meanings of the words we use. Therefore, so long as we are discussing meanings, we shall

refer to that which is being talked about as the *denotation* of an utterance. We may not be able to point to the city of Winnipeg each time we speak of it, but the denotation of the word "Winnipeg" can be understood as the prairie city of that name in southern Manitoba. The extensional meaning of "dog" can't be pointed to if there are no dogs about, but the word "dog" denotes a class of animals which includes dog^1 (Fido), dog^2 (Rex), dog^3 (Rover) . . . dog^n.

The *intensional meaning* of a word or expression is that which is suggested (connoted) inside one's head. Roughly speaking, whenever we express the meaning of words by uttering other words, we are giving connotations or intensional meaning.

Utterances may have, of course, both extensional and intensional meaning. If they have no intensional meaning at all—that is, if they start no notions whatever spinning about in our heads—they are meaningless noises, like foreign languages that we do not understand.

Some utterances, moreover, may get many notions spinning about in our heads but still have no extensional meaning. The statement "Angels watch over my bed at night" has no extensional meaning. But this does not mean that no angels watch over my bed at night. When we say that the

statement has no extensional meaning, we are merely saying that we cannot see, touch, photograph, or in any scientific manner detect the presence of angels. The result is that, if an argument begins on the subject of whether or not angels watch over my bed, *there is no way of ending the argument to the satisfaction of all disputants,* the Christians and the non-Christians, the pious and the agnostic, the mystical and the scientific. Therefore, whether we believe in angels or not, knowing in advance that any argument on the subject will be both endless and futile, we can avoid getting into fights about it.

On the other hand, when statements have extensional content, as when we say, "This room is fifteen feet long," arguments can come to a close. No matter how many guesses there are about the length of the room, all discussion ceases when someone produces a tape measure. This, then, is the important difference between extensional and intensional meanings: namely, when utterances have extensional meanings, discussion can be ended and agreement reached; when utterances have intensional meanings only and no extensional meanings, arguments may, and often do, go on indefinitely. Such arguments can only result in conflict. Among individuals, they may break up friendships; in society, they often split organizations into bitterly opposed groups; among nations, they may aggravate existing tensions so seriously as to become real obstacles to the peaceful settling of disputes.

Arguments of this kind may be termed "non-sense arguments," because they are based on utterances about which *no sense data can be collected.* (Needless to say, there are occasions when the hyphen may be omitted— that depends on one's feeling toward the particular argument under consideration.) In the exercises, the reader is requested to list examples of "non-sense arguments." Even the foregoing example of the angels may give offense to some people, in spite of the fact that no attempt is made to deny or affirm the existence of angels. You can imagine, therefore, the uproar that might result from giving a number of examples, from theology, politics, law, art, economics, literary criticism, and other fields in which it is not customary to distinguish clearly sense from non-sense.

The "One Word, One Meaning" Fallacy

Everyone, of course, who has ever given any thought to the meanings of words has noticed that words are always shifting and changing in meaning. Usually, people regard this as a misfortune, leading to "sloppy thinking" and "confusion." To remedy this condition, they are likely to suggest that we should all agree on one meaning for each word and use it only with that meaning. Thereupon it may occur to them that we simply cannot make people agree in this way, even if we could set up an ironclad dictatorship under a committee of lexicographers who could place censors in every newspaper office and tape recorders in every home. The situation, therefore, appears hopeless.

Such an impasse is avoided when we start with a new premise altogether—one of the premises upon which modern linguistic thought is based: namely, *that no word ever has exactly the same meaning twice.* The extent to which this premise fits the facts can be demonstrated in a number of ways. First, if we accept the proposition that the contexts of an utterance determine its meaning, it becomes apparent that since no two contexts are ever *exactly* the same, no two meanings can ever be exactly the same. How can we *fix the meaning* even for so common an expression as "to believe in" when it can be used in such sentences as the following?

I *believe* in you (I have confidence in you).
I *believe* in democracy (I accept the principles implied by the term democracy).
I *believe* in Santa Claus (It is my opinion that Santa Claus exists).

Secondly, we can take for an example a word of "simple" meaning like "kettle." But when Lynne says "kettle," its intensional meanings to her are the common characteristics of all the kettles Lynne remembers. When Peter says "kettle," however, its intensional meanings to him are the common characteristics of all the kettles he remembers. *No matter how small or how negligible the differences may be between Lynne's "kettle" and Peter's "kettle," there is some difference.*

Finally, let us examine utterances in terms of extensional meanings. If Pat, Christy, Donna, and Jeff each say "my personal computer," we would have to point to *four different personal computers* to get the extensional meaning in each case: Pat's new Apple 2e, Christy's old IBM, Donna's MacIntosh, and the undenotable intended personal computer that Jeff plans some day to buy: "My personal computer, when I buy one, will have graphics capabilities." Also, if Pat says "my personal computer" today and again "my personal computer" tomorrow, the extensional meaning is different in the two cases because the personal computer is not *exactly* the same from one day to the next (nor from one minute to the next): slow processes of wear, change, and decay are going on constantly. Although we can say that the differences in the meanings of a word on one occasion, on another occasion a minute later, and on still another occasion another minute later are *negligible*, we cannot say that the meanings are *exactly* the same.

We cannot know what a word means before it is uttered. All we can know in advance of its utterance is *approximately* what it will mean. After the utterance, we interpret what has been said in the light of both verbal and physical contexts, then act or understand according to our interpretation. That is why, when a friend looks up from a book and asks, "What does 'complimentary' mean?" we often ask that he read the sentence in which the word appears. From the context of the sentence we can determine which meaning of "complimentary" is most fitting.

An examination of the verbal context of an utterance, as well as an examination of the utterance itself, directs us to its intensional meanings; an examination of the physical context directs us to the extensional meanings. When David says to James, "Bring me that book, will you?" James looks in the direction of David's pointed finger (physical context) and sees a desk piled with books (physical context); he thinks back over their previous conversation (verbal context) and knows which of those books is being referred to.

Interpretation, therefore, must be based on the totality of contexts. If it were otherwise, we should not be able to account for the fact that even if we fail to say what we mean in some situations, or fail to use the right or customary words, people can very frequently understand us. For example:

A: Gosh, look at that second baseman go!
B: (Looking): You mean the shortstop?
A: Yes, that's what I mean.

A: There must be something wrong with the oil line; the engine has started to balk.
B: Don't you mean gas line?
A: Yes, didn't I say gas line?

Contexts often indicate our meanings so clearly that we do not even have to say what we mean in order to be understood.

The Ignoring of Contexts

In the course of argument, people frequently complain about words meaning different things to different people. Instead of complaining, they should accept it as a matter of course. It would be startling indeed if the word "justice," for example, were to have the same meaning to each of the nine justices of the United States Supreme Court; then we should get nothing but unanimous decisions. It would be even more startling if "justice" meant the same to the robber as to the robbed. If we can get deeply into our consciousness the principle that no word ever has the same meaning twice, we will develop the habit of automatically examining contexts, and this enables us to understand better what others are saying. As it is, however, we are all too likely to have automatic, or signal, reactions to certain words and read into people's remarks meanings that were never intended. Then we waste energy in angrily accusing people of intellectual dishonesty or abuse of words, when their only sin is that they use words in ways unlike our own, as they can hardly help doing, especially if their background has been widely different from ours. There are cases of intellectual dishonesty and of the abuse of words, of course, but they do not always occur in the places where people think they do.

In the study of history of cultures other than our own, contexts take on special importance. To say, "There was no running water or electricity in the house," does not condemn an English house in 1570, but says a great deal against a house in Chicago today. Again, if we wish to understand the Constitution of the United States, it is not enough, as our historians now tell us, merely to look up all the words in the dictionary and to read the interpretations written by Supreme Court justices. We must see the Constitution in its *historical context:* the conditions of life, the current ideas, the fashionable prejudices, and the probable interests of the people who drafted the Constitution. After all, the words "United States of America" stood for quite a different-sized nation and a different culture in 1790 from what they stand for today. When it comes to very big subjects, the range of contexts to be examined—verbal, social, and historical—may become very large indeed.

The Interaction of Words

All this is not to say, however, that we might just as well throw away the dictionary, since contexts are so important. Any word in a sentence—any sentence in a paragraph, any paragraph in a larger unit—whose meaning is revealed by its context *is itself part of the context of the rest of the text.* To look up a word in a dictionary, therefore, frequently explains not only the word itself, but the rest of the sentence, paragraph, conversation, or essay in which it is found. *All words within a given context interact upon one another.*

Realizing, then, that a dictionary is a historical work, we should understand the dictionary thus: "The word *mother* has most frequently been used in the past among English-speaking people to indicate *a female parent.*" From this we can safely infer, "If that is how it has been used, that is what it probably means in the sentence I am trying to understand." This is what we normally do, of course; after we look up a word in the dictionary, *we reexamine the context to see if the definition fits.* If it doesn't; if the context reads, "Mother began to form in the bottle," the context—and the dictionary—may bear closer scrutiny, as the word in question may have multiple meanings.[1]

---

[1]One of the more obscure meanings of the noun "mother" is " a slimy membrane . . . that develops on the surface of alcoholic liquids undergoing . . . fermentation . . ." (Webster's *New Collegiate Dictionary*).

CHAPTER 5

The Double Task of Language

Tens of thousands of years have elapsed since we shed our tails, but we are still communicating with a medium developed to meet the needs of arboreal man. . . . We may smile at the linguistic illusions of primitive man, but may we forget that the verbal machinery on which we so readily rely, and with which our metaphysicians still profess to probe the Nature of Existence, was set up by him, and may be responsible for other illusions hardly less gross and not more easily eradicable?

C. K. OGDEN and I. A. RICHARDS

Connotations

REPORT LANGUAGE, as we have seen, is *instrumental* in character—that is, instrumental in getting work done. But language is also used for the direct *expression* of a speaker's feelings. Considering language from the point of view of the *hearer*, we can say that report language *informs* us, but that expressive uses of language such as judgments and presymbolic functions *affect* us—that is, affect our feelings. Affective language has the character of a kind of force.

A spoken insult, for example, may provoke a return insult, just as a blow may provoke a return blow; a loud and peremptory command compels, just as a push compels; talking and shouting are as much a display of energy as pounding the chest. The first of the affective elements in speech is the *tone of voice*—its loudness or softness, its pleasantness or unpleasantness, its variations in volume and intonation during the course of the utterance.

Another affective element in language is *rhythm*. Rhythm is the name we give to the effect produced by the repetition of auditory (or kinesthetic) stimuli at fairly regular intervals. From the boom-boom of a drum to the nuances of cultivated poetry and music there is a continuous development and refinement of man's responsiveness to rhythm. To produce rhythm is to arouse attention and interest; so affective is rhythm, indeed, that it catches our attention even when we do not want our attention distracted. *Rhyme* and *alliteration* are, of course, ways of emphasizing rhythm in language, through repetition of similar sounds at regular intervals. Political-slogan writers and advertisers therefore have a special fondness for rhyme and alliteration: "Tippecanoe and Tyler Too," "Fifty-four-forty or Fight," "Keep Cool with Coolidge," "Better Buy Buick," "I Like Ike," "All the Way with L.B.J.," "McD.L.T." These are rather absurd expressions so far as information is concerned, but by their sound they set up small rhythmic echoes in one's head that make them annoyingly difficult to forget.

In addition to tone of voice and rhythm, another extremely important affective element in language is the aura of feelings, pleasant or unpleasant, that surrounds practically all words. It will be recalled that, in Chapter 4, a distinction was made between denotations (or extensional meaning), pointing to things, and connotations (or intensional meaning), consisting of "ideas," "notions," "concepts," and feelings suggested in the mind. These connotations can be divided into two kinds, the *informative* and the *affective*.

Informative Connotations

The informative connotations of a word are its socially agreed-upon, "impersonal" meanings, *insofar as meanings can be given at all by additional words.* For example, if we talk about a "pig," we cannot give the exten-

During the Boer War, the Boers were described in the British press as "sneaking and skulking behind rocks and bushes." The British forces, when they finally learned from the Boers how to employ tactics suitable to warfare on the South African veldt, were described as "cleverly taking advantage of cover." During the Vietnam War, retreat by U.S. forces was sometimes termed "strategic withdrawal."

A Note on Verbal Taboo

In every language, there seem to be certain "unmentionables"—words of such strong affective connotations that they cannot be used in polite discourse. In English, the first of these to come to mind are, of course, words dealing with excretion and sex. We ask waiters and salesclerks where the "lounge" or "rest room" is, although we usually have no intention of lounging or resting. "Powder room" is another euphemism for the same facility, also known as "toilet," which itself is an earlier euphemism. Indeed, it is impossible in polite society to state, without having to resort to baby talk or a medical vocabulary, what a "rest room" is for. (It is "where you wash your hands.")

Words referring to anatomy and sex—and words even vaguely suggesting anatomical and sexual matters—have even stronger affective connotations, especially in American and British culture. Polite ladies and gentlemen of the nineteenth century could not bring themselves to say "breast," "leg," or "thigh"—not even of chicken—so the terms "white meat" and "dark meat" were substituted. It was thought inelegant to speak of "going to bed," so "to retire" was used instead. When D. H. Lawrence's first novel, *The White Peacock* (1911) was published, the author was widely criticized for having used the word "stallion," even though its context was innocuous. Taboos and the euphemisms we use as substitutes do change, of course: a novel by Henry James or Edith Wharton uses the phrase "making love" in a way different from the way we use the term now. To Americans at the turn of the century, "making love" meant "wooing" or "courting"—these, in turn, are both words not in current use. Currently, we use "making love" as a more acceptable, romantic alternative to clinical or vulgar expressions for sexual union.

Amusing as these verbal taboos sometimes are, they may also produce serious problems, since they may prevent frank discussion of sexual or physical matters. Finding the nontechnical vocabulary of sex too coarse and shocking, and being unfamiliar with the medical or technical vocabulary, many people are simply unable to seek or use information about such "sensitive" issues.

When scientists first learned about AIDS, for example, the vague, hesitant vocabulary used to explain how the disease was transmitted confused many people. Gradually, the vocabulary became more specific as newspapers, magazines, and other publications began using a less technical, common vocabulary to convey the critical facts needed by specific groups and audiences at risk for the disease. Nevertheless, some people have objected to, or have been shocked by, the appearance in print of explicit sexual terms designed to ensure that people of all ages know enough about AIDS to help prevent its spread.

Money is another subject about which communication is inhibited. It is acceptable to mention *sums* of money, such as $10,000 or $2.50. But it is considered in bad taste to inquire directly into other people's financial affairs, unless such an inquiry is really necessary in the course of business. When creditors send bills, they almost never mention money, although that is what they are writing about. There are many circumlocutions: "We beg to call your attention to what may be an oversight on your part." "We would appreciate your early attention to this matter." "May we look forward to an early remittance?"

The fear of death carries over, quite understandably in view of the widespread confusion of symbols with things symbolized, into fear of the *words* having to do with death. Many people, therefore, instead of saying someone has "died," substitute such expressions as "passed away," "gone to his reward," "departed," "bought the farm," or "gone west." In Japanese, the word for death, *shi*, happens to have the same pronunciation as the word for the number four. This coincidence results in many linguistically awkward situations, since people avoid "*shi*" in the discussion of numbers and prices, and use "*yon*," a word of different origin, instead.

The stronger verbal taboos have, however, a genuine social value. When we are extremely angry and we feel the need of expressing our anger in violence, the uttering of these forbidden words may provide a relatively harmless verbal substitute for going berserk and smashing furniture; they may act as a kind of safety valve in our moments of crisis.

It is difficult to explain why some words should have such powerful affective connotations while others with the same informative connotations do not. Some of our verbal reticences, especially the religious ones, have the authority of the Bible: "Thou shalt not take the name of the Lord thy God in vain; for the Lord will not hold him guiltless that taketh his name in vain" (Exodus 21:7). "Gee," "gosh almighty," and "gosh darn" are ways to avoid saying "Jesus," "God Almighty," and "God damn." Carrying the biblical injunction one step further, we also avoid taking the name of the devil in vain by means of such expressions as "the deuce," "the dickens," and "Old Nick." It appears that among all the people of the world, among the civilized as well as the primitive, there is a feeling that the names of the gods are too holy, and the names of evil spirits too terrifying, to be invoked lightly.

The primitive confusion of word with thing, of symbol with thing symbolized, manifests itself in some parts of the world in a belief that the name of a person is *part of* that person. To know someone's name, therefore, is to have power over him. Because of this belief, it is customary among some peoples for children to be given at birth a "real name" known only to the parents and never used, as well as a nickname or public name to be called by in society. In this way a child is protected from being put in anyone's power. The story of Rumpelstiltskin is a European illustration of this belief in the power of names.

Thomas Mann, in *Joseph and His Brethren*, gives the following dramatic account of the power of names, according to ancient Jewish belief:

[Joseph, speaking of a lion.] "But if he had come, with lashing tail, and roared after his prey, like the voice of the chanting seraphim, yet thy child would have been little affrighted or not at all before his rage. . . . For knoweth not my father that the beasts fear and avoid man, for that God gave him the spirit of understanding and taught him the orders into which single things fall; doth he not know how Shemmael shrieked when the man of earth knew how to name the creation as though he were its master and framer. . .? And the beasts too they are ashamed and put the tail between their legs because we know them and have power over their names and can thus render powerless the roaring might of the single one, by naming him. If now he had come, with long slinking tread, with his hateful nose, mewing and spitting, terror would not have robbed me of my senses, nor made me pale before his riddle. 'Is thy name Blood-Thirst?' I would have asked of him making merry at his expense. 'Or Springing Murder?' But there I would have sat upright and cried out: 'Lion! Lo, Lion art thou, by nature and species, and thy riddle lieth bare before me, so that I speak it out and with a laugh it is plain.' And he would have blinked before the name and gone meekly away before the word, powerless to answer unto me. For he is quite unlearned and knows nought of writing tools."

Words With Built-in Judgments

The fact that some words simultaneously arouse both informative and affective connotations gives a special complexity to discussions involving religious, racial, national, and political groups. To many people, the word "communist" has both the informative connotation of "one who believes in communism" and the affective connotation of "one whose ideals and purposes are altogether repellent." Words applying to occupations of which one disapproves ("pickpocket," "racketeer," "prostitute") and those applying to believers in philosophies of which one disapproves ("atheist," "radical," "heretic," "materialist," "fundamentalist") likewise often communicate *simultaneously* a fact and a judgment on that fact. Such words may be called "loaded"—that is, their affective connotations may strongly shape people's thoughts.

In some parts of the United States, there is a strong prejudice against certain ethnic groups, such as Mexican-Americans, whether immigrant or

American-born. The strength of this prejudice is revealed by the fact that polite people and the press have stopped using the word "Mexican," using the term "Hispanic" instead to avoid any negative connotations. There are also terms such as "Chicano" and "Latino" that Mexican-American and Spanish-speaking groups have chosen to describe themselves.

Names that are "loaded" tend to influence behavior toward those to whom they are applied. Currently, the shop doorways and freeway underpasses of American cities are sheltering tens of thousands of people who have no work and no homes. These people used to be referred to as "bums"—a word that suggests not only a lack of employment but a lack of desire to work, people who are lazy, satisfied with little, and who have no desire to enter the mainstream of the American middle class or subscribe to its values. Thus, to think of these people as "bums" is to think that they are only getting what they deserve. With the search for new names for such people—"street people," "homeless," "displaced persons"—we may find new ways of thinking about their situation that may in turn suggest new ways of helping deal with it. Similarly, "problem drinker" has replaced "drunkard" and "substance abuser" has replaced "junkie." "Developmentally disabled" has replaced "retarded," which in turn replaced "idiot."

The negative connotations of words sometimes change because of deliberate changes in the way they are used. Michael Harrington, the American socialist, has said that "socialist" became a political dirty word in the 1930s and 1940s in the United States when opposing politicians and editorialists repeatedly linked "socialism" and "communism," obscuring what adherents to the two philosophies saw as distinctions between them. In the 1964 presidential campaign, it was said by his opponents that Senator Barry Goldwater was "too conservative" to be made president. The negative connotations of "conservative" had receded by 1988; in that presidential campaign, then Vice President George Bush repeatedly amplified the negative connotations of the word "liberal" and then accused his opponent, Michael Dukakis, of being one.

The meaning of words also changes from speaker to speaker, from hearer to hearer, and from decade to decade. An elderly Japanese woman of my acquaintance used to squirm at the mention of the word "Jap." "Whenever I hear that word," she used to say, "I feel dirty all over." She was reacting to the negative connotations as it was used during the Second World War and earlier. More recently, "JAP" is an acronym for "Jewish-American princess," heard as an insult by an entirely different ethnic group.

A black friend of mine recalls hitchhiking as a young man in the 1930s through an area of the country where very few blacks lived. He was given a ride by a white couple, who fed him and gave him a place to sleep in their home. However, they kept referring to him as "little nigger," which upset him profoundly. He finally asked them not to call him by that "insulting term," a request they had difficulty understanding, as they had not meant to offend him. One way my friend might have explained his point further would have been to say, "Excuse me, but in the part of the country I come from, white people who wish to show contempt for my race call us 'niggers.' I assume this is not your intention."

In recent times, the negative connotations of the word "nigger" are more widely understood. This is partly the result of efforts by black Americans and others to educate the public. Early in 1942, when I was living in Chicago and teaching at the Illinois Institute of Technology, I was invited to become a columnist for the *Chicago Defender*—at that time the most militant of Negro newspapers. I say "Negro" rather than "black" because this was 1942 and it was the mission of that newspaper to make people proud of being "Negro." The word "Negro" at that time was used with dignity and pride. In its editorial policy, the *Defender* saw to it that the word was used in that way. It was always capitalized. Later, during the civil rights movement of the 1950s and 1960s, a wider effort was made to make just this point in the mind of the American public as a whole, first substituting "Negro" for "colored," "nigger," "nigrah," and, later, substituting "black" for "Negro." "Black" is now the word most frequently chosen by people of African origin in the United States to describe themselves, and the word "Negro" is considered by many to be old-fashioned and condescending. Most recently, it has been proposed that "African-American" be substituted for "black." *Those who believe that the meaning of a word is innately part of the word risk offending or being offended because of having ignored differences in context or current usage.*

The conflicts that erupt over words are invariably an index to social concerns over the reality that the words refer to. Much debate has arisen over the issue of sexual discrimination in language. Is it fair, many people ask, that the word "man" should stand for all human beings, male and female? Should we say, "Everyone should cast his vote," when half the voters are women? Are there biases that are unfair to women—and to men—built into the English language? If so, what can or should be done about it?

The problem can be better understood if we look at the disputed words in the contexts in which they appear. In some contexts, the extensional meaning of "man" as a synonym for the species *Homo sapiens* covers both sexes, without any discrimination implied: men, women and children; Englishmen, Chinese, Eskimos, Aborigines, next-door neighbors, and so forth. In other contexts, "man" refers only to the male: "There is a man at the door." The problems with connotation occur in a context such as: "The work team is short ten men." In such a case the employer may be inclined to look for ten more males to hire, even when the work can be done equally well by women.

The Chinese ideograph [人], also used in Japanese, stands for "man" in the generic sense: "person," "human being." A different ideograph [男] is used for "man" in the sense of "male human being." Since women traditionally have been assigned subordinate roles in both Chinese and Japanese cultures, discrimination against women cannot be said to be due solely to the peculiarities of language.

For those who have no difficulty with the different meanings of "man," or who like the maleness they find in the generic term, the language needs no modification. But what about those who are dissatisfied with the masculine connotations of "man"? What about the woman on the softball team who insists on being called "first baseperson" or the committee leader who styles herself "chairperson"? What about the woman named "Cooperman" who wanted to change her name to "Cooperperson" and petitioned a court to legalize the change? (Her petition was denied.) Can the language accommodate them?

Fortunately, the language is flexible enough for people to make personal adjustments to meet their own standards. "Human beings" or "humans" or "people" are acceptable substitutes for the generic "man," though rhetorically they may not always sound as good. Instead of saying "Man is a tool-using animal," we can say, "Human beings are tool-using animals."

Once it becomes apparent that we can construct any sentence we please without incurring possible sexual stereotypes, a further question remains: Should we demand that all writers adopt a "nonsexist" vocabulary and always use it—for example, the neutral plural? On this point history offers some guidance.

Most of the attempts made to force living language into a doctrinaire program have failed resoundingly. Jonathan Swift once spoke out acidly against the use of the word "mob" as a corrupt shortening of the Latin term *mobile vulgus*. Dr. Samuel Johnson resisted, to no avail, the admission of the word "civilization" into his dictionary because it seemed to him a barbarism, despite its respectable Latin root. In this century, Mussolini tried to eliminate the informal *tu* in Italian (the second person singular pronoun, whose English counterpart, "thou," has disappeared in ordinary English usage). He covered Italy with posters commanding Italians to use the *voi* form instead. His campaign failed. The social forces that created the words in the first place could not be changed by logic, fiat, or program. Language has usually proven stronger than the individual.

It must not be forgotten that language, created over centuries and inherited with our culture, does not exert its tyranny uniformly over all who use it. In the novel *Kingsblood Royal* by Sinclair Lewis, actually a tract against racial prejudice, the central character is a vicious racial bigot—but he is careful never to use the word "nigger."

Similarly, an individual who uses "sexist" terms uncritically may have all kinds of discriminatory attitudes towards women, or he—or she—may be entirely free of them. The presence or absence of such terms has no necessary connection with the presence or absence of the corresponding attitudes.

This does not mean that writers who are sensitive to sexual bias in language should resign themselves to what they consider a sorry state of affairs. They can carry out their own programs within their own speech and writing. These efforts are not without risk of accidentally engendering new, unintended meanings. For example, in revising the words of hymns, the Episcopal Church changed "Christian Men, Rejoice!" to "Christian Friends, Rejoice!" However, as Sara Mosle pointed out in *The New Republic*, the theological implications of extending joy only to friends—what about Christian enemies, or even strangers?—were entirely inappropriate to the message of the hymn. "How long would it be before Christmas cards read 'Peace on Earth, good will towards friends?' A different proposition altogether from the brotherly (or sisterly) benediction to all mankind."[1]

The calling of attention to sex discrimination contained within language, a campaign conducted in a similar way to that by which "Negro" and then "black" were successfully substituted for "colored," has served to raise society's awareness of the problem of built-in bias in language, even though it has not yet transformed the language. Even if such efforts fail to dislodge all forms of gender bias in the language, the effort to correct the problem is, in itself, worthwhile. As the poet John Ciardi has observed:

In the long run the usage of those who do not think about the language will prevail. Usages I resist will become acceptable. It will not do to resist uncompromisingly. Yet those who care have a duty to resist. Changes that occur against such resistance are tested changes. The language is better for them—and for the resistance.

One other curious fact needs to be recorded about the words we apply to such hotly debated issues as race, religion, political heresy, and economic dissent. Every reader is acquainted with people who, according to their own flattering descriptions of themselves, "believe in being frank" and like to "tell it like it is." By "telling it like it is," such people usually mean calling anything or anyone by the term which has the strongest and most disagreeable affective connotations. Why people should pin medals on themselves for "candor" for performing this nasty feat has often puzzled me. Sometimes it is necessary to violate verbal taboos as an aid to clearer thinking, but, more often, to insist upon "telling it like it is" is to provide our minds with a greased runway down which we may slide back into unexamined and reactive patterns of evaluation and behavior.

[1]"Washington Diarist," *The New Republic*, Nov. 21, 1988

Everyday Uses of Language

The language of everyday life, then, differs from "reports" such as those discussed in Chapter 3. As in reports, we have to be accurate in choosing words that have the informative connotations we want; otherwise the reader or hearer will not know what we are talking about. But, in addition, we have to choose words with the affective connotations we want so that readers or listeners will be interested or moved by what we are saying and feel towards things the way we do. This double task confronts us in almost all ordinary conversation, oratory, persuasive writing, and literature. Much of this task, however, is performed intuitively; without being aware of it, we choose the tone of voice, the rhythms, and the affective connotations appropriate to our utterance.

We exercise somewhat more conscious control over the informative connotations of our utterances. Improvement in our ability to understand language, as well as in our ability to use it, depends, therefore, not only upon sharpening our sense for the informative connotations of words, but *also sharpening our insight into the affective elements in language through social experience, through contact with many kinds of people in many kinds of situations, and through literary study.*

The following, finally, are some of the things that can happen in any given speech event—writing, speaking, listening, reading:

1. The informative connotations may be inadequate or misleading, but the affective connotations may be sufficiently well directed so that we are able to interpret correctly. For example, when someone says, "Imagine who I saw today! Old What's-his-name—oh, you know who I mean—Whoosis, that fellow who lives on, oh—what's the name of that street!" there are means, certainly not clearly informative, by which we manage to understand who is being referred to.

2. The informative connotations may be correct enough and the extensional meanings clear, but the affective connotations may be inappropriate, misleading, or ludicrous. This happens frequently when people try to write elegantly: "Jim ate so many bags of *Arachis hypogaea*, commonly known as peanuts, at the ball game today that he was unable to do justice to his evening repast."

3. Both informative and affective connotations may "sound all right," but there may be no "territory" corresponding to the "map." For example: "He lived for many years in the beautiful hill country just south of Chicago." There is no hill country just south of Chicago.

4. Both informative and affective connotations may be used *consciously* to create "maps" of "territories" that do not exist. There are many reasons why we should wish on occasion to do this. Of these, only two need be

mentioned now. The first reason is to enable us to plan for the future. For example, we can say, "Let us suppose there is a bridge at the foot of this street; then the heavy traffic on High Street would be partly diverted over the new bridge; shopping would be less congested on High Street. . . . " Having visualized the condition that would result, we can recommend or oppose the bridge according to whether or not we like the probable results. Second, we may wish to give pleasure:

> Yet mark'd I where the bolt of Cupid fell:
> It fell upon a little western flower,
> Before milk-white, now purple with love's wound,
> And maidens call it Love-in-idleness.
> Fetch me that flower; the herb I show'd thee once:
> The juice of it on sleeping eyelids laid
> Will make or man or woman madly dote
> Upon the next live creature that it sees.
> SHAKESPEARE, *A Midsummer Night's Dream*

CHAPTER 6

The Language of Social Cohesion

Two little dogs sat by the fire
Over a fender of coal dust;
Said one little dog to the other little dog,
"If you don't talk, why, I must."

MOTHER GOOSE

Are words in phatic communion [a type of speech in which ties of union are created by a mere exchange of words] used primarily to convey meaning, the meaning which is symbolically theirs? Certainly not! They fulfill a social function and that is their principal aim, but they are neither the result of intellectual reflection, nor do they necessarily arouse reflection in the listener.

BRONISLAW MALINOWSKI

Noises as Expression

WHAT COMPLICATES the problems of interpretation is the fact that informative uses of language are intimately fused with older and deeper functions of language. In fact, we have every reason to believe that the ability to use noises as symbols was developed only recently in the course of our evolution. Long before we developed language as we know it, we probably made, like the lower animals, all sorts of animal cries expressive of such internal conditions as hunger, fear, triumph, and sexual desire. We can recognize a variety of such noises, and the conditions of which they are symptoms, in our domestic animals. Gradually, in human beings, these noises seem to have become more and more differentiated; consciousness expanded. Grunts and gibberings became language. But, although we developed symbolic language, the habit of making noises *expressing* our internal conditions has remained. The result is that we use language in *presymbolic* ways; that is, as the equivalent of screams, howls, purrs, and gibbering. These presymbolic uses of language coexist with our symbolic systems, and we still have constant recourse to them in the talking we do in everyday life.

The presymbolic character of much of our talk is most clearly illustrated in cries expressive of strong feeling of any kind. If, for example, we carelessly step off a curb when a car is coming, it doesn't much matter whether someone yells, "Look out!" or "Kiwotsuke!" or "Hey!" or "Prends garde!" or simply screams, so long as whatever noise made is uttered loud enough to alarm us. It is the fear expressed in the *loudness* and the *tone* of the cry that conveys the necessary sensations, and not the words. Similarly, commands given sharply and angrily usually produce quicker results than the same commands uttered tonelessly. The quality of the voice itself has a power of expressing feelings that are almost independent of the symbols used. We can say, "I hope you'll come to see us again," in a way that clearly indicates that we hope the visitor never comes back. Or again, if a young woman with whom we are strolling says, "The moon is bright tonight," we are able to tell by the tone whether she is making a meteorological observation or indicating that she wants to be kissed.

Infants understand the love, the warmth, or the irritation in a mother's voice long before they are able to understand her words. Most children retain this sensitivity to presymbolic elements in language. It even survives in some adults; they are the people credited with "intuition" or "unusual tact." Their talent lies in their ability to interpret tones of voice, facial expressions, body language, and other symptoms of the internal condition of the speaker. They listen not only to *what* is said, but to *how* it is said. On the other hand, people who have spent much of their lives in the study of *written* symbols (scientists, intellectuals, accountants) are often relatively deaf to everything but the surface sense of the words. If a young woman wants a person of this kind to kiss her, she usually has to tell him in so many words or actions.

Noises for Noise's Sake

Sometimes we talk simply for the sake of hearing ourselves talk; that is, for the same reason that we play golf or dance. The activity gives us a pleasant sense of being alive. Children prattling and adults singing in the bathtub alike are enjoying the sound of their voices. Sometimes large groups make noises together, as in group singing, recitation, or chanting, for similar presymbolic reasons. In all this, the significance of the words used is almost completely irrelevant. We often, for example, may sing mournfully about a desire to be carried back to a childhood home in old Virginny, when in actuality we have never been there and haven't the slightest intention of going.

What we call social conversation is again largely presymbolic in character. When we are at a reception or dinner party, for example, we all have to talk—about anything: the weather, the performance of the Green Bay Packers, John Updike's latest novel, Cher's latest film. Rarely, except among very good friends, are the remarks made during these conversations ever important enough to be worth making for their informative value. Nevertheless, it is regarded as rude to remain silent. Indeed, in such matters as greetings and farewells: "Good morning"—"Lovely day"—"And how's your family these days?"—"It was a pleasure meeting you"—"Look us up the next time you're in town"—"Have a nice day"—it is regarded as a social error not to say these things even if we do not mean them. There are numberless daily situations in which we talk simply because it would be impolite not to. Every social group has its own form of this kind of talking—the art of conversation, small talk, or the mutual kidding that Americans love so much. From these social practices it is possible to assert that, as a general principle, *the prevention of silence is itself an important function of speech.*

This presymbolic talk for talk's sake is, like the cries of animals, a form

Frantic escape from the burden of silence

of activity. We talk together about nothing at all and thereby establish friendships. The purpose of the talk is not the communication of information, as the symbols used would seem to imply ("I see the Dodgers are out in the lead again"), but the establishment of communion. Human beings have many ways of establishing communion among themselves: breaking bread together, playing games together, working together. But talking together is the most easily arranged of all these forms of collective activity. The *togetherness* of the talking, then, is the most important element in social conversation; the subject matter is only secondary.

There is a principle at work, therefore, in the selection of subject matter. Since the purpose of this kind of talk is the establishment of communion, *we are careful to select subjects about which agreement is immediately possible.* Consider, for example, what happens when two strangers feel the necessity or the desire to talk to each other:

"Nice day, isn't it?"

"It certainly is." (*Agreement on one point has been established. It is safe to proceed.*)

"Altogether, it's been a fine summer."

"Indeed it has. We had a nice spring, too." (*Agreement on two points having been established, the second party invites agreement on a third point.*)

"Yes, it was a lovely spring." (*Third agreement reached.*)

The togetherness, therefore, is not merely in the talking itself, but in the opinions expressed. Having agreed on the weather, we go on to further agreements—that it is nice farming country around here, that it certainly is scandalous how prices are going up, that New York is certainly an interesting place to visit but it would be awful to have to live there, and so on. *With each new agreement, no matter how commonplace or obvious, the fear and suspicion of the stranger wears away, and the possibility of friendship enlarges.* When further conversation reveals that we have friends or political views or artistic tastes or hobbies in common, a friend is made, and genuine communication and cooperation can begin.

The Value of Unoriginal Remarks

Early in 1942, a few weeks after the beginning of World War II and at a time when rumors of Japanese spies were widely current, I had to wait two or three hours in a railroad station in Oshkosh, Wisconsin, a city in which I was a stranger. I became aware as time went on that the other people waiting in the station were staring at me suspiciously and feeling uneasy about my presence. One couple with a small child were staring with special uneasiness and whispering to each other. I therefore took occasion to remark to the husband that it was too bad that the train should be late on so cold a night. The man agreed. I went on to remark that it must be especially difficult to travel with a small child in winter when train schedules were so uncertain. Again the husband agreed. I then asked the child's age and remarked that the child looked very big and strong for his age. Again agreement, this time with a slight smile. The tension was relaxing.

After two or three more exchanges, the man asked, "I hope you don't mind my bringing it up, but you're Japanese, aren't you? Do you think the Japs have any chance of winning this war?"

"Well," I replied, "your guess is as good as mine. I don't know any more than I read in the papers. [This was true.] But the way I figure it, I don't see how the Japanese, with their lack of coal and steel and oil and their limited industrial capacity, can ever beat a powerfully industrialized nation like the United States."

My remark was admittedly neither original nor well informed. Hundreds of radio commentators and editorial writers were saying much the same thing during those weeks. But just because they were, the remark *sounded familiar* and was *on the right side*, so that it was easy to agree with. The man agreed at once, with what seemed like genuine relief. How much the wall of suspicion had been broken down was indicated in his next question, "Say, I hope your folks aren't over there while the war is going on."

"Yes, they are. My father and mother and two young sisters are over there."

"Do you ever hear from them?"

"How can I?"

"Do you mean you won't be able to see them or hear from them till after the war is over?" Both he and his wife looked troubled and sympathetic.

There was more to the conversation, but the result was that within ten minutes after it had begun they had invited me to visit them sometime in their city and have dinner with them in their home. And the other people in the station, seeing me in conversation with people who *didn't* look suspicious, ceased to pay any attention to me and went back to reading their newspapers or staring at the ceiling.

This account is the result of later reflection. It should be added that I was by no means *consciously* applying the principles of this chapter during the incident. I was simply groping, as anyone else might have done, for a way to relieve my own loneliness and discomfort in the situation.

Maintenance of Communication Lines

Such presymbolic uses of language not only establish new lines of communication but keep old lines open. Old friends like to talk even when they have nothing special to say to each other. In the same way that long-distance telephone operators, ship radio officers, and army signal corps outposts chatter with each other even when there are no official messages to communicate, so do people who live in the same household or work in the same office continue to talk to each other even when there is nothing much to say. The purpose in both cases seems to be partly to relieve tedium, but partly, and more importantly, to keep the lines of communication open.

Hence the situation between many a married couple:

Wife: Honey, why don't you ever talk to me?
Husband (*interrupted in his reading of Schopenhauer or* The Racing Form): What's that?
Wife: Why don't you talk to me?
Husband: But there isn't anything to say.
Wife: You don't love me.
Husband (*thoroughly interrupted, and somewhat annoyed*): Oh, don't be silly. You know I do. (*Suddenly consumed by a passion for logic.*) Do I run around? Don't I bring my paycheck home? Don't I work my head off for you and the kids?
Wife: But still I wish you'd say something.
Husband: Why?
Wife: Well, because.

Of course, in one way the husband is right. His actions are an extensional demonstration of his love, and he believes they speak louder than words. But in a different way, the wife is right. How does one know that the lines of communication are still open unless one keeps them working? A sound engineer who says into a microphone, "One. . .two. . .three . . .four. . .testing. . ." isn't saying anything much. But it is nevertheless important at times that it be said.

Presymbolic Language in Ritual

Sermons, political caucuses, conventions, pep rallies, and other ceremonial gatherings illustrate the fact that all groups—religious, political, patriotic, scientific, and occupational—like to gather together at intervals for the purpose of sharing certain accustomed activities, wearing special costumes (vestments in religious organizations, regalia in lodges, uniforms in patriotic societies), eating together (banquets), displaying the flags, ribbons or emblems of their group, and marching in processions. Among these ritual activities is always included a number of speeches, either traditionally worded or specially composed for the occasion, whose principal function is *not* to give the audience new information, *not* to create new ways of feeling, but something else altogether.

What this something else is, we shall analyze more fully in Chapter

7, "The Language of Social Control." We can analyze now, however, one aspect of language as it appears in ritual speeches. Let us look at what happens at a "pep rally" such as precedes college football games. The members of "our team" are "introduced" to a crowd that already knows them. Called upon to make speeches, the players mutter a few incoherent and often ungrammatical remarks, which are received with wild applause. The leaders of the rally make fantastic promises about the mayhem to be performed on the opposing team the next day. The crowd utters "cheers," which normally consist of animalistic noises arranged in extremely primitive rhythms. *No one comes out any wiser or better informed than before.*

To some extent, religious ceremonies are equally puzzling at first glance. The priest or clergy in charge utter set speeches, *often in a language incomprehensible to the congregation* (Hebrew in orthodox Jewish synagogues, until recently Latin in the Roman Catholic Church, Sanskrit in Chinese and Japanese temples), with the result that, as often as not, no information whatsoever is communicated to those present.

If we approach these linguistic events as students of language trying to understand what is happening, and if we examine our own reactions when we enter into the spirit of such occasions, we cannot help observing that, whatever the words used in ritual utterance may signify, we often do not think very much about their signification during the course of the ritual. Most of us, for example, have often repeated the Lord's Prayer, sung "The Star-Spangled Banner," or recited the "Pledge of Allegiance" without thinking about the words at all. As children, we are taught to repeat such sets of words before we can understand them, and many of us continue to say them for the rest of our lives without bothering about their meaning. We cannot regard such utterances as meaningless, because they have a genuine effect upon us. We may come out of church, for example, with no clear memory of what the sermon was about, but with a sense nevertheless that the service has somehow done us good.

What is the good that is done us in ritual utterances? It is the *reaffirmation of social cohesion:* The Christian feels closer to his fellow Christians, the Elk feels more united with his brother Elks, the American feels more American and the Frenchman more French as a result of these rituals. Societies are held together by such bonds of common reactions to sets of linguistic stimuli.

Ritualistic utterances, therefore, whether made up of words that had symbolic significance at other times, of words in foreign or obsolete tongues, or of meaningless syllables, may be regarded as consisting in large part of presymbolic uses of language: that is, accustomed sets of noises which convey no information, but to which feelings (in this case, group feelings) are attached. Such utterances rarely make sense to anyone not a member of the group. The abracadabra of a lodge meeting is absurd to anyone not a member of the lodge. When language becomes ritual, its effect becomes, to a considerable extent, independent of whatever signification the words once possessed.

Advice to the Literal-Minded

Presymbolic communications have this characteristic in common: their effectiveness does not depend on the use of words. They can even be performed without recognizable speech at all. Group feeling may be established, for example, among animals by collective barking or howling and among human beings by college cheers, community singing, and other collective noise-making activities. Indications of friendliness such as we give when we say "Good morning" or "Nice day, isn't it?" can be given by smiles, gestures, or, as among animals, by nuzzling or sniffing. Frowning, laughing, smiling, jumping up and down, can satisfy a large number of needs for expression, without the use of verbal symbols. But the use of verbal symbols is more customary among human beings, so that instead of expressing our feelings by knocking a man down, we verbally blast him to perdition; instead of forming social groups by huddling together like puppies, we write constitutions and bylaws for the vocal expression of our cohesion.

To understand the presymbolic elements that enter into our everyday language is extremely important. We cannot restrict our speech to the asking and giving of factual information; we cannot confine ourselves strictly to statements that are literally true, or we should often be unable to say even "Pleased to meet you" when the occasion demanded. The intellectually persnickety are always telling us that we "ought to say what we mean" and "mean what we say," and "talk only when we have something to talk about." Of course these are impossible prescriptions.

Ignorance of the existence of these presymbolic uses of language is not so common among uneducated people (who often perceive such things intuitively) as it is among the educated. The educated often listen to the chatter at parties and receptions, and conclude from the triviality of the conversation that all the guests (except themselves) are fools. They may discover that people often come away from church services without any clear memory of the sermon and conclude that churchgoers are either fools or hypocrites. They may hear the political oratory of the opposition party, wonder "how anybody can believe such rot," and conclude therefore that people in general are so unintelligent that democracy is unworkable. Almost all such gloomy conclusions about the stupidity or hypocrisy of our friends and neighbors are unjustifiable on such evidence, because they usually come from applying the standards of symbolic language to linguistic events that are either partly or wholly presymbolic in character.

One further illustration may make this clearer. Let us suppose that we are on the roadside struggling with a flat tire. A friendly youth comes up

and asks, "Got a flat tire?" If we insist upon interpreting his words literally, we will regard this as an extremely silly question and our answer may
be, "Can't you see I have, you dumb ox?" If we pay no attention to what
the words say, however, and understand his meaning, we will return his
gesture of friendly interest by showing equal friendliness, and in a short
while he may be helping us to change the tire. In a similar way, many
situations in life as well as in literature demand that we pay no attention
to what the words say, since the meaning may often be a great deal more
intelligent and intelligible than the surface *sense* of the words themselves.

The example of the flat tire appeared in the 1941 version of this book,
Language in Action. It was commented on and elaborated by Dr. Karl
Menninger in *Love Against Hate* (1942), in which he offered the following
translation of "Got a flat tire?" in terms of its psychological meaning:

"Hello—I see you are in trouble. I'm a stranger to you, but I might be
your friend now that I have a chance to be if I had any assurance that my
friendship to you would be welcomed. Are you approachable? Are you a
decent fellow? Would you appreciate it if I helped you? I would like to do
so, but I don't want to be rebuffed. This is what my voice sounds like.
What does your voice sound like?" Why does not the youth simply say
directly, "I would be glad to help you"? Menninger explains: "But people
are too timid and mutually distrustful to be so direct. *They want to hear
one another's voices. People need reassurance that others are just like themselves.*" (Italics added.)

CHAPTER 7

The Language of Social Control

The effect of a parade of sonorous phrases upon human conduct has never been adequately studied.   THURMAN W. ARNOLD

Making Things Happen

THE MOST INTERESTING and perhaps least understood of the relations between words and things is the relation between words and future events.
When we say, for example, "Come here!" we are not describing the extensional world about us, nor are we merely expressing our feelings; we are
trying to *make something happen*.

What we call "commands," "pleas," "requests," and "orders" are the
simplest ways we have of making things happen by means of words. There
are, however, more roundabout ways. When we say, for example, "Our
candidate is a great American," we are of course uttering an enthusiastic
"purr" about that candidate, but we may also be trying to influence how
other people vote. Again, when we say, "Our war against the enemy is
God's war. God wills that we must triumph," we are saying something
that cannot be scientifically verified; nevertheless, it may influence others
to help in the prosecution of the war. Or if we merely state as a fact, "Milk
contains calcium," we may be influencing others to buy milk.

Consider, too, such a statement as "I'll meet you tomorrow at two
o'clock in front of Union Station." Such a statement about *future* events
can only be made, it will be observed, in a system in which symbols are
independent of things symbolized. The future, like the recorded past, is a
specifically human dimension. To a dog, the expression "hamburger *tomorrow*" is meaningless—at best it will look at you expectantly, hoping
for the extensional hamburger to appear *now*. Squirrels, to be sure, store
food for next winter, but the fact that they store food regardless of whether
their needs are adequately provided for demonstrates that such behavior
(usually called "instinctive") is governed neither by symbols nor by other
interpreted stimuli. Human beings are unique in their ability to react
meaningfully to such expressions as "next Saturday" or "twenty years from
now, I promise to pay." That is to say, a map can be made despite the fact
that the territory it stands for is not yet an actuality. Guiding ourselves by
means of such maps of territories-to-be, we can impose a certain predictability upon future events.

With words, therefore, we influence and to an enormous extent *control
future events*. It is for this reason that writers write; preachers preach;
employers, parents, and teachers scold; propagandists send out news re-
leases; politicians give speeches. All of them, for various reasons, are trying
to influence our conduct—sometimes for our own good, sometimes for
their own. These attempts to control, direct, or influence the future actions
of fellow human beings with words may be termed *directive uses of language*.

If directive language is to direct effectively, it cannot be dull or uninteresting. If it is to influence our conduct, it must make use of the affective element available in language: dramatic variations in tone of voice,

rhyme and rhythm, purring and snarling, words with strong affective connotations, endless repetition. If meaningless noises will move the audience, meaningless noises must be made; if facts move them, facts must be given; if noble ideals move them, we must make our proposals appear noble; if they will respond only to fear, we must scare them stiff.

The nature of the affective means used in directive language is limited, of course, by the nature of our aims. If we are trying to direct people to act more kindly toward each other, we obviously do not want to arouse feelings of cruelty or hate. If we are trying to direct people to think and act more intelligently, we obviously should not use subrational appeals. If we are trying to direct people to lead better lives, we use affective appeals that arouse their finest feelings. Included among directive utterances, therefore, are many of the greatest and most treasured works: the Christian and Buddhist scriptures, the writings of Confucius, Milton's *Areopagitica*, and Lincoln's Gettysburg Address.

There are, however, occasions when it is felt that language is not sufficiently affective by itself to produce the results wanted. We supplement directive language, therefore, by *nonverbal affective appeals* of many kinds. We supplement the words "Come here" by gesturing with our hands. Advertisers are not content with saying in words how beautiful their products will make us; they supplement their words by the use of color, sound, or motion. The affective appeal of sermons and religious exhortations may be supplemented by costumes, incense, processions, choir music, and church bells. A political candidate seeking office reinforces his or her speech-making with a considerable array of nonverbal affective appeals: brass bands, flags, parades, barbecues, and formal dinners.

Now, if we want people to do certain things and don't care *why they do them*, then no affective appeals are excluded. Some political candidates want us to vote for them regardless of our reasons for doing so. Therefore, if we hate the rich, they will snarl at the rich for us; if we dislike labor unions, they will snarl at union members. Some business firms want us to buy their products regardless of our reasons for doing so; therefore, if delusions and fantasies will lead us to buy their products, they will seek to produce delusions and fantasies; if we want to be attractive to the other sex, they will promise instant seductiveness; if we admire beautiful people, they will associate beautiful people with their products, whether they are selling shaving cream, automobiles, summer resorts, or hardware.

The Implied Promises of Directive Language

Aside from simply attracting attention or creating pleasant sensations, *directive utterances say something about the future.* They are "maps," either explicitly or by implication, of *"territories" that are to be.* They direct us to do certain things with the stated or implied promise that if we do these

things, certain consequences will follow: "If you adhere to the Bill of
Rights, your civil rights too will be protected." "If you vote for me, I will
have your taxes reduced." "Take Choco-Lax and enjoy that glorious feeling
that goes with regularity." "Live according to these religious principles,
and you will have peace in your soul." "Read this magazine, and you will
keep up with important current events." Needless to say, some of these
promises are kept, and some are not. Indeed, we encounter promises daily
that are obviously incapable of being kept.

There is no sense in objecting, as some people do, to advertising and
political propaganda—the only kind of directives they worry about—on
the grounds that they are based on "emotional appeals." Unless directive
language has affective power of some kind, it is useless. We do not object
to campaigns that tell us, "Give to the Community Chest and enable poor
children to enjoy better care," although that is an "emotional appeal." Nor
do we resent being reminded of our love of home, friends, and nation when
people issue moral or patriotic directives at us. The important question to
be asked of any directive utterance is, "Will things happen as promised if
I do as I am directed? If I accept your philosophy, will I achieve peace of
mind? If I vote for you, will my taxes be reduced? If I use Dove Soap, will
my beloved come back to me?"

We rightly object to advertisers who make false or misleading claims
and to politicians who ignore their own promises. Life being as uncertain
and as unpredictable as it is, we are constantly trying to find out what is
going to happen next so that we may prepare ourselves. Directive utterances undertake to tell us how we can bring about desirable events and
avoid undesirable events. If we can rely upon what directive utterances tell
us about the future, the uncertainties of life are reduced. When, however,
directive utterances are of such a character that things do *not* happen as
predicted—when, after we have done as we were told, peace in the soul
has not been found, taxes have not been reduced, the beloved has not returned — there is disappointment. Such disappointments may be trivial or
grave; in any event, they are so common that we do not even bother to
complain about most of them. They are, nevertheless, all serious in their
implications. Each of them serves, in greater or lesser degree, to break
down that mutual trust that makes cooperation possible and knits people
together into a society.

All of us, therefore, who utter directive language, with its concomitant
promises, stated or implied, are morally obliged to be as certain as possible
that we are arousing no false expectations. Politicians promising the immediate abolition of poverty, national advertisers suggesting that tottering
marriages can be restored to bliss by a change in the brand of laundry
detergent used in the family, newspapers threatening the collapse of the
nation if the party they favor is not elected—all such utterers of non-sense
are, for the reasons stated, menaces to the social order. It does not matter

much whether such misleading directives are uttered in ignorance and error or with conscious intent to deceive, because the disappointments they cause are all similarly destructive of mutual trust among human beings.

The Foundations of Society

What we call society is a vast network of mutual agreements. We agree to drive on the right-hand side of the road, and others agree to do the same; we agree to deliver specified goods, and others agree to pay us for them; we agree to observe the rules of an organization, and the organization agrees to let us enjoy its privileges. This complicated network of agreements, into which almost every detail of our lives is woven and upon which most of our expectations in life are based, consists essentially of *statements about future events which we are supposed, with our own efforts, to bring about*. Without such agreements, there would be no such thing as society. We all would be huddling in caves, not daring to trust anyone, and life would be, as the English philosopher Thomas Hobbes put it, "nasty, brutish, and short." With such agreements, and a will on the part of the vast majority of people to live by them, behavior begins to fall into relatively predictable patterns; cooperation becomes possible; peace and freedom are established.

Therefore, in order that we shall continue to exist as human beings, we *must* impose patterns of behavior on each other. We must make citizens conform to social and civic customs; we must make spouses faithful, soldiers courageous, judges just, priests pious, and teachers solicitous for the welfare of their pupils. In early stages of culture, the principal means of imposing patterns of behavior was, of course, physical coercion. But such control can also be exercised, as human beings must have discovered extremely early in history, by *words*—that is, by directive language. Therefore, directives about matters which society as a whole regards as essential to its own safety are made especially powerful, so that no individual in that society will fail to be impressed with a sense of obligation. To make doubly sure, society further reinforces the directives by the assurance that punishment, possibly including imprisonment and death, may be visited upon those who fail to heed the words.

Directives With Collective Sanction

These directive utterances with collective sanction, which try to impose patterns of behavior upon the individual in the interests of the whole group, are among the most interesting of linguistic events. Not only are they usually accompanied by ritual; they are usually the central purpose of ritual. There is probably no kind of utterance that we take more seriously, that affects our lives more deeply. Constitutions of nations and of organizations, legal contracts, and oaths of office are utterances of this kind; in marriage vows, confirmation exercises, induction ceremonies, and initiations, they are the essential constituent. Those terrifying verbal jungles called "laws" are simply the systematization of such directives, accumulated and modified through the centuries. In its laws, society makes its mightiest collective effort to impose predictability upon human behavior.

Directive utterances made under collective sanction may exhibit any or all of the following features:

1. Such language is almost always phrased in *words that have affective connotations*, so that people will be appropriately impressed and awed. Archaic and obsolete vocabulary or stilted phraseology quite unlike the language of everyday life is employed. For example: "Wilt thou, John, take this woman for thy lawful wedded wife?" "This lease, made this tenth day of July, A.D. One Thousand Nine Hundred and Ninety, between Samuel Smith, hereinafter called the Lessor, and Jeremiah Johnson, hereinafter called Lessee, WITNESSETH, that Lessor, in consideration of covenants and agreements hereinafter contained and made on the part of the Lessee, hereby leases to Lessee for a private dwelling, the premises known and described as follows, to wit. . ."

2. Such directive utterances are often accompanied by appeals to supernatural powers, who are called upon to help carry out the vows, or to punish us if we fail to carry them out. An oath, for example, ends with the words, "So help me God." Prayers, incantations, and invocations accompany the utterance of important vows in practically all cultures, from the most primitive to the most civilized.

3. If God does not punish us for failing to carry out our agreements, it is made clear, either by statement or implication, that our society will. For example, we all realize that we can be imprisoned for desertion, nonsupport, or bigamy; sued for "breach of contract"; "defrocked" for activities contrary to priestly vows; "cashiered" for "conduct unbecoming an officer"; "impeached" for "betrayal of public trust"; executed or imprisoned for "murder."

4. The formal and public utterance of the vows may be preceded by preliminary disciplines of various kinds: courses of training in the meaning of the vows one is undertaking; fasting and self-mortification, as before entering the priesthood; initiation ceremonies involving physical torture, as upon being inducted into the warrior status among some primitive people or even into membership in some college fraternities.

5. The utterance of the directive language may be accompanied by other activities or gestures, all calculated to impress the occasion on the mind. For example, everybody in a courtroom stands up when a judge is about

to open a court; huge processions and extraordinary costumes accompany coronation ceremonies; academic gowns are worn for commencement exercises; for many weddings, an organist and a soprano are procured and special clothes are worn.

6. The uttering of the vows may be immediately followed by feasts, dancing, and other joyous manifestations. Again, the purpose seems to be to reinforce still further the effect of the vows. For example, there are wedding parties and receptions, graduation dances, banquets for the induction of officers, and, even in the most modest social circles, some form of "celebration" when a member of the family enters into a compact with society. In primitive cultures, initiation ceremonies for chieftains may be followed by feasting and dancing that last for days or weeks.

7. In cases where the first utterance of the vows is not made a special ceremonial occasion, the effect on the memory is usually achieved by frequent repetition. The flag ritual ("I pledge allegiance to the flag of the United States. . .") is repeated daily in some schools. Mottoes, which are briefly stated general directives, are exhibited frequently; sometimes they are stamped on dishes, sometimes engraved on a warrior's sword, sometimes inscribed in prominent places such as gates, walls, and doorways, where people can see them and be reminded of their duties.

The common feature of all these activities that accompany directive utterances, as well as of the affective elements in the language of directive utterances, is the deep effect they have on the memory. Every kind of sensory impression may be aroused, from the severe pain of initiation rites to the pleasures of banqueting; music, splendid clothing, and ornamental surroundings may be employed; every emotion from the fear of divine punishment to pride in being made the object of special public attention may be aroused. This is done in order that the individual who enters into a compact with society—that is, the individual who utters the "map" of the not-yet-existent "territory"—shall never forget to try to bring that "territory" into existence.

For these reasons, such occasions as when a cadet receives his commission, when a Jewish boy has his *bar mitzvah*, when a priest takes vows, when a police officer receives a badge, when a foreign-born citizen is sworn in as a citizen of the United States, or when a president takes the oath of office—these are events the person experiencing them never forgets. Even if, later on, a person realizes that he has not fulfilled his vows, he cannot shake off the feeling that he should have done so. All of us, of course, use and respond to these ritual directives. The phrases and speeches to which we respond reveal our deepest religious, patriotic, social, professional, and political allegiances more accurately than do the citizenship papers or membership cards that we carry in our pockets or the badges that we wear on our coats. A person who has changed religions after reaching adulthood will often, on hearing a ritual familiar from childhood, feel an urge to return to that earlier form of worship. In such ways, then, do human beings use words to reach out into the future and control each other's conduct.

It should be said that many of our social directives and the rituals accompanying them are antiquated and somewhat insulting to adult minds. Rituals intended to scare people into good behavior are unnecessary to people who already have a sense of social responsibility. For example, a five-minute marriage ceremony performed at the city hall for a mature, responsible couple may "take" much better than a full-dress church wedding for an immature couple. In spite of the fact that the strength of social directives obviously lies in the willingness, the maturity, and the intelligence of the people to whom the directives are addressed, there still is a widespread tendency to rely on the efficacy of ceremonies themselves. This tendency is due, of course, to a lingering belief in word-magic, the notion that, by *saying* things repeatedly or in specified ceremonial ways, we can cast a spell over the future and force events to turn out the way we said they would. ("There'll always be an England!") An interesting manifestation of this superstitious attitude toward words and rituals is to be found among those who seem to believe that the way to educate schoolchildren in citizenship is to stage more frequent flag-saluting ceremonies rather than to increase the time allotted for the factual study of democratic institutions and the day-to-day exercise of democratic practices.

What Are "Rights"?

What, extensionally, is the meaning of the word "my" in such expressions as "my real estate," "my book," "my automobile"? Certainly the word describes no characteristics of the objects named. A check changes hands and "your" automobile becomes "mine," but no change results in the automobile. What has changed?

The change is, of course, in our *social agreements covering our behavior* toward the automobile. Formerly, when it was "yours," you felt free to use it as you liked, while I did not. Now that it is "mine," I use it freely and you may not. The meaning of "yours" and "mine" lies not in the external world, but in *how we intend to act*. And when society as a whole recognizes my "right of ownership" (by issuing me, for example, a certificate of title), it agrees to protect me in my intentions to use the automobile, and to frustrate, by police action if necessary, the intentions of those who may wish to use it without my permission. Society makes this agreement with me in return for my obeying its laws and paying my share of the expenses of government.

Cannot, then, all assertions of ownership and statements about "rights" be understood as directives? Does not "this is mine" mean "I am going to use this object; you keep your hands off"? Cannot "Every child has a *right* to an education" be translated "*Give* every child an education"? And is not the difference between "moral" or "human rights" and "legal" or "civil rights" the difference between agreements which people believe *ought* to be made, and those which, through collective, legislative sanction, *have been* made?

Directives and Disillusionment

A few cautions may be added before we leave the subject of directive language. First, it should be remembered that, since words cannot "say all" about anything, the promises implied in directive language are never more than "outline maps" of "territories-to-be." The future will fill in those outlines, often in unexpected ways. Sometimes the future will bear no relation to our "maps" at all, in spite of all our endeavors to bring about the promised events. We swear always to be good citizens, always to do our duty, and so on, but we never quite succeed in being good citizens *every* day of our lives or in performing *all* our duties. A realization that directives cannot *fully* impose any pattern on the future saves us from having impossible expectations and therefore from suffering needless disappointments.

Second, one should distinguish between directive utterances and informative ones. Such statements as "A Boy Scout is clean and chivalrous and brave" or "Police officers are defenders of the weak" *set up goals* and do not necessarily describe the present situation. This is extremely important, because all too often people understand such definitions as being descriptive and are thereupon shocked, horrified, and disillusioned upon encountering a Boy Scout who is not chivalrous or police officers who are brutal. They decide that they are "through with Boy Scouts" or "disgusted with all police," which, of course, is nonsense.

A third source of disappointment and disillusionment arising from the improper understanding of directives results from reading into directives promises that they do not make. A common instance is provided by advertisements of over-the-counter medicines that people buy under the impression that the cure or prevention of colds was promised. Under the watchful eye of the Federal Trade Commission, the writers of these ads carefully avoid saying that their preparations will prevent or cure anything. Instead they say that they "help reduce the severity of infection," "help relieve the symptoms of a cold," or "help guard against sniffling and other discomforts." If, after reading these advertisements, you feel that prevention or cure of colds has been promised, you are exactly the kind of sucker they are looking for. (Of course, if you buy the product knowing clearly what was promised and what was not, that is a different matter.)

Another way of reading into directives things that were not said is by believing promises to be more specific and concrete than they really are. When, for example, a candidate for political office promises to "help the farmer," and you vote for him, and then you discover that he helps the *cotton* farmer without helping the *potato* farmer—and you grow potatoes—you cannot exactly accuse the politician of having broken a promise. Or, if another candidate promises to "protect union labor," then after election works for legislation that infuriates officials of your union—calling it "legislation to protect union members from their own racketeering leadership"—again you cannot exactly complain about a promise being broken, since the action may have been taken in accord with the politician's sincere notion of "helping union labor." The ambiguities of campaign oratory are notorious.

Politicians are often accused of breaking their promises. No doubt many of them do, although they sometimes make promises that later circumstances prevent them from keeping. But it must be remarked that they often do not promise as much as their constituents think they do. The platforms of the major parties are almost always phrased at high levels of abstraction (they "mean all things to all men," as the cynical say), but they are often understood by voters to be more specific (that is, at lower levels of abstraction) than they are. If one is disillusioned by the acts of a politician, sometimes the politician is to blame, but sometimes the voter is to blame for having entertained the illusion to start with—for having confused different levels of abstraction.

CHAPTER 8

The Language of Affective Communication

What I call the "auditory imagination" is the feeling for syllable and rhythm, penetrating far below the conscious levels of thought and feeling, invigorating every word; sinking to the most primitive and forgotten, returning to the origin and bringing something back, seeking the beginning and the end. It works through meanings, certainly, or not without meanings in the ordinary sense, and fuses the old and obliterated and the trite, the current, and the new and surprising, the most ancient and the most civilized mentality.   T. S. ELIOT

"What's all this about 'one man, one vote'?" asked the Nottingham miner. "Why, one bloody man, one bloody vote," Bill replied. "Well, why the 'ell can't they say so?"   HUGH WALPOLE

One must know and recognize not merely the direct but the secret power of the word.   KNUT HAMSUN

THE LANGUAGE of reports is instrumental in getting done the work necessary for life, but it does not tell us anything about what life feels like in the living. We can communicate scientific facts to each other without knowing or caring about each other's feelings, but before love, friendship, and community can be established among us so that we *want* to cooperate and become a society, there must be a flow of sympathy between one person and another. This flow of sympathy is established by means of the affective uses of language. Most of the time, after all, we are not interested in keeping our feelings out of our discourse, but rather we are eager to express them as fully as we can. Affective language is used to express the feelings of the speaker and to communicate them by creating similar feelings in the listener. Let us examine, then, some more of the ways in which language can be made to work affectively.

Verbal Hypnotism

First, it should be pointed out again that fine-sounding speeches, long words, and the general *air* of saying something important are affective in result, regardless of what is being said. Often, when we are hearing or reading impressively worded sermons, speeches, political addresses, essays, or "fine writing," we stop being critical altogether, and simply allow ourselves to feel as excited, sad, joyous, or angry as the author wishes us to feel. Like snakes under the influence of a snake charmer's flute, we are swayed by the musical phrases of the verbal hypnotist. If the author is one to be trusted, there is no reason why we should not enjoy ourselves in this way now and then. But to listen or read like this all the time is a debilitating habit.

To return to our earlier analogy, there is a kind of churchgoer who habitually listens in this way, who enjoys any sermon, no matter what the moral principles recommended, no matter how poorly organized or developed, no matter how shabby its rhetoric, so long as it is delivered in an impressive tone of voice with proper musical and physical settings. Such listeners are by no means to be found only in churches. I have frequently been upset when, after having spoken on problems about which I wished to arouse thoughtful discussion, someone from the audience has remarked, "That was such a lovely address, professor. You have such a nice voice."

Some people, that is, never listen to *what* is being said, since they are interested only in what might be called the gentle inward massage that the *sound* of words gives them. Just as cats and dogs like to be stroked, so do some human beings like to be stroked verbally at fairly regular intervals; it is a form of rudimentary sensual gratification. Because listeners of this kind are numerous, intellectual shortcomings are rarely a barrier to a successful career in public life, on the stage or the networks, in the ministry, or on the lecture platform.

More Affective Elements

The affective power of repetition of similar sounds, as in catchy titles and slogans, has already been mentioned. Somewhat higher on the scale are repetitions not only of sounds but of grammatical structures, as in:

> First in war,
> first in peace,
> first in the hearts of his countrymen. . .

> Government of the people,
> by the people,
> for the people. . .

Elements of discourse such as these are, from the point of view of scientific reporting, extraneous; but without them, these phrases would not have impressed people. Lincoln could have signified just as much for informative purposes had he said "government of, by, and for the people," or even more simply, "a people's government." But he was not writing a scientific monograph. He hammers the word "people" at us three times, and with each apparently unnecessary repetition he arouses deeper and more affecting connotations of the word. While this is not the place to discuss in detail the complexities of the affective qualities of language that reside in sound alone, it is important to remember that many of the attractions of literature and oratory have a simple phonetic basis—rhyme, alliteration, assonance, crossed alliteration, and the subtleties of rhythm. All these sound effects are used to reinforce, whenever possible, the other affective devices.

Another affective device is the *direct address* to the listener or reader, as: "Keep off the grass. This means YOU!" The most painful example of this device is, of course, the spurious friendliness and intimacy with which the announcer of television commercials "personally" addresses each of several million listeners. But direct appeal to an audience is by no means limited to the advertising poster and television announcer. It softens the impersonality of formal speeches, so that a speaker or writer who feels a special urgency about his message, can hardly help using it. It occurs, therefore, in the finest rhetoric as well as in the simplest. An interesting variant of the "you" device occurs in the college classroom, when the learned professor says, "You will recall what Kropotkin says in his *Mutual Aid: A Factor in Evolution. . .* ," knowing full well that Mr. Merkle, sprawling in his chair at the back of the class, has never even heard of Kropotkin before. Thanks to the computer, many people receive "personal" letters with their own names in the body of the letter from companies seeking sales or politicians seeking votes—another variant of spurious intimacy.

Almost as common as the "you" device is the "we" device. The writer in this case allies the reader with himself, in order to carry the reader along in seeing things as the writer does: "*We* shall now consider. . ." "Let *us* take, for example. . ." "*Our* duty is to go forward. . ." This device is particularly common in the more polite forms of exhortation used by preachers and teachers, though recently the use of the first person "I" has appeared. The "we" device is also often heard in kindergarten and the lower elementary grades, where teachers use it to sugarcoat their disciplinary directives: "Now, Ricky, now, Stephanie, we don't fight and call each other names here. We'll all say we're sorry and sit down and be friends again, *won't we*?" (Children usually believe that the word "cooperate" means "obey.")

In such rhetorical devices as the *periodic sentence*, there is distortion of grammatical order for affective purposes. A periodic sentence is one in which the completion of the thought is, for the sake of the slight dramatic effect that can be produced by keeping the reader in suspense for a while, delayed. Then there are such devices as *antithesis*, in which strongly opposed notions are placed together or even laid side by side in parallel phonetic or grammatical constructions, so that the reader feels the contrast and is stirred by it: "Born a serf, he died a king." "The sweetest songs are those that tell of saddest thought." "The hungry judges soon the sentence sign, /And wretches hang that jurymen may dine."

Metaphor and Simile

As we have seen, words have affective connotations in addition to their informative value, and this accounts for the fact that statements of this kind: "I've been waiting *ages* for you—you're an hour late!" "He's got *tons* of money!" "I'm so tired I'm simply *dead!*"—which are nonsensical if interpreted literally—nevertheless "make sense." The inaccuracy or inappropriateness of the informative connotations of our words are often irrelevant from the point of view of affective communication. Therefore we may refer to the moon as "a piece of cheese," "a lady," "a silver ship," "a fragment of angry candy," or anything else, so long as the words arouse the desired feelings toward the moon or toward the whole situation in which the moon appears. This, incidentally, is the reason literature is so difficult to translate from one language to another: a translation that follows informative connotations will often falsify the affective connotations, and vice versa, so that readers who know both the language of the original and the language of the translation are almost sure to be dissatisfied, feeling either that the "spirit of the original has been sacrificed" or else that the translation is "full of inaccuracies."

In translations, a further problem is presented by the fact that a well-understood metaphor in one culture may have entirely different meanings in another part of the world. The United Nations once made a short movie in which an owl was shown, to indicate wisdom. It completely misfired in certain Asian countries where the movie was shown, and the footage had to be reshot. Why? Because in those countries it was found that the owl was a traditional image of stupidity and an object of amusement.

During the long time in which *metaphor* and *simile* were regarded as "ornaments" of speech—that is, as if they were like embroidery, which improves the appearance of linen but adds nothing to its utility—the psychology of such communicative devices was neglected. We tend to assume, in ways that will be discussed more fully in later chapters, that things that create in us the same responses are identical with each other. If, for example, we are revolted by the conduct of an acquaintance at dinner and we have had such a sense of revulsion before only when watching pigs at a trough, our first, unreflecting reaction is naturally to say, "He is a pig." So far as our feelings are concerned, the man and the pig are identical with each other. Again, the soft winds of spring may produce in us agreeable sensations; the soft hands of young women also produce agreeable sensations; therefore, "Spring has soft hands." This is the basic process by which we arrive at metaphor. Metaphors are not "ornaments of discourse"; they are direct expressions of evaluations and are bound to occur whenever we have strong feelings to express. They are to be found in special abundance, therefore, in primitive speech, in folk speech, in the speech of the unlearned, in the speech of children, and in the professional argot of theater people, of gangsters, and of those in other lively occupations.

So far as our feelings are concerned, there is no distinction between animate and inanimate objects. Our fright *feels* the same whether it is a creature or object that we fear. Therefore, in the expression of our feelings, a car may "lie down and die," the wind "kisses" our cheeks, the waves are "angry" and "roar" against the cliffs, the roads are icy and "treacherous," the mountains "look down" on the sea, machine guns "spit," revolvers "bark," volcanoes "vomit" fire, and the engine "gobbles" fuel. This special kind of metaphor is called *personification* and is ordinarily described in textbooks of rhetoric as "making animate things out of inanimate." It is better understood, however, if we describe it as *a reaction that does not distinguish between the animate and the inanimate.*

Simile

However, even at rudimentary stages of evaluation it becomes apparent that calling a person a pig does not take sufficiently into consideration the differences between the person and the pig. Further reflection compels one to say, in modification of the original statement, "He is *like* a pig." Such an expression is called a *simile*—the pointing out of the similarities in our feelings toward the person and the pig. The simile, then, is something of a compromise stage between the direct, unreflective expression of feeling and the report, but of course closer to the former than the latter.

Adequate recognition has never been given to the fact that what we call slang and vulgarism works on exactly the same principles as poetry does. Slang makes constant use of metaphor and simile: "sticking his neck out," "out like a light," "way out on a limb," "baloney (no matter how thin you slice it)," "punch-drunk," "keep your shirt on," "as phony as a three-dollar bill." Clarence "Pinetop" Smith, one of the founders of the boogie-woogie style of piano playing, used to admonish his friends: "Take it easy, greasy; there's a long way to slide!"

The imaginative process by which phrases such as these are coined is the same as that by which poets arrive at poetry. In poetry, there is the same love of seeing things in scientifically outrageous but emotionally expressive language:

> The hunched camels of the night
> Trouble the bright
> And silver waters of the moon.   FRANCIS THOMPSON

> The snow doesn't give a soft white
> damn Whom it touches.   e. e. cummings

> . . . the leaves dead
> Are driven, like ghosts from an enchanter fleeing,
> Yellow, and black, and pale, and hectic red,
> Pestilence-stricken multitudes.   PERCY BYSSHE SHELLEY

> Sweet are the uses of adversity,
> Which like the toad, ugly and venomous,
> Wears yet a precious jewel in his head;
> And this our life, exempt from public haunt,
> Finds tongues in trees, books in the running brooks,
> Sermons in stones, and good in everything.   WILLIAM SHAKESPEARE

> I saw Eternity the other night
> Like a great ring of pure and endless light.   HENRY VAUGHAN

What is called slang, therefore, might well be regarded as the poetry of everyday life, since it performs much the same function as poetry; that is, it vividly expresses people's feelings about life and about the things they encounter in life.

Dead Metaphor

Metaphor, simile, and personification are among the most useful communicative devices we have, because, by their quick affective power, they often make unnecessary the inventing of new words for new things or new feelings. They are so commonly used for this purpose, indeed, that we resort to them constantly without realizing that we are doing so. For example, when we talk about the "head" of a cane, the "face" of a cliff, the "bowels" of a volcano, the "arm" of the sea, the "hands" of a watch, the "branches" of a river or an insurance company, we are using metaphor. A sales representative "covers" an area; an engine "knocks"; people write "rubber" checks that "bounce"; a theory is "built up" and then "knocked down"; a government "drains" the taxpayers, and negotiators "hammer out" an agreement. Even in so unpoetical a source as the financial page of a newspaper, metaphors are to be found: stock is "watered," shares are "liquidated," prices are "slashed" or "stepped up," markets are "flooded," the exchange is "bullish"; in spite of government efforts to "hamstring" business and "strangle" enterprise, there are sometimes "melons" to be "sliced"; although this is—but here we leave the financial page—"pure gravy" for some, others are left "holding the bag." The "rings" both of "drug rings" and "hydrocarbon rings" are metaphorical, as are the "chains" in chain stores and chain reactions.

Metaphors are so useful that they often pass into the language as part of its regular vocabulary. Metaphor is probably the most important of all the means by which language develops, changes, grows, and adapts itself to our changing needs. Sometimes, however, metaphors get overworked— "ball-and-chain" (spouse), "head-shrinker," "a horse of a different color," "a fine kettle of fish"—so that they turn into linguistic deadwood (another metaphor!), or *clichés*.[1] When metaphors are successful, they "die"—that is, they become so much a part of our regular language that we cease thinking of them as metaphors at all.

To object to arguments, as is often done, on the ground that they are based on metaphors or on "metaphorical thinking" is rarely just. The question is not whether metaphors are used, but whether the metaphors represent useful similarities.

Allusion

Still another affective device is *allusion*. If we say, for example, when standing on a bridge in St. Paul, Minnesota, in the early morning:

> Earth has not anything to show more fair;
> Dull would he be of soul who could pass by
> A sight so touching in its majesty. . .

we are evoking, in the mind of anyone familiar with the poem, such feelings as William Wordsworth expressed at the sight of London in the early morning light in September 1802, and we are applying them to St. Paul. Thus, by a kind of implied simile, we can give expression to our feelings.

---

[1] The word "cliché" conceals still another metaphor; see its etymology as given in *Webster's Third New International Dictionary*.

Allusion, then, is an extremely quick way of expressing and also of creating shades of feeling in our hearers. With a Biblical allusion ("Hasten ye, O generation of vipers, and pay me heed"), we can often arouse reverent or penitential attitudes; with a historical allusion, such as saying that New York is "the modern Babylon," we can say quickly and effectively that we feel New York to be a luxurious and extremely wicked city, doomed to destruction because of its sinfulness; by a literary allusion, we can evoke the exact feelings found in a given story or poem as a way of feeling toward the event before us.

But allusions work as affective devices only when the listener is familiar with the history, literature, people, or events alluded to. Family jokes (which are allusions to events or memories in the family's experience) have to be explained to outsiders; classical allusions in literature have to be explained to people not familiar with the classics. Nevertheless, whenever a group of people—the members of a single family or the members of a whole civilization—have memories and traditions in common, extremely subtle and efficient affective communications become possible through the use of allusion.

The foreigner, even one who may have studied English before coming to America, will fail to detect the sources of the allusions in such expressions as, "He's an Archie Bunker type" (referring to a television character) or, "He communicates good, like a semanticist should" (referring to an ungrammatical cigarette ad). The number of times we find it necessary to stop and explain things when we converse with foreigners indicates the degree to which we rely upon allusions in everyday discourse.

One of the reasons, therefore, that the young in every culture are made to study the literature and history of their own linguistic or national groups is that they may be able to understand and share in the communications of the group. Those who fail to understand passing allusions to well-known figures in European or American history, to well-known lines in Chaucer, Shakespeare, Milton, Wordsworth, or the King James version of the Bible, or to well-known characters in Dickens, Thackeray, or Mark Twain, may be said to be outsiders to an important part of the traditions of English-speaking people. The study of history and of literature, therefore, is not merely the idle acquisition of social polish, as some practical-minded folk are fond of believing, but a necessary means both of increasing the efficiency of our communications with others and of increasing our understanding of what others are trying to communicate to us.

Irony, Pathos, and Humor

A somewhat more complex device, upon which much of humor, pathos, and irony depends, is the use of a metaphor, simile, or allusion that is very obviously inappropriate to the subject at hand. The result of the incongruous comparison is a feeling of conflict, a conflict between our more obvious feelings toward that which we are talking about and the feelings aroused by the expression. In such a case, the conflicting feelings resolve themselves into a third, new feeling. Let us suppose, returning to our example above, that we are looking at an extremely ugly part of St. Paul, so that our obvious feelings are those of distaste. Then we arouse, with the Wordsworth quotation, the feeling of beauty and majesty. The result is a feeling suggested neither by the sight of the city alone nor by the allusion alone, but one that is a product of the *conflict* of the two—a sharp sense of incongruity that compels us either to laugh or to weep, depending on the rest of the context. There are many complex shades of feeling that can hardly be aroused in any other way. If a village poet is referred to as the "Mudville Milton," for example, the conflict between the inglorious connotations of "Mudville" and the glorious connotations of "Milton" produces an effect of the ludicrous, so that the poet is exposed to contempt (although, if Craigenputtock can produce a Carlyle, there is no reason why Mudville should not produce a Milton). The rather complex device that we have been discussing may be represented graphically by a diagram borrowed from mathematics:

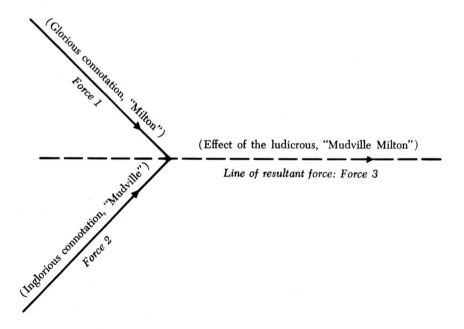

The Affectiveness of Facts

The following account of an automobile accident is quoted from the Chicago *Sun-Times:*

One [victim], Alex Kuzma, 63, of 808 North Maplewood Avenue, was hit with such impact that his right forearm was carried off on the car of the hit-run motorist who struck him. Kuzma was struck Sunday as he crossed Chicago Avenue at Campbell Avenue. Witnesses saw the car slow down, douse its headlights and speed away. After searching futilely for the dead man's missing arm, police expressed belief it must have lodged in some section of the speeding auto.

There are few readers who will not have some kind of affective reaction to this story—at least a mild horror at the gruesomeness of the accident and some indignation at the driver who failed to stop after striking someone. Facts themselves, *especially at lower levels of abstraction*, can be affective without the use of special literary devices to make them more so.

There is, however, one important difference between the affectiveness of facts and the other affective elements in language. In the latter, the writer or speaker is expressing personal feelings; in the former, he or she is suppressing personal feelings—that is to say, stating things in a way that would be verifiable by all observers, regardless of one's feelings.

Often, as in the example given, a report with accurately stated facts is more affective in result than outright and explicit judgments. By bringing the report down to even lower levels of abstraction—describing the blood on the victim's face and torn clothing, the torn ligaments hanging out of the remaining stump of his arm, and so on—one can make it even more affective. Instead of telling the reader, "It was a ghastly accident!" *we can make the reader say it for himself.* The reader is, so to speak, *made to participate in the communicative act by being left to draw his own conclusions.* A skillful writer is often, therefore, one who is especially expert at selecting the facts that are sure to move his or her readers in the desired ways. We are more likely to be convinced by such descriptive and factual writing than by a series of explicit judgments, because the writer does not ask us to take his or her word for it that the accident was ghastly. Such a conclusion becomes, in a sense, our own reaction rather than that of the reporter.

Levels of Writing

Reliance on the affectiveness of facts—that is, reliance on the reader's ability to arrive at the judgment we want him or her to arrive at—varies considerably, of course, with the audience and with the subject being treated.

In this light, it is interesting to compare magazines and stories at different levels: the "pulp" and "confession" magazines, the "slicks" (*Ladies' Home Journal, Cosmopolitan, McCall's,* and so on), and the "quality" magazines (*Harper's,* the *Atlantic,* the *New Yorker,* and *Commentary,* for example). In the magazines of mass appeal, the writers rarely rely on readers' ability to arrive at their own conclusions. In order to save any possible strain on the reader's intelligence, the writers *make the judgments for us.*

The "slicks" do this less than the "pulps," while, in the "quality" group, the tendency is to rely a great deal on the reader: to give no judgments at all when the facts "speak for themselves," or to give enough facts with every judgment so that the reader is free to make a different judgment.

The following passages from *True Confessions* give an example of judgments made for the reader so that he or she doesn't have to figure them out:

Telling Mrs. Peters and Mrs. Jenks, watching grief engulf them, was nightmare enough, but telling Edie was worst of all. She just stood there in frozen silence, her eyes wide with horror and disbelief, her face getting whiter and whiter.

"I did everything possible to save them!" I cried. "It was an accident—an unpreventable accident!"

But Edie's eyes were bitterly accusing as she choked, "*Accident!* If you hadn't insisted on taking them, there would have been no accident!" Tears streamed down her ravaged face and her voice rose hysterically. "I never want to see you again as long as I live! You—*you murderer!*" she screamed.

I stared at her for what seemed a lifetime of horror before I turned and fled, a million shrieking demons screaming in my ear, *She's right! You're a murderer! Murderer!*

The coroner's verdict called the boat's overloading "a tragic error of judgment.". . . But nothing could lighten that feeling of guilt in my heart or remove the sound of Edie's voice screaming, "Murderer!" It rang in my ears day and night, making work impossible—sleep even more impossible. Until I sought forgetfulness in the only way I could find it—by getting blind drunk and staying that way.

I was lurching through the door of a cheap bar weeks later when. . .

.   .   .   .

Jim was big and strong with huge shoulders and a great shock of yellow hair. Just looking at him made me excited and breathless. His great laugh could stir me to laughter. The touch of his hand filled me with a sweet, frightening delight. The day he invited me to the senior prom I thought I'd die of happiness.

Then I told Mother. I can still see her thin, fine-featured face pinched as if with frost. There was cold retreat in her eyes, and the wry smile on her lips made my heart turn over. . . .

The prose style of Ernest Hemingway is perhaps the classic example of the opposite technique—a highly sophisticated one, needless to say—of stating externally observable facts in the form of bare reports and of letting the reported facts have their impact on the reader. The following passage is the famous ending of *A Farewell to Arms:*

I went into the room and stayed with Catherine until she died. She was unconscious all the time, and it did not take her very long to die.

Outside the room, in the hall, I spoke to the doctor, "Is there anything I can do tonight?"

"No. There is nothing to do. Can I take you to your hotel?"

"No, thank you. I am going to stay here a while."

"I know there is nothing to say. I cannot tell you—"

"No," I said. "There's nothing to say."

"Good-night," he said. "I cannot take you to your hotel?"

"No, thank you."

"It was the only thing to do," he said. "The operation proved—"

"I do not want to talk about it," I said.

"I would like to take you to your hotel."

"No, thank you."

He went down the hall. I went to the door of the room.

"You can't come in now," one of the nurses said.

"Yes I can," I said.

"You can't come in yet."

"You get out," I said. "The other one too."

But after I had got them out and shut the door and turned off the light it wasn't any good. It was like saying good-by to a statue. After a while I went out and left the hospital and walked back to the hotel in the rain.

What Literature Is For

From what has been said, our first and most obvious conclusion is that, since the expression of individual feelings is central to literature, affective elements are of the utmost importance in all literary writing. In the evaluation of a novel, poem, play, or short story, as well as in the evaluation of sermons, moral exhortations, political speeches, and directive utterances generally, the usefulness of the given piece of writing as a "map" of actual "territories" is often secondary—sometimes quite irrelevant. If this were not the case, *Gulliver's Travels*, *Alice in Wonderland*, *The Scarlet Letter*, or Emerson's *Essays* would have no excuse for existence.

Second, when we say that a given piece of affective writing is true, we do not mean "scientifically true." We may merely mean that we agree with the sentiment; we may also mean that we believe that an attitude has been accurately expressed; again, we may mean that the attitudes evoked seem such as will lead us to better social or personal conduct.

The word "true" has many meanings. People who feel that science and literature or science and religion are in necessary conflict do so because they habitually think in opposites of black and white, true and false, good and evil. To such people, if science is "true," then literature or religion is nonsense; if literature or religion is "true," science is merely "pretentious ignorance." What should be understood when people tell us that certain statements are "scientifically true" is that they are useful and verifiable formulations, suitable for the purposes of organized cooperative workmanship. What should be understood when people tell us that the plays of Shakespeare or the poems of Milton or Dante are eternally true is that they produce in us attitudes toward our fellow human beings, an understanding of ourselves, or feelings of deep moral obligation that are valuable to humanity under any conceivable circumstances.

Third, let us consider an important shortcoming of the language of reports and of scientific writing. John Smith in love with Mary Jones is not William Brown in love with Jane Adams; William Brown in love with Jane Adams is not Henry Jones in love with Maria Gonzales; Henry Jones in love with Maria Gonzales is not Robert Browning in love with Elizabeth Barrett. Each of these situations is unique; no two loves are exactly alike—in fact, no love even between the same people is *exactly* the same from day to day. Science, seeking as always laws of the widest possible applicability and the greatest possible generality, would abstract from these situations *only what they have in common*. But each of these lovers is conscious only of the *uniqueness* of his or her own feelings: each feels, as we all know, that he or she is the first one in the world ever to have so loved. Literature creates the sense of what life feels like in the living.

How is that sense of difference conveyed? It is here that affective uses of language play their most important part. The infinity of differences in our feelings toward all the many experiences that we undergo are too subtle to be reported; they must be expressed. And we express them by the complicated manipulation of tones of voice, of rhythms, of connotations, of affective facts, of metaphors, of allusions, of every affective device of language at our command.

Frequently, the feelings to be expressed are so subtle or complex that a few lines of prose or verse are not enough to convey them. It is sometimes necessary, therefore, for authors to write entire books, carrying their readers through numbers of scenes, situations, and adventures, pushing their sympathies now this way and now that, arousing in turn their fighting spirit, their tenderness, their sense of tragedy, their laughter, their superstitions, their cupidity, their sensuousness, their piety. Sometimes it is only in such ways that the *exact* feelings an author wants to express can be recreated in his readers. This, then, is the reason that novels, poems, dramas, stories, allegories, and parables exist: to convey such propositions as "Life is tragic" or "Susanna is brilliant," not by telling us so, but by putting us through a whole series of experiences that make us feel toward life or toward Susanna as the author did. *Literature is the most exact expression of feelings, while science is the most exact kind of reporting.* Poetry, which condenses the affective resources of language into patterns of infinite rhythmical subtlety, may be said to be *the language of expression at its highest degree of efficiency.*

Symbolic Experience

In a very real sense, then, people who have read good literature have lived more than people who cannot or will not read. To read *Gulliver's Travels* is to have the experience, with Jonathan Swift, of turning sick at one's stomach at the conduct of the human race; to read *Huckleberry Finn* is to feel what it is like to drift down the Mississippi River on a raft; to read Byron is to suffer with him his rebellions and neuroses and to enjoy with him his nose-thumbing at society; to read *Native Son* is to know how it feels to be frustrated in the particular way in which many blacks in Chicago have been frustrated. This is the great task that affective communication performs: it enables us to feel how others felt about life, even if they lived thousands of miles away and centuries ago. It is not true that we have only one life to live; if we can read, we can live as many more lives and as many kinds of lives as we wish.

Here, the reader may object by asking, are we not twisting language somewhat to talk about "living" other lives than one's own? In one sense, the objection is correct; two different meanings of the word "live" are involved in the expressions "living one's own life" and "living other people's lives in books." Human life, however, is "lived" at more than one level; we inhabit both the extensional world and the world of words (and other symbols). "Living other people's lives in books" means, as we shall use the expression here, *symbolic experience*—sometimes called "vicarious experience."

In the enjoyment and contemplation of a work of literary or dramatic art—a novel, a play, a moving picture—*we find our deepest enjoyment when the leading characters in the story to some degree symbolize ourselves.* Watching Meryl Streep venturing out into the veldt in *Out of Africa,* Jennifer Smith's pulse quickens, as if she herself were living an adventure—and *symbolically,* she is. In other words, she identifies herself with Meryl Streep and her role in the story. Sylvester Stallone fighting a villain is watched by thousands of fans who clench their fists as if *they* were doing the fighting—which they are, *symbolically.* As we identify ourselves with the people in the story, the dramatist or the novelist puts us through *organized sequences of symbolic experiences.*

The differences between actual and symbolic experiences are great—one is not scarred by watching a motion-picture battle, nor is one nourished by watching people in a play having dinner. Furthermore, actual experiences come to us in highly disorganized fashion: meals, arguments with the landlady, visits to the doctor about one's fallen arches, and so on, interrupt the splendid course of romance. The novelist, however, *abstracts* only the events relevant to the story and then *organizes* them into a meaningful sequence. This business of abstracting (selecting) events and organizing them so that they bear some meaningful relationship to each other and to the central theme of a novel or play constitutes the storyteller's art. Plot construction, development of character, narrative structure, climax, denouement, and all the other things one talks about in technical literary criticism have reference to this organizing of symbolic experiences so that the whole complex of symbolic experiences (that is, the finished story or play) will have the desired impact on the reader.

All literary and dramatic enjoyment, whether of nursery tales, of films, or of "great literature," appears to involve to some degree the reader's imaginative identification of himself with the roles portrayed and his projection of himself into the situations described in the story.[2] Whether a reader is able to identify himself with the characters of a story depends both on the maturity of the story and the maturity of the reader. If a mature reader finds difficulty identifying himself with the hero of a cowboy story, it may be because he finds the hero too simple-minded a character to serve as an acceptable symbol for himself, and the villains and the events too improbable to serve as symbols for his own enemies and his own problems.

However, the simple-mindedness of the people and the improbability of the events of cowboy or detective movies contribute much to their popularity on television. We live in a complex civilization, in which the vast majority of us lead peaceful, unaggressive lives. When we are troubled by problems—when sales fall off or profits decline or our jobs are threatened or shipments do not arrive on time or customers complain—many, many things may be to blame: manufacturers, wholesalers, the stock market, the labor unions, high taxes, high rentals, the railroads, the government, local zoning regulations, or the problems of communication inevitable in large and complex societies. As a rule, there is no single villain or group of villains, no one agency, that can be the object of our wrath when things go wrong. Hence, the world of the television drama is comforting to come home to when the day's work is done: the "good guys" and the "bad guys" are clearly distinguishable, and all troubles are dissolved in a happy ending when the "bad guys" are defeated or dead after a heroic gunfight or car chase.

One reason for calling some people immature is that they are incapable of confronting defeat, tragedy, or unpleasantness of any kind. Such persons usually cannot endure an "unhappy ending" *even in a set of symbolic experiences.* Hence the widespread passion for happy endings in popular literature, so that even stories about unhappy events have to be made, in the end, to come out all right. The immature constantly need to be reassured that everything will always come out all right.

Readers who mature as they grow older, however, steadily increase the depth and range and subtlety of their symbolic experiences. Under the guidance of skilled writers who have accurately observed the world and have been able to organize their observations in significant ways, the mature reader may symbolically experience murder, guilt, religious exalta-

---

[2] At what age does the capacity for imaginative identification of oneself with the roles portrayed in a story begin? I would suggest, on the basis of very limited observation, that it begins around age two or earlier. An interesting test case is to read the story of the Three Bears to a very small child to see when he or she begins to identify with Baby Bear or with Goldilocks.

tion, bankruptcy, the loss of friends, the discovery of gold mines or new philosophical principles, or the sense of desolation following a locust invasion in North Dakota. Each new symbolic experience means the enrichment of the reader's insight into people and events.

As we progress in our reading, our consciousness widens. Gradually, the "maps" which we have inside our heads become fuller, more accurate pictures of the actual "territories" of human character and behavior under many different conditions and in many different times. Gradually, too, our increased insight gives us sympathy with our fellow human beings everywhere. The pharaohs of Egypt, the Tibetan priest behind his ceremonial mask, the Roman political exile, and the embittered inner-city youth are presented to us by the novelist, the poet, and the playwright, at levels of vivid and intimate description, so that we learn how they lived, what they worried about, and how they felt. When the lives of other people, of whatever time and place, are examined in this way, we discover to our amazement that they are all people. This discovery is the basis of all civilized human relationships. If we remain uncivilized—whether in community, industrial, national, or international relationships—it is largely because most of us have not yet made this discovery. Literature is one of the important instruments to that end.

Science and Literature

By means of scientific communication, with its international systems of weights and measures, international systems of botanical and zoological nomenclature, international mathematical symbols, we are enabled to exchange information with each other, pool our observations, and acquire collective control over our environment. By means of affective communication—by conversation and gesture when we can see each other, but by literature and other arts when we cannot—we come to understand each other, to cease being brutishly suspicious of each other, and gradually to realize the profound community that exists between us and our fellow human beings. Science, in short, makes us able to cooperate; the arts enlarge our sympathies so that we become willing to cooperate.

BOOK TWO
Language and Thought

He [the student of politics] must also be on his guard against the old words, for the words persist when the reality that lay behind them has changed. It is inherent in our intellectual activity that we seek to imprison reality in our description of it. Soon, long before we realize it, it is we who become the prisoners of the description. From that point on, our ideas degenerate into a kind of folklore which we pass to each other, fondly thinking we are still talking of the reality around us.

Thus we talk of free enterprise, of capitalist society, of the rights of free association, of parliamentary government, as though all of these words stand for the same things they formerly did. Social institutions are what they do, not necessarily what we say they do. It is the verb that matters, not the noun.

If this is not understood, we become symbol worshipers. The categories we once evolved and which were the tools we used in our intercourse with reality become hopelessly blunted. In these circumstances the social and political realities we are supposed to be grappling with change and reshape themselves independently of the collective impact of our ideas. We become the creature and no longer the partner of social realities. As we fumble with outworn categories our political vitality is sucked away and we stumble from one situation to another, without chart, without compass, and with the steering wheel lashed to a course we are no longer following.

This is the real point of danger for a political party and for the leaders and thinkers who inspire it. For if they are out of touch with reality, the masses are not.   ANEURIN BEVAN, *In Place of Fear*

Prologue

The Story of A-Town and B-Ville: A Semantic Parable

ONCE UPON A TIME, said the professor, there were two small communities, spiritually as well as geographically situated at a considerable distance from each other. They had, however, this problem in common: both were hard hit by a recession, so that in each of the towns there were about one hundred heads of families unemployed.

The leaders of A-town, the first community, were substantial and sound-thinking business people. The unemployed tried hard, as unemployed people usually do, to find jobs; but the situation did not improve. The city leaders had been brought up to believe that there is always enough work for everyone, if you only look for it hard enough. Comforting themselves with this doctrine, the leaders could have shrugged their shoulders and turned their backs on the problem, except for the fact that they were genuinely kindhearted. They could not bear to see the unemployed workers and families starving. In order to prevent hardship, they felt that they had to provide these people with some means of sustenance. Their principles told them, nevertheless, that if people were given something for nothing, it would demoralize their character. Naturally this made the city fathers even more unhappy, because they were faced with the horrible choice of (1) letting the unemployed starve, or (2) destroying their moral character.

The solution they finally hit upon, after much debate and soul-searching, was this. They decided to give the unemployed families "welfare payments" of five hundred dollars a month. (They considered using the English term "dole," but with their characteristic American penchant for euphemism, they decided on the less offensive term.) To make sure that the unemployed would not take their unearned payments too much for granted, however, they decided that the "welfare" was to be accompanied by a moral lesson, to wit: the obtaining of the assistance would be made so difficult, humiliating, and disagreeable that there would be no temptation for anyone to go through the process unless it was absolutely necessary; the moral disapproval of the community would be turned upon the recipients of the money at all times in such a way that they would try hard to get "off welfare" and "regain their self-respect." Some even proposed that people on welfare be denied the vote, so that the moral lesson would be

Words forming thought and vice versa

more deeply impressed upon them. Others suggested that their names be published at regular intervals in the newspapers. The city fathers had enough faith in the goodness of human nature to expect that the recipients would be grateful, since they were getting something for nothing, something for which they hadn't worked.

When the plan was put into operation, however, the recipients of the welfare checks proved to be an ungrateful, ugly bunch. They seemed to resent the cross-examinations and inspections at the hands of the "welfare investigators," who, they said, took advantage of a person's misery to snoop into every detail of private life. In spite of uplifting editorials in the A-town *Tribune* telling them how grateful they ought to be, the recipients of welfare refused to learn any moral lessons, declaring that they were "just as good as anybody else." When, for example, they permitted themselves the rare luxury of a movie, a six-pack of beer, or an evening of bingo, their neighbors looked at them sourly, as if to say, "I work hard and pay my taxes just in order to support loafers like you in idleness and pleasure." This attitude, which was fairly characteristic of those members of the community who still had jobs, further embittered the welfare recipients, so that they showed even less gratitude as time went on and were constantly on the lookout for insults, real or imaginary, from people who might think that they weren't as good as anybody else. A number of them took to moping all day long; one or two even committed suicide. Others, feeling that they had failed to provide, found it hard to look their families in the face. Children whose parents were "on welfare" felt inferior to classmates whose parents were not "public charges." Some of these children developed inferiority complexes that affected not only their grades at school, but their lives and self-concepts after they left school. Drug abuse and alcoholism increased. Finally, several welfare recipients felt they could stand their loss of self-respect no longer and decided, after many efforts to gain honest jobs, that they would earn money by their own efforts even if they had to rob. They did so and were caught and sent to the state penitentiary.

The recession, therefore, hit A-town very hard. The welfare policy had averted starvation, no doubt, but suicide, personal quarrels, unhappy homes, the weakening of social organizations, the maladjustment of children, and finally, crime, had resulted. A culture in which recipients felt themselves unworthy, and felt little responsibility or control over their own lives, was created. The town was divided in two, the "haves" and the "have-nots," so that there was class hatred. People shook their heads sadly and declared that it all went to prove over again what they had known from the beginning, that giving people something for nothing inevitably demoralizes their characters. The citizens of A-town gloomily waited for prosperity to return, with less and less hope as time went on.

The story of the other community, B-ville, was entirely different. B-ville was a relatively isolated town, too far out of the way to be reached by Rotary Club speakers and other dispensers of conventional wisdom. One of the city commissioners, however, who was something of an economist, explained to the other commissioners that unemployment, like sickness, accident, fire, tornado, or death, hits unexpectedly in modern society, irrespective of the victim's merits or deserts. He went on to say that B-ville's homes, parks, streets, industries, and everything else B-ville was proud of, had been built by the work and taxes of these same people who were now unemployed. He then proposed to apply a principle of insurance: if the contribution these unemployed people had previously made to the community could be regarded as a form of "premium" paid to the community against a time of misfortune, payments now made to them to prevent their starvation could be regarded as "insurance claims." He therefore proposed that all persons of good repute who had worked in the community in some line of useful endeavor, whether as machinists, clerks, or bank managers, be regarded as "citizen policyholders," having "claims" against the city in the case of unemployment for five hundred dollars a month until such time as they might again be employed. Naturally, he had to talk very slowly and patiently, since the idea was entirely new to his fellow commissioners. But he described his plan as a "straight business proposition," and finally they were persuaded. They worked out in detail, to everyone's satisfaction, the conditions under which citizens should be regarded as policyholders in the city's social insurance plan, and decided to give checks for five hundred dollars a month to the heads of each of B-ville's indigent families.

B-ville's "claim adjusters," whose duty it was to investigate the claims of the citizen "policyholders," had a much better time than A-town's "welfare investigators." While the latter had been resentfully regarded as snoopers, the former, having no moral lesson to teach but simply a business transaction to carry out, treated their clients with businesslike courtesy and got the same amount of information as the welfare investigators had, with considerably less difficulty. There were no hard feelings.

It further happened, fortunately, that news of B-ville's plans reached a liberal newspaper editor in the big city at the other end of the state.

This writer described the plan in a leading feature story headed "B-VILLE LOOKS AHEAD. Adventure in Social Pioneering Launched by Upper Valley Community." As a result of this publicity, inquiries about the plan began to come to the city hall even before the first checks were mailed out. This led, naturally, to a considerable feeling of pride on the part of the commissioners, who, being boosters, felt that this was a wonderful opportunity to put B-ville on the map.

Accordingly, the commissioners decided that instead of simply mailing out the checks as they had originally intended, they would publicly present the first checks at a monster civic ceremony. They invited the governor, who was glad to come to bolster his none-too-enthusiastic support in that locality; the president of the state university; the state senator from their district; and other functionaries. They decorated the National Guard Armory with flags and got out the American Legion Fife and Drum Corps, the Boy Scouts, and other civic organizations.

At the big celebration, each family who was to receive a "social insurance check" was marched up to the platform to accept it, and the governor and the mayor shook hands with each of them as they came trooping up in their best clothes. Fine speeches were made; there was much cheering and shouting; pictures of the event showing the recipients of the checks shaking hands with the mayor, and the governor patting the heads of the children, were not only published in the local papers but broadcast on the evening news.

The recipients of these insurance checks, therefore, felt personally honored, that B-ville was a wonderful little town, and that they could face unemployment with greater courage and assurance since the community was so supportive of them. The men and women found themselves being kidded in a friendly way by their acquaintances for having been "up there with the big shots," shaking hands with the governor, and so on. The children at school found themselves envied for having been on television. All in all, B-ville's unemployed did not commit suicide, were not haunted by a sense of failure, did not turn to crime and drugs, did not manifest personal maladjustments, did not develop class hatred as the result of their five hundred dollars a month. . . .

At the conclusion of the professor's story, the discussion began:

"That just goes to show," said the Advertising Executive, who was known as a realistic thinker, "what good promotional work can do. B-ville's city council had real advertising sense, and that civic ceremony was a masterpiece. . . . made everyone happy . . . put over the scheme in a big way. Reminds me of the way we do things in our business: as soon as we called horse-mackerel "tuna-fish," we developed a big market for it. I suppose if you called welfare 'insurance,' you could actually get people to like it, couldn't you?"

"What do you mean, 'calling' it insurance?" asked the Social Worker. "B-ville's scheme wasn't welfare at all. It *was* insurance."

"Good grief! Do you realize what you're saying?" cried the Advertising Executive in surprise. "Are you implying that those people had any *right* to that money? All I said was that it's a good idea to *disguise* welfare as insurance if it's going to make people happier. But it's still welfare, no matter what you *call* it. It's all right to kid the public along to reduce discontent, but we don't need to kid ourselves as well!"

"But they *do* have a right to that money! They're not getting something for nothing. It's insurance. They did something for the community, and that's their prem—"

"Say, are you crazy?"

"Who's crazy?"

"You're crazy. Welfare is welfare, isn't it? If you'd only call things by their right names. . . . "

"But, confound it, insurance is insurance, isn't it?"

P.S. Those who have concluded that the point of the story is that the Social Worker and the Advertising Executive were "only arguing about different names for the same thing" are asked to reread the story and explain what they mean by (1) "only" and (2) "the same thing."

CHAPTER 9

How We Know
What We Know

The crucial point to be considered in a study of language behavior is the relationship of language and reality, between words and not-words. Except as we understand this relationship, we run the grave risk of straining the delicate connection between words and facts, of permitting our words to go wild, and so of creating for ourselves fabrications of fantasy and delusion.   WENDELL JOHNSON

Bessie, the Cow

THE UNIVERSE IS in a perpetual state of flux. The stars are in constant motion, growing, cooling, exploding. The earth itself is not unchanging; mountains are being worn away, rivers are altering their channels, valleys are deepening. All life is also a process of change, through birth, growth, decay, and death. Even what we used to call "inert matter"—chairs and tables and stones—is not inert, as we now know, for, at the submicroscopic level, they are whirls of electrons and protons. If a table looks today very much as it did yesterday or as it did a hundred years ago, it is not because it has not changed, but because the changes have been too minute for our coarse perceptions.

To modern science, there is no "solid matter." If matter looks "solid" to us, it does so only because its motion is too rapid or too minute to be felt. It is solid only in the sense that a rapidly rotating color chart is "white" or a rapidly spinning top is "standing still." Our senses are extremely limited, so that we constantly have to use instruments such as microscopes, telescopes, speedometers, stethoscopes, and seismographs to detect and record occurrences that our senses are not able to record directly. The way in which we happen to see and feel things is the result of the peculiarities of our nervous system. There are "sights" we cannot see, and, as even children know today with their high-frequency dog whistles, "sounds" that we cannot hear. It is absurd, therefore, to imagine that we ever perceive anything "as it really is."

Inadequate as our senses are, with the help of instruments they tell us a great deal. The discovery of microorganisms with the use of the microscope has given us a measure of control over bacteria; we cannot see, hear, or feel radio waves, but we can create and transform them to useful purpose. Most of our conquest of the external world, in engineering, in chemistry, and in medicine, is due to our use of mechanical contrivances of one kind or another to increase the capacity of our nervous systems. In modern life, our unaided senses are not half enough to get us about in the world. We cannot even obey speed laws or compute our gas and electric bills without mechanical aids to perception.

To return, then, to the relations between words and what they stand for, let us say that there is before us "Bessie," a cow. Bessie is a living organism, constantly changing, constantly ingesting food and air, transforming it, getting rid of it again. Her blood is circulating, her nerves are sending messages. Viewed microscopically, she is a mass of variegated corpuscles, cells, and bacterial organisms; viewed from the point of view of modern physics, she is a perpetual dance of electrons. What she is in her entirety, we can never know; even if we could at any precise moment say what she was, at the next moment she would have changed enough so that our description would no longer be accurate. It is impossible to say completely what Bessie or anything else really *is*. Bessie is no static "object," but a dynamic *process*.

The Bessie that we experience, however, is something else again. We experience only a small fraction of the total Bessie: the lights and shadows of her exterior, her motions, her general configuration, the noises she makes, and the sensations she presents to our sense of touch. *And because of our previous experience, we observe resemblances in her to certain other animals to which, in the past, we have applied the word "cow."*

The Process of Abstracting

The "object" of our experience, then, is not the "thing in itself," but *an interaction between our nervous systems (with all their imperfections) and something outside them.* Bessie is unique—there is nothing else in the universe exactly like her in all respects. But our nervous systems, automatically *abstracting* or selecting from the Bessie-in-process those features of hers in which she resembles other animals of like shape, functions, and habits, *classify* her as "cow."

When we say, then, that "Bessie is a cow," we are only noting the process-Bessie's resemblances to other "cows" and *ignoring differences.* What is more, we are leaping a huge chasm: from the dynamic process-Bessie, a whirl of electrochemico-neural eventfulness, to a relatively static "idea," "concept," or *word*, "cow". The reader is referred to the diagram entitled "The Abstraction Ladder" on page 101.[1]

As the diagram illustrates, the "object" we see is an abstraction of the lowest level, but it is still an abstraction, since it leaves out characteristics of the process that is the real Bessie. The *word* "Bessie" (cow$_1$) is the lowest *verbal* level of abstraction, leaving out further characteristics—the differences between Bessie yesterday and Bessie today, between Bessie today and Bessie tomorrow—and selecting only the similarities. The word "cow" selects only the similarities between Bessie (cow$_1$), Daisy (cow$_2$), Rosie (cow$_3$), and so on, and therefore leaves out still more about Bessie. The word "livestock" selects or abstracts only the features that Bessie has in common with pigs, chickens, goats, and sheep. The term "farm asset" abstracts only the features Bessie has in common with barns, fences, livestock, furniture, generating plants, and tractors, and is therefore on a very high level of abstraction.

Our concern here with the process of abstracting may seem strange, since the study of language is all too often restricted to matters of pronunci-

---

[1] The "Abstraction Ladder" is based on the "Structural Differential," a diagram originated by Alfred Korzybski to explain the process of abstracting. For a further explanation both of the diagram and of the process it illustrates, see his *Science and Sanity: An Introduction to Non-Aristotelian Systems and General Semantics* (1933), especially Chapter 25.

ABSTRACTION LADDER
Start reading from the bottom up

8. "wealth"

8. The word "wealth" is at an extremely high level of abstraction, omitting *almost* all reference to the characteristics of Bessie.

7. "asset"

7. When Bessie is referred to as an "asset," still more of her characteristics are left out.

6. "farm assets"

6. When Bessie is included among "farm assets," reference is made only to what she has in common with all other salable items on the farm.

5. "livestock"

5. When Bessie is referred to as "livestock," only those characteristics she has in common with pigs, chickens, goats, etc., are referred to.

4. "cow"

4. The word "cow" stands for the characteristics we have abstracted as common to cow_1, cow_2, cow_3 . . . cow_n. Characteristics peculiar to specific cows are left out.

3. "Bessie"

3. The word "Bessie" (cow_1) is the *name* we give to the object of perception of level 2. The name *is not* the object; it merely *stands for* the object and omits reference to many of the characteristics of the object.

2.

2. The cow we perceive is not the word, but the object of experience, that which our nervous system abstracts (selects) from the totality that constitutes the process-cow. Many of the characteristics of the process-cow are left out.

1. The cow ultimately consists of atoms, electrons, etc., according to present-day scientific inference. Characteristics (represented by circles) are infinite at this level and ever-changing. This is the *process level.*

ation, spelling, vocabulary, grammar, and such. The methods by which composition and oratory are taught in many school systems seem to be largely responsible for this widespread notion that the way to study words is to concentrate one's attention exclusively on words.

But as we know from everyday experience, learning language is not simply a matter of learning words; it is a matter of correctly relating our words to the things and happenings for which they stand. We learn the language of baseball by playing or watching the game *and studying what goes on.* It is not enough for children to learn to *say* "cookie" or "dog"; they must be able to use these words in their proper relationship to nonverbal cookies and nonverbal dogs before we can grant that they are learning the language. As Wendell Johnson has said, "The study of language begins properly with a study of what language is about."

Once we begin to concern ourselves with what language is about, we are at once thrown into a consideration of how the human nervous system works. When we call Beau (the Boston terrier), Pedro (the chihuahua), Snuffles (the English bulldog), and Shane (the Irish wolfhound)—creatures that differ greatly in size, shape, appearance, and behavior—by the same name, "dog," our nervous system has obviously gone to work *abstracting* what is common to them all, ignoring for the time being the differences among them.

Why We Must Abstract

This process of abstracting, of leaving characteristics out, is an indispensable convenience. To illustrate by still another example, suppose that we live in an isolated village of four families, each owning a house. A's house is referred to as *maga;* B's house is *biyo;* C's is *kata,* and D's is *pelel.* This is quite satisfactory for ordinary purposes of communication in the village, unless a discussion arises about building a new house—a spare one, let us say. We cannot refer to the projected house by any one of the four words we have for the existing houses, since each of these has too specific a meaning. We must find a *general* term, at a higher level of abstraction, that means "something that has certain characteristics in common with *maga, biyo, kata,* and *pelel,* and yet is not A's, B's, C's, or D's. Since this is much too complicated to say each time, an *abbreviation* must be invented. So we choose the noise, *house.* Out of such needs do our words come—they are a form of shorthand. The invention of a new abstraction is a great step forward, since it *makes discussion possible*—as, in this case, not only the discussion of a fifth house, but of all future houses we may build or see in our travels or dream about.

A producer of educational films once remarked to me that it is impossible to make a shot of "work." You can shoot Joe hoeing potatoes, Susan polishing her car, Bill spraying paint on a barn, but never just "work."

Words defining words

"Work," too, is a shorthand term, standing, at a higher level of abstraction, for a characteristic that a multitude of activities, from dishwashing to navigation to running an advertising agency to governing a nation, have in common. The special meaning that "work" has in physics is also clearly derived from abstracting the common characteristics of many different kinds of work. ("A transference of energy from one body to another, resulting in the motion or displacement of the body acted upon, in the direction of the acting force and against resistance." Funk and Wagnalls, *Standard College Dictionary.*)

The indispensability of this process of abstracting can again be illustrated by what we do when we "calculate." The word "calculate" originates from the Latin word *calculus*, meaning "pebble," and derives its present meaning from such ancient practices as putting a pebble into a box for each sheep as it left the fold, so that one could tell, by checking the sheep returning at night against the pebbles, whether any had been lost. Primitive as this example of calculation is, it will serve to show why mathematics works. Each pebble is, in this example, an abstraction representing the "oneness" of each sheep—its numerical value. And because we are abstracting from extensional events on clearly understood and uniform principles, the numerical facts about the pebbles are also, barring unforeseen circumstances, numerical facts about the sheep. Our x's and y's and other mathematical symbols are abstractions made from numerical abstractions, and are therefore abstractions of still higher level. And they are useful in predicting occurrences and in getting work done because, since they are abstractions properly and uniformly made from starting points in the extensional world, the relations revealed by the symbols will be, again barring unforeseen circumstances, relations existing in the extensional world.

On Definitions

Definitions, contrary to popular opinion, tell us nothing about things. They only describe people's linguistic habits; that is, they tell us what words people use under what conditions. Definitions should be understood as *statements about language.*

House. This word, at the next higher level of abstraction, can be substituted for the more cumbersome expression, "Something that has characteristics in common with Bill's bungalow, Jordan's cottage, Mrs. Smith's guest home, Dr. Jones's mansion . . . "

Red. A feature that rubies, roses, ripe tomatoes, robins' breasts, uncooked beef, and lipsticks have in common is abstracted, and this word expresses that abstraction.

Kangaroo. Where the biologist would say "herbivorous mammal, a marsupial of the family Macropodidae," ordinary people say "kangaroo."

Now it will be observed that while the definitions of "house" and "red" given here point *down* the abstraction ladder (see the charts) to *lower* levels of abstraction, the definition of "kangaroo" remains at the same level. That is to say, in the case of "house," we could if necessary go and *look* at Bill's bungalow, Jordan's cottage, Mrs. Smith's guest home, and Dr. Jones's mansion, and figure out for ourselves what features they seem to have in common; in this way, we might begin to understand under what conditions to use the word "house." But all we know about "kangaroo" from the above is that where some people say one thing, other people say another. That is, when we stay at the *same* level of abstraction in giving a definition, we do not give any information, unless, of course, the listener or reader is already sufficiently familiar with the defining words to work down the abstraction ladder. Dictionaries, in order to save space, have to assume in many cases such familiarity with the language on the part of the reader. But where the assumption is unwarranted, definitions at the same level of abstraction are worse than useless. Looking up "indifference" in some pocket dictionaries, we find it defined as "apathy": we look up "apathy" and find it defined as "indifference."

Even more useless, however, are the definitions that go *up* the abstraction ladder to *higher* levels of abstraction—the kind most of us tend to make automatically. Try the following experiment on an unsuspecting friend:

"What is meant by the word *red?*"
"It's a color."
"What's a color?"
"Why, it's a quality things have."
"What's a *quality?*"
"Say, what are you trying to do, anyway?"

You have pushed him into the clouds. If, on the other hand, we habitually go *down* the abstraction ladder to *lower* levels of abstraction when we are asked the meaning of a word, we are less likely to get lost in verbal mazes; we will tend to "have our feet on the ground" and know what we are talking about. This habit displays itself in an answer such as this:

"What is meant by the word *red?*"
"Well, the next time you see some cars stopped at an intersection, look at the traffic light facing them. Also, you might go to the fire department and see how their trucks are painted."

Thus, some of the most helpful definitions are those that include examples with which readers or listeners may be familiar. A writer provides details—verbal images, examples, illustrations—so readers can understand more thoroughly, so readers will have more opportunities to link their own experiences to what they read.

"Let's Define Our Terms"

An extremely widespread instance of an unrealistic (and ultimately superstitious) attitude toward definitions is found in the common academic prescription, "Let's define our terms so that we shall all know what we are talking about." As we have already seen in Chapter 4, the fact that a golfer, for example, cannot define golfing terms is no indication that he cannot understand and use them. Conversely, the fact that we can define a large number of words is no guarantee that we know what objects or operations they stand for in concrete situations. Having defined a word, people often believe that some kind of understanding has been established, ignoring the fact that the words in the definition often conceal even more serious confusions and ambiguities than the word defined. If we happen to discover this fact and try to remedy matters by defining the defining words, and then, finding ourselves still confused, we go on to define the words in the definitions of the defining words, we quickly find ourselves in a hopeless snarl. The only way to avoid this snarl is to keep definitions to a minimum and to point to extensional levels wherever necessary; in writing and speaking, this means giving specific examples of what we are talking about.

Operational Definitions

Another way to keep extensional levels in mind, when definitions are called for, is to use what physicist P. W. Bridgman called "operational definitions." As he says:

To find the length of an object, we have to perform certain physical operations. The concept of length is therefore fixed when the operations by which length is measured are fixed. . . . In general, we mean by any concept nothing more than a set of operations; *the concept is synonymous with the corresponding set of operations.*[2]

The operational definition, then, as Anatol Rapoport explains, is one that tells you *"what to do* and *what to observe* in order to bring the thing defined or its effects within the range of one's experience." He gives the following simple example of how to define "weight": go to a railroad station or drugstore, look for a scale, stand on it, put in a penny, read the number at which the pointer comes to rest. *That* is your weight. But suppose different scales give different readings? Then your weight can be said to be within the range of, say, 140 to 145 pounds. With more accurate scales you might get closer readings, such as 142 pounds plus-or-minus one. *But there is no "property" called weight that exists apart from the operations of measuring it.* As Rapoport says, "If the only way we can be aware of the amount of weight is by means of the scale, then the very definition of weight has to be in terms of the scale."[3]

Such, then, is the scientific, or "operational" point of view toward definition—one that attempts rigidly to exclude non-extensional, non-sense statements. We can extend this idea from science to the problems of everyday life and thought. Just as there is no such thing as "length" apart from the operations by which length is measured, there is likewise no "democracy" apart from the sum total of democratic *practices*, such as universal franchise, freedom of speech, equality before the law, and so on. Similarly, there is no such thing as "brotherhood" apart from brotherly behavior, nor "charity" apart from charitable actions.

The operational point of view does much to keep our words meaningful. When people say things like "Let's have no more of *progressive* methods in our schools," "Let's get back to *sound business principles* in running our county government," "Let's try to do the *Christian* thing," "Let's restore *family values*," we are entitled to ask, "What do you mean—extensionally speaking?" To ask this question often—of ourselves as well as of others—is to do our bit toward reducing the vast amount of non-sense that is written, spoken, and shouted in this incredibly garrulous world.

The best examples in everyday life of operational definitions are to be found in cookbooks, which describe the *operations* by means of which the entity defined may be extensionally experienced. Thus: "*Steak Diane.* Slice tenderloin beef very thin and give it a few whacks with a meat mallet to flatten it even more; sprinkle with salt and pepper to taste. Have your pan very hot . . . " (*The Sunset Cook Book*). Writers and speakers would do well to study cookbooks occasionally to increase the clarity and verifiability of their utterances.

[2] *The Logic of Modern Physics* (1927), p. 5.
[3] *Operational Philosophy* (1953), p. 25.

Chasing Oneself in Verbal Circles

In other words, the kind of "thinking" we must be extremely wary of is that which *never* leaves the higher verbal levels of abstraction, the kind that never points *down* the abstraction ladder to lower levels of abstraction and from there to the extensional world:

"What do you mean by *democracy?*"
"Democracy means the preservation of human rights."
"What do you mean by *rights?*"
"By rights I mean those privileges God grants to all of us—I mean man's inherent privileges."
"Such as?"
"Liberty, for example."
"What do you mean by *liberty?*"
"Religious and political freedom."
"And what does that mean?"
"Religious and political freedom is what we enjoy under a democracy."

Of course it is possible to talk meaningfully about democracy, as Jefferson and Lincoln have done, as Frederick Jackson Turner does in *The Frontier in American History*, as Karl R. Popper does in *The Open Society and Its Enemies*, as Robert Dahl does in *Pluralist Democracy in the United States; Conflict and Consent*—to name only a few examples that come to mind. Speakers who never leave the higher levels of abstraction, however, may fail to notice when they are saying something and when they are not.

This is by no means to say, however, that we must never make extensionally meaningless noises. When we use directive language, when we talk about the future, when we utter ritual language or engage in social conversation, and when we express our feelings, we often make utterances that have no extensional verifiability. It must not be overlooked that our highest ratiocinative and imaginative powers are derived from the fact that symbols *are* independent of things symbolized, so that we are free not only to go quickly from low to extremely high levels of abstraction (from "canned peas" to "groceries" to "commodities" to "national wealth") and to manipulate symbols even when the things they stand for cannot be so manipulated ("If all the freight cars in the country were hooked up to each other in one long line . . . "), but we are also free to manufacture symbols at will, even if they stand only for abstractions made from other abstractions and not anything in the extensional world. Mathematicians, for example, often play with symbols and ideas that have no extensional content just to find out what can be done with them; this is called "pure mathematics." And pure mathematics is far from being a useless pastime, because mathematical systems that are elaborated with no extensional application in mind often prove later to be applicable in useful and unforeseen ways.

Mathematicians, however, when they are dealing with extensionally meaningless symbols, usually know what they are doing. *We*, likewise, must know what we are doing.

Nevertheless, all of us (including mathematicians), when we speak the language of everyday life, often make meaningless noises without knowing that we are doing so. We have already seen what confusion this can lead to. The fundamental purpose of the abstraction ladder, as shown both in this chapter and the next, is to make us aware of the process of abstracting.

The Distrust of Abstractions

We may, using our abstraction ladder, allocate statements as well as words to differing levels of abstraction. "Mrs. Levin makes good potato pancakes" may be regarded as a statement at a fairly low level of abstraction, although, to be sure, it leaves out many elements, such as (1) the meaning of "goodness" in potato pancakes, and (2) the infrequent occasions when her pancakes fail to turn out well. "Mrs. Levin is a good cook" is a statement at a higher level of abstraction, covering Mrs. Levin's skill not only with potato pancakes, but also with roasts, pickles, noodles, strudels, and so on, nevertheless omitting *specific* mention of what she can accomplish. "Chicagoans are good cooks" is a statement at a still higher level of abstraction; it can be made (if at all) only from observation of the cooking of a statistically significant number of Chicagoans. "The culinary art has reached a high state in America" would be a still more highly abstract statement and, if made at all, would have to be based not only on observation of the Mrs. Levins of Chicago, New York, San Francisco, Denver, Albuquerque, and Atlanta, but also on observation of the quality of meals served in hotels and restaurants, the quality of training in high school and college departments of home economics, the quality of writings on culinary art in American books and magazines, and many other relevant factors.

Unfortunately, though understandably, there is a tendency in our times to speak with contempt of "mere abstractions." The ability to climb to higher and higher levels of abstraction is a distinctively human trait without which none of our philosophical or scientific insights would be possible. In order to have a science of chemistry, one *has* to be able to think of "H_2O," leaving out of consideration for the time being the wetness of water, the hardness of ice, the pearliness of dew, and the other extensional characteristics of H_2O at the objective level. In order to have a study called "ethics," one has to be able to think of what elements in ethical behavior have in common under different conditions and in different civilizations; one has to abstract that which is common to the behavior of the ethical carpenter, the ethical politician, the ethical businessman, and the ethical soldier—and that which is common to the laws of conduct of the Buddhist, the Orthodox Jew, the Confucian, the Christian. Thinking that is most abstract can also be that which is most generally useful. The famous injunction of Jesus, "And as ye would that men should do to you, do ye also to them likewise," is, from this point of view, a brilliant generalization of more particular directives—a generalization at so high a level of abstraction that it appears to be applicable to all people in all cultures.

But high-level abstractions acquire a bad reputation because they are so often used, consciously or unconsciously, to confuse and befuddle people. Depriving blacks of their votes in violation of the Constitution of the United States was at one time spoken of as "preserving states' rights." The consequences of such free, and often irresponsible, use of high-level abstractions in public controversy and special pleading is that a significant portion of the population has grown cynical about *all* abstractions.

But, as the abstraction ladder has shown, *all we know are abstractions.* What you know about the chair you are sitting in is an abstraction from the totality of the chair. When you eat white bread you cannot tell by the taste whether or not it has been "enriched by vitamin B" as it says on the wrapper; you simply have to trust that the process (from which the words "vitamin B" are abstracted) was performed. What you know about your spouse—even a spouse of thirty years—is again an abstraction. Distrusting all abstractions simply does not make sense.

The test of abstractions then is not whether they are "high-level" or "low-level" abstractions, but *whether they are referable to lower levels.* If one makes a statement about "culinary arts in America," one should be able to refer the statement down the abstraction ladder to particulars of American restaurants, American domestic science, American techniques of food preservation, down to Mrs. Levin in her kitchen. If one makes a statement about "civil rights in Wisconsin," one should know something about national, state, and local statutes; one should also know something about the behavior of police officers, magistrates, judges, academic authorities, hotel managers, and the general public in Wisconsin, all of whose acts and whose decisions affect that minimum of decent treatment in the courts, in politics, and in society that we call "civil rights." A preacher, a professor, a journalist, or a politician whose high-level abstractions can systematically and surely be referred to lower-level abstractions is not only talking but saying something.

"Dead-Level Abstracting"

The late professor Wendell Johnson of the University of Iowa, in *People in Quandaries*, discusses a linguistic phenomenon that he calls "dead-level abstracting." Some people, it appears, remain more or less permanently stuck at certain levels of the abstraction ladder, some on the lower levels, some on the very high levels. There are those, for example, who go in for "persistent low-level abstracting":

Probably all of us know certain people who seem able to talk on and on without ever drawing any very general conclusions. For example, there is the back-fence chatter that is made up of he said and then I said and then she said and I said and then he said, far into the afternoon, ending with, "Well, that's *just* what I told him!" Letters describing vacation trips frequently illustrate this sort of language, detailing places seen, times of arrival and departure, the foods eaten and the prices paid, whether the beds were hard or soft, etc.

A similar inability to get to higher levels of abstraction characterizes certain types of mental patients who suffer, as Johnson says, "a general blocking of the abstracting process." They go on indefinitely, reciting insignificant facts, never able to pull them together to frame a generalization that would give a meaning to the facts.

Other speakers remain stuck at higher levels of abstraction, with little or no contact with lower levels. Such language remains permanently in the clouds. As Johnson says:

It is characterized especially by vagueness, ambiguity, even utter meaninglessness. Simply by saving various circulars, brochures, free copies of "new thought" magazines, etc. . . . it is possible to accumulate in a short time quite a sizable file of illustrative material. Much more, of course, is to be found on library shelves, on newsstands, and in radio programs. Everyday conversation, classroom lectures, political speeches, commencement addresses, and various kinds of group forums and round-table discussions provide a further abundant source of *words cut loose from their moorings.* [Italics supplied.]

(I once heard of a course in esthetics given at a large midwestern university in which an entire semester was devoted to Art and Beauty and the principles underlying them, and during which the professor, even when asked by students, persistently declined to name specific paintings, symphonies, sculptures, or objects of beauty to which his principles might apply. "We are interested," he would say, "in principles, not in particulars.")

There are psychiatric implications to dead-level abstracting on higher levels, too, because when maps proliferate wildly without any reference to a territory, the result can only be delusion. But whether at higher or lower levels, dead-level abstracting is, as Johnson says, always dull:

The low-level speaker frustrates you because he leaves you with no directions as to what to do with the basketful of information he has given you. The high-level speaker frustrates you because he simply doesn't tell you what he is talking about. . . . Being thus frustrated, and being further blocked because the rules of courtesy (or of attendance at class lectures) require that one remain quietly seated until the speaker has finished, there is little for one to do but daydream, doodle, or simply fall asleep.

It is obvious, then, that interesting speech and writing, as well as clear thinking and psychological well-being, require the constant interplay of higher-level and lower-level abstractions, and the constant interplay of the verbal levels with the nonverbal ("object") levels. In science, this interplay goes on constantly, hypotheses being checked against observations, predictions against extensional results. (Scientific *writing*, however, as exemplified in technical journals, offers some appalling examples of *almost* dead-level abstracting, which is the reason so much of it is hard to read. Nevertheless, the interplay between verbal and nonverbal experimental levels does continue, or else we would not have science.)

The work of good novelists and poets also represents this constant interplay between higher and lower levels of abstraction. A "significant" novelist or poet is one whose message has a high level of *general* usefulness in providing insight into life, but he gives his generalizations an impact and persuasiveness through an ability to observe and describe actual social situations and states of mind. A memorable literary character, such as Sinclair Lewis's George F. Babbitt, has *descriptive* validity (at a low level of abstraction) as the picture of an individual, as well as a *general* validity as a picture of a "typical" American businessman of his time.

The great political leader is also one in whom there is interplay between higher and lower levels of abstraction. The ward heeler knows politics only at lower levels of abstraction: what promises or what acts will cause what people to vote as desired; his loyalties are not to principles (high-level abstractions) but to persons (for example, political bosses) and immediate advantages (low-level abstractions). The so-called impractical political theorist knows the high-level abstractions ("democracy," "civil rights," "social justice") but is not well enough acquainted with facts at lower levels of abstraction to get elected county registrar of deeds. But the political leaders to whom states and nations remain permanently grateful are those who are able, somehow or other, to achieve simultaneously higher-level aims ("freedom," "national unity," "justice") *and* lower-level aims ("better prices for potato farmers," "higher wages for textile workers," "judicial reform," "soil conservation").

The interesting writer, the informative speaker, the accurate thinker, and the sane individual operate on all levels of the abstraction ladder, moving quickly and gracefully and in orderly fashion from higher to lower, from lower to higher, with minds as lithe and deft and beautiful as monkeys in a tree.

CHAPTER 10

The Little Man Who Wasn't There

As I was going up the stair
I met a man who wasn't there.
He wasn't there again today.
I wish, I wish he'd stay away.

HUGHES MEARNS

Everybody is familiar with the fact that the ordinary man does not see things as they are, but only sees certain fixed types. . . . Mr. Walter Sickert is in the habit of telling his pupils that they are unable to draw any individual arm because they think of it as an arm; and because they think of it as an arm they think they know what it ought to be.

T. E. HULME

How Not to Start a Car

THE FOLLOWING NEWSPAPER story is presented in the hope that the reader will find it as instructive (and as depressing) as I did:

> More than one motorist has secretly wished he could do what Samuel Rios, 30, was accused of doing yesterday. Driving at 12:30 A.M. through Williamsburg, he swung around a corner and accidentally sideswiped a sedan parked at the curb in front of 141 Hopkins Street. Furious, police charged, Rios stopped, took the jack handle from his car trunk, and slam-banged the offending obstacle from windshield to tail-lights.
> *New York Post*

People in primitive societies often act in similar ways. They may "punish" the rock which caused them to stumble. When crops fail or rocks fall upon them, they make a deal with—offer sacrifices to—the "spirits" of vegetation or of the rocks, in order to obtain better treatment from them in the future. We too have reactions of similar kinds: sometimes, tripping over a chair, we kick it and call it names; some people, indeed, when they fail to get letters, get angry at the mail carrier. In all such behavior, we confuse the abstraction that is *inside* our heads with that which is *outside* and act as if the abstraction *were* the event in the outside world. We create in our heads an imaginary chair that maliciously trips us, and "punish" the extensional chair that bears ill will to nobody; we create an imaginary mail carrier who is holding back our mail, and bawl out the extensional mail carrier who would gladly bring us letters if there were any to bring.

Confusing Levels of Abstraction

In a wider sense we are confusing levels of abstraction—confusing that which is inside our heads with that which is outside—all the time. For example, we talk about a yellow pencil as if the yellowness were a property of the pencil, and not a product, as we have seen, of the interaction of something outside our skins with our own perceptions. We confuse, that is to say, the two lowest levels of the abstraction ladder (see page 101) and treat them as one. Properly speaking, we ought not to say, "The pencil is yellow," which is a statement that places the yellowness in the pencil; we might say instead, "I see something that has characteristics which lead me to call it 'pencil.' This thing that I call pencil has a further characteristic that leads me to call it 'yellow.'" We don't have to be that pedantic, of course, in the language of everyday life, but it should be observed that the latter statements take into consideration the part our nervous systems play in creating whatever pictures of reality we have in our heads while the former statement does not.

This habit of confusing that which is inside our skins and that which is outside is essentially a relic of prescientific patterns of thinking. The more complicated civilization becomes, the more conscious we must be that our nervous systems automatically leave out characteristics of the events before us. If we are not aware of characteristics left out, if we are not conscious of the process of abstracting, we make *seeing and believing a single process*. If, for example, you react to the third rattlesnake you encounter in your life as if it were identical with the abstraction you have in your head as the result of the two rattlesnakes you have seen, you may not be far afield in your reactions.

But words, as we have illustrated by means of the abstraction ladder, exist at still higher levels of abstraction than the objects of experience. The more words at extremely high levels of abstraction we hear or read, the more conscious we must be of the process of abstracting. For example, the word "rattlesnake" leaves out nearly every important feature of an actual rattlesnake. But if the word is vividly remembered as central to a complex of terrifying experiences, the word itself is capable of arousing the same feelings as a real rattlesnake. There are people, therefore, who turn pale at the *word*.

This, then, is the origin of word-magic. The word "rattlesnake" and the actual creature are felt to be one and the same thing, because they arouse the same feelings. This sounds like nonsense, of course, and it is nonsense. But from the point of view of a prescientific logic, it has its justification. As Lucien Lévy-Bruhl explains, primitive "logic" works on such a principle. The creature frightens us; the word frightens us; therefore the creature and the word are "the same"—not actually the same, perhaps, but there is a "mystical connection" between the two. This sense of "mystical connection" is Lévy-Bruhl's term for what we have called "necessary connection" in discussing naive attitudes towards symbols in Chapter 2. As a consequence of this naiveté, a "mystical power" is attributed to words. There come to be "fearful words," "unspeakable words"—words taking on the characteristics of what they stand for. The word "grammarian" is said to have referred at one time to a person who had magical power—one who was versed in "gramarye" and therefore could manipulate to advantage the mystical power of words.

The commonest form of this confusion of levels of abstraction, however, is illustrated by our reacting to the "conservative" to whom we have just been introduced ("I want you to meet Mr. Lee Buck, who is active in our new conservative movement on campus") as if he were identical with the abstraction "conservative" inside our heads. "If he is a conservative, he is OK"—or "He is a dangerous reactionary"—we are likely to say to ourselves, confusing the extensional conservative with our abstraction "conservative," which is the product not simply of the previous "conservatives" we have met, but also of all that we have been *told and have read* about "conservatives."

The Nature of Prejudice

To make the principles clearer, we shall use an example that is loaded with prejudices for many people: "Mr. Miller is a *Jew*." To such a statement, some "non-Jews" instantaneously have marked hostile reactions, for example, putting themselves on guard against what they expect to be Mr. Miller's sharp financial practices or excluding him from tenancy in an apartment complex or from membership in a fraternity or country club. That is to say, they may confuse this high-level abstraction, "Jew," and its accompanying erroneous connotations, with the extensional Mr. Miller and behave towards Mr. Miller as if he were identical with that abstraction. "Jew" is only one of thousands upon thousands of abstractions that may be applied to Mr. Miller, to whom such terms as "left-hander," "parent," "amateur golfer," "history teacher," "teetotaler," "Bostonian," and so on may possibly be equally applied. But the prejudiced person is unaware of all but the one abstraction—perhaps in most contexts the least relevant one—"Jew."

Moreover, the word "Jew" is perhaps one of the most complicated abstractions in the language—that is, one of the most difficult to refer systematically down the abstraction ladder to lower levels. Does "Jew" refer to a race, a religion, a nationality, a state of mind, a loosely knit community? If not these, what?

Being a Jew is not necessarily a matter of religion. Some high officials of Israel seldom set foot in a synagogue, except on special state occasions. Are they Jews? What about the fanatical Neturai of Karta sect of Jerusalem, whose members, in addition to three regular daily services, hold a

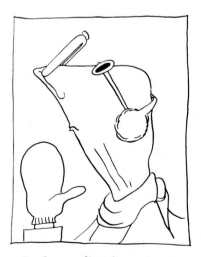

Intolerance listening to reason

midnight prayer and vigil for the coming of the Messiah—and refuse to recognize the Jewish state or to bear arms for it? Major conferences and conventions of American Jews in recent years have included sessions on the question "What is a Jew?"

For the purposes of immigration to Israel, a Jew is a person born of a Jewish mother or converted to the faith. After the 1988 elections in Israel, when asked by the Likud party to participate in a coalition government, three tiny, religious-based minority political parties demanded revision of the "Law of Return," which grants automatic Israeli citizenship to Jews who request it. The parties' demand that only persons converted in orthodox branches of the faith be eligible for Israeli citizenship shook American Jewish communities based in the Conservative and Reform branches of Judaism. Many American Jews protested strongly, saying the change would amount to Israel questioning their "Jewishness." The resulting storm of controversy apparently contributed to the decision by the leading party, Likud, to form another coalition with Labor rather than join with the religious parties.

Let us return now to our hypothetical Mr. Miller, who has been introduced as a "Jew." To a person for whom the affective connotations of this word are very much alive, and who habitually confuses that which is inside his nervous system with that which is outside, Mr. Miller may be a man "not to be trusted." If Mr. Miller succeeds in business, such a person may say it only "proves" that "Jews are smart," while if Mr. Johansen succeeds in business, it only proves that Mr. Johansen is smart.

But Mr. Miller may be, for all we know, rich or poor, a wife-beater or a saint, a stamp collector or a violinist, a farmer or a physicist, a lens-grinder or an orchestra leader. If, as the result of our automatic reactions, we put ourselves on guard about our *money* immediately upon meeting Mr. Miller, we may offend a man from whom we might have profited financially, morally, or spiritually, or we may fail to notice his attempts to run off with our wife—that is, we shall act with complete inappropriateness to the *actual* situation at hand. Mr. Miller is not identical with our notion of "Jew," *whatever our notion of "Jew" may be.* The "Jew," created by intensional definition of the word, *simply is not there.*

Indeed, to say that some people are blinded by prejudice seems to be more than a metaphor. Ralph Ellison calls his central character, who is black, "the invisible man," in his novel of that name. This is to suggest that many whites, on encountering someone black, see only the abstraction "black" that they carry in their heads; busy with this "little man that isn't there," they never notice the actual individual.

Something similar may be said about the typical Western attitude toward the "Arab." The Arab world is anything but homogeneous, though the word—and cartoon images of oil-rich sheiks—are often carelessly used in a way that suggests it is. Lebanese Christians and Moslems fought a bloody civil war against each other, showing that even among Arabs there are often intense hatreds that erupt from time to time. We also find that the Arabs of Syria have a fierce rivalry with the Arabs of Iraq, and that, not infrequently, Arabs are tall, blond, and blue-eyed. The term "Arab" as it is often used by the Westerner must be regarded as brother to the term "Jew" as it is used by the prejudiced or the ignorant. This does not mean that the term "Arab" should be discarded; it should be used more accurately. According to Edward Atiyah, an expert on the Arab world, the term may have three meanings. (1) It may designate the nomadic people who inhabit the Jordanian, Arabian, Syrian, and North African deserts, known as the *Bedu* or *Bedouin*. (2) It may designate the people of the Arabian peninsula (often referred to as "the Arabians"), both the nomads and the city-dwellers; in this sense, the word denotes an ethnic group— the present-day Saudis, Yemenites, Kuwaitis, and other descendants of the original Arab homeland. (3) Finally, the word "Arab" may mean a culture group—a *bloc* of Arabic-speaking communities stretching continuously from the Persian Gulf in the east to the Atlantic in the west.

In this vast area, the proportion of nomads to sedentary population is very small, the majority of people being *fellahin* (farmers) and inhabitants of the ancient and famous cities—Aleppo, Damascus, Beirut, Latakia, Cairo, Alexandria, Baghdad, Jerusalem, Tunis, Algiers—once the centers of world civilization. Another common error is the assumption that the people of Iran are Arabs, when in fact they belong to a different cultural group, speak a different language (Farsi, or Persian), and have, through history, often been rivals of the Arabs. Hence, if we wish to speak with some precision and without giving offense to a group of people whose importance in the world is growing daily, we should learn at least to distinguish among these different abstractions and to avoid applying the word "Arab" as if it corresponded to the stereotype many of us know from misleading adventure movies and novels.

John Doe, the "Criminal"

Another instance of the confusion of levels of abstraction is to be found in cases like this: Let us say that here is a man, John Doe, who is introduced as one "who has just been released after three years in the penitentiary." This is already on a fairly high level of abstraction, but it is nevertheless a *report*. From this point, however, many people *immediately and unconsciously* climb to still higher levels of abstraction: "John Doe is an *ex-convict*. . . . he's a *criminal!*" But the word "criminal" is not only on a much higher level of abstraction than "the man who spent three years in the penitentiary," but it is also, as we have seen in Chapter 3, a *judgment*, with the implication, "He committed a crime in the past and will probably commit more crimes in future." The result is that when John Doe applies

for a job and is forced to state that he has spent three years in the penitentiary, prospective employers, automatically confusing levels of abstraction,
may say to him, "You can't expect me to give jobs to criminals!"

John Doe, for all we know from the report, may have undergone a
complete reformation or, for that matter, may have been unjustly imprisoned in the first place; nevertheless, he may wander in vain, looking for a
job. If, in desperation, he finally says to himself, "If everybody is going to
treat me like a criminal, I might as well act like one," such treatment may
be said to have contributed to his plight.

The reader is familiar with the way in which rumor grows as it spreads.
Many of the exaggerations are due to this inability on the part of some
people to refrain from climbing to higher levels of abstraction—from reports to inferences to judgments—and then confusing the levels. According
to this kind of "reasoning":

> *Report:* "Mary Smith didn't get in until three last Saturday night."
> *Inference:* "I bet she was out fooling around!"
> *Judgment:* "She's a tramp. I never did like her looks. I knew it the moment I
> first laid eyes on her."

Basing our actions towards our fellow human beings on such hastily
abstracted judgments often makes life miserable not only for others, but
for ourselves.

As a final example of this type of confusion, *notice the difference between what happens when someone says, "I have failed three times,"
and the effect of saying, "I am a failure!"*

Delusional Worlds

Consciousness of abstracting prepares us in advance for the fact that things
that look alike are *not* alike, for the fact that things that have the same
name are *not* the same, for the fact that judgments are *not* reports. In
short, it prevents us from acting like idiots. Without consciousness of abstracting—or rather, without the habit of *delaying reactions*, which is the
product of a deep awareness that seeing is not believing—we are unpre-
pared for the differences between roses and paper roses, between the dramatization in TV commercials and real events, between the intensional
"criminal" and the extensional John Doe.

Such delayed reactions are a sign of maturity. It happens, however,
that as the result of miseducation, bad training, frightening experiences in
childhood, obsolete traditional beliefs, propaganda, and other influences
in our lives, all of us have what might be termed "areas of insanity" or
perhaps better, "areas of infantilism," in which we are at the mercy of
ingrained, inappropriate semantic reactions. There are certain subjects

about which we can never, as we say, "think straight," because we are "blinded by prejudice." Some people, for example, as the result of a childhood experience, cannot help being frightened by the mere sight of a police officer—any police officer; the terrifying "police officer" inside their heads "is" the extensional police officer outside, who probably has no designs that anyone could regard as terrifying. Some people turn pale at the sight of a spider—any spider—even one safely enclosed in a bottle. Some people automatically become hostile at the *words* "un-American," "gun control," "communist," "conservative," "liberal," Palestinian, or Jew.

The picture of reality created inside our heads by the lack of consciousness of the abstracting process is not at all a "map" of an existing "territory." It is a delusional world. In this never-never land, all "Jews" are out to cheat you; all "capitalists" are overfed tyrants, smoking expensive cigars and gnashing their teeth at labor unions; all "welfare mothers" are lazy, satisfied to receive handouts from the government; all "liberals" are out to raise taxes and make government grow bigger. In this world, too, all snakes are poisonous; automobiles can be disciplined by being bashed with a tire-iron, and every stranger with a foreign accent is not to be trusted. Some of the people who spend too much of their time in such delusional worlds eventually get locked up, but, needless to say, there are many still at large.

How do we reduce such infantilism in our thought? One way is to know deeply that there is no "necessary connection" between words and what they stand for. For this reason, the study of a foreign language is always good for us. Other ways have already been suggested: to be aware of the process of abstracting and *to realize fully that words never "say all" about anything.* The abstraction ladder—an adaptation of a diagram originated by Alfred Korzybski to illustrate visually the relationship between words, perceptions, and "objects"—is designed to help us understand and remain conscious of the process of abstracting.

If our ideas and beliefs are held with an awareness of abstracting, they can be changed if found to be inadequate or erroneous. But if they are held without an awareness of abstracting—if our mental maps are believed *to be the territory*—they are prejudices. As teachers or parents, we cannot help passing on to the young a certain amount of misinformation and error, however hard we may try not to. But if we teach them to be habitually conscious of the process of abstraction, we give them the means by which to free themselves from whatever erroneous notions we may have inadvertently taught them.

to distinguish it as a *dobo;* your other neighbor, who likes to see snakes killed, distinguishes it as a *busa.* What we call things and where we draw the line between one class of things and another depend upon the interests we have and the purposes of the classification. For example, animals are classified in one way by the meat industry, in a different way by the leather industry, in another different way by the fur industry, and in a still different way by the biologist. None of these classifications is any more final than any of the others; each of them is useful for its purpose.

This holds, of course, regarding everything we perceive. A table "is" a table to us, because we can understand its relationship to our conduct and interests; we eat at it, work on it, lay things on it. But to a person living in a culture where no tables are used, it may be a very strong stool, a small platform, or a meaningless structure. If our culture and upbringing were different, that is to say, our world would not even look the same to us.

Many of us, for example, cannot distinguish between pickerel, pike, salmon, smelt, perch, crappie, halibut, and mackerel; we say that they are "just fish, and I don't like fish." To a seafood connoisseur, however, these distinctions are real, since they mean the difference to him between one kind of good meal, a very different kind of good meal, or a poor meal. To a zoologist, who has other and more general ends in view, even finer distinctions assume great importance. When we hear the statement, then, "This fish is a specimen of pompano, *Trachinotus carolinus,*" we accept this as being "true," even if we don't care, not because that is its "right name," but because that is how it is *classified* in the most complete and most general system of classification that people scientifically interested in fish have evolved.

When we name something, then, we are classifying. *The individual object or event we are naming, of course, has no name and belongs to no class until we put it in one.* To illustrate again, suppose that we were to give the extensional meaning of the word "Korean." We would have to point to all "Koreans" living at a particular moment and say, "The word 'Korean' denotes at the present moment these persons: A_1, A_2, A_3, . . . A_n." Now, let us say, a child, whom we shall designate as Z, is born among these "Koreans." *The extensional meaning of the word "Korean," determined prior to the existence of Z, does not include Z.* Z is a new individual belonging to no classification, since all classifications were made without taking Z into account. Why, then, is Z also a "Korean"? *Because we say so.* And, saying so—fixing the classification—we have determined to a considerable extent future attitudes toward Z. For example, Z will always have certain rights in Korea; in other nations he will be regarded as an "alien" and will be subject to laws applicable to "aliens."

In matters of "race" and "nationality," the way in which classifications work is especially apparent. For example, I am by birth a "Canadian," by "race" a "Japanese," and am now an "American." Although I was legally admitted to the United States on a Canadian passport as a "non-quota immigrant," I was unable to apply for American citizenship until after 1952. Until 1965, American immigration law used classifications based on "nationality" and on "race." A Canadian entering the United States as a permanent resident had no trouble getting in, unless he happened to be of Oriental extraction, in which case his "nationality" became irrelevant and he was classified by "race." If the quota for his "race"—for example, Japanese—was filled (and it often was), and if he could not get himself classified as a non-quota immigrant, he was not able to get in at all. (Since 1965, race and national origin have been replaced with an emphasis on "family reunification" as the basis for American immigration law, and race is no longer explicitly mentioned.) Are all these classifications "real"? Of course they are, *and the effect that each of them has upon what he may or may not do constitutes their "reality."*

I have spent my entire life, except for short visits abroad, in Canada and the United States. I speak Japanese haltingly, with a child's vocabulary and an American accent; I do not read or write it. Nevertheless, because classifications seem to have a kind of hypnotic power over some people, I am occasionally credited with (or accused of) having an "Oriental mind." Since Buddha, Confucius, General Tojo, Mao Tse-tung, Pandit Nehru, Rajiv Gandhi, and the proprietor of the Golden Pheasant Chop Suey House all have "Oriental minds," it is difficult to know whether to feel complimented or insulted.

When is a person "black"? By the definition once widely accepted in the United States, any person with even a small amount of "Negro blood"—that is, whose parents or ancestors were classified as "Negroes"—is "black." *It would be exactly as justifiable to say that any person with even a small amount of "white blood" is "white."* Why say one rather than the other? Because the former system of classification *suits the convenience*

Labeling

of those making the classification. (The classification of blacks and other minorities in this country has often suited the convenience of whites.) Classification is not a matter of identifying "essences." It is simply a reflection of social convenience or necessity—and different necessities are always producing different classifications.

There are few complexities about classifications at the level of dogs and cats, knives and forks, cigarettes and candy, but when it comes to classifications at high levels of abstraction, for example, those describing conduct, social institutions, philosophical and moral problems, serious difficulties occur. When one person kills another, is it an act of murder, an act of temporary insanity, an act of homicide, an accident, or an act of heroism? As soon as the process of classification is completed, our attitudes and our conduct are, to a considerable degree, determined. We hang the murderer, we treat the insane, we absolve the victim of circumstance, we pin a medal on the hero.

The Blocked Mind

We need not concern ourselves here with the injustices done to "Jews," "Roman Catholics," "Republicans," "redheads," "chorus girls," "sailors," "Southerners," "Yankees," and so on, by snap judgments or, as it is better to call them, fixed reactions. "Snap judgments" suggests that such errors can be avoided by thinking more slowly; this, of course, is not the case, for some people think very slowly with no better results. What we are concerned with is the way in which we block the development of our own minds by automatic reactions.

In the grip of such reactions, some people may say, "A Jew's a Jew. There's no getting around that"—confusing the denoted, extensional Jew with the fictitious "Jew" inside their heads. Such persons, the reader will have observed, can usually be made to admit, on being reminded of certain "Jews" whom they admire—perhaps Albert Einstein, Sandy Koufax, Jascha Heifetz, Benny Goodman, Woody Allen, Henry Kissinger, or Kitty Dukakis—that "there are exceptions, of course." They have been compelled by experience, that is to say, to take cognizance of at least a few of the multitude of Jews who do not fit their preconceptions. At this point, however, they continue triumphantly, "But exceptions only prove the rule?"[1]—which is another way of saying, "Facts don't count."

People who "think" in this way may identify some of their best friends as "Jewish"; but to explain this they may say, "I don't think of them as

---

[1] This extraordinarily fatuous saying originally meant, "The exception tests the rule"— *Exceptio probat regulum.* This older meaning of the word "prove" survives in such an expression as "automobile proving ground."

Jews at all. They're just friends." In other words, the fictitious "Jew" inside their heads remains unchanged *in spite of their experience.*

People like this may be said to be impervious to new information. They continue to vote Republican or Democratic, no matter what the Republicans or Democrats do. They continue to object to socialists, no matter what the socialists propose. They continue to regard mothers as sacred, no matter who the mother. A woman who had been given up on both by physicians and psychiatrists as hopelessly insane was being considered by a committee whose task it was to decide whether or not she should be committed to an asylum. One member of the committee doggedly refused to vote for commitment. "Gentlemen," he said in tones of deepest reverence, "you must remember that this woman is, after all, a mother." Similarly, some people continue to hate Protestants or Catholics, no matter which Protestant or Catholic. Ignoring characteristics left out in the process of classification, they overlook—when the term Republican is applied to the party of Abraham Lincoln, the party of Warren Harding, the party of Richard Nixon, and the party of Ronald Reagan—the rather important differences among them.

Cow₁ Is Not Cow₂

How do we prevent ourselves from getting into such intellectual blind alleys, or, finding we are in one, how do we get out again? One way is to remember that practically all statements in ordinary conversation, debate, and public controversy taking the form "Republicans are Republicans," "Business is business," "Boys will be boys," "Woman drivers are woman drivers," and so on, are *not true.* Let us put one of these blanket statements back into a context in life.

> "I don't think we should go through with this deal, Bill. Is it altogether fair to the railroad company?"
> "Aw, forget it! *Business is business,* after all."

Such an assertion, although it looks like a "simple statement of fact," is not simple and is not a statement of fact. The first "business" *denotes* the transaction under discussion; the second "business" invokes the *connotations* of the word. The sentence is a *directive,* saying, "Let us treat this transaction with complete disregard for considerations other than profit, as the word 'business' suggests." Similarly, when a father tries to excuse the mischief done by his sons, he says, "Boys will be boys"; in other words, "Let us regard the actions of my sons with that indulgent amusement customarily extended toward those whom we call 'boys,' " though the angry neighbor will say, of course, "Boys, my eye! They're little hoodlums; that's what they are!" Such assertions are not informative statements but directives, directing us to classify the object or event under discussion in given ways, in order that we may feel or act as suggested by the terms of the classification.

There is a simple technique for preventing such directives from having their harmful effect on our thinking. It is the suggestion made by Korzybski that we add "index numbers" to our terms, thus: Englishman$_1$, Englishman$_2$ . . . ; cow$_1$, cow$_2$, cow$_3$ . . . ; communist$_1$, communist$_2$, communist$_3$. The terms of the classification tell us what the individuals in that class have in common; *the index numbers remind us of the characteristics left out*. A rule can then be formulated as a general guide in all our thinking and reading: police officer$_1$ *is not* police officer$_2$; mother-in-law$_1$ *is not* mother-in-law$_2$, and so on. This rule, if remembered, prevents us from confusing levels of abstraction and forces us to consider the facts on those occasions when we might otherwise find ourselves leaping to conclusions which we may later have cause to regret.

"Truth"

Many semantic problems are, ultimately, problems of classification and nomenclature. Take, for example, the extensive debate over abortion. To opponents of legalized abortion, the unborn entity within a woman's womb is a "baby." Because abortion foes *want* to end abortion, they insist that the "baby" *is* a human being with its own legal rights and that therefore *"abortion is murder."* They call themselves "pro-life" to emphasize their position. Those who *want* individual women to be able to choose whether or not to end a pregnancy call that same unborn entity a "fetus" and insist that the "fetus" *is not* a viable human being capable of living on its own, and claim that a woman has a "right" to make such a choice. Partisans of either side have accused the other of "perverting the meanings of words" and of "not being able to understand plain English."

The decision finally rests not upon appeals to past authority, but upon *what society wants*. In the case *Roe v. Wade*, the Supreme Court found that a "right"—specifically, a right to privacy—permits women to make a private, medical decision before a certain stage of pregnancy. If society again wants doctors prosecuted for performing abortions, as they often were before 1973, it will obtain a new decision from Congress or the Supreme Court that abortion "is" murder or that the unborn entity "is" a human being. Either way, society will ultimately get the decision it collectively wants, even if it must wait until the present members of the Supreme Court are dead and an entirely new court is appointed. When the desired decision is handed down, people will say, "Truth has triumphed." *Society, in short, regards as "true" those systems of classification that produce the desired results.*

The scientific test of "truth," like the social test, is strictly practical, except for the fact that the "desired results" are more severely limited. The results desired by society may be irrational, superstitious, selfish, or humane, but the results desired by scientists are only that our systems of classification produce predictable results. Classifications, as amply indicated already, determine our attitudes and behavior toward the object or event classified. When lightning was classified as "evidence of divine wrath," no courses of action other than prayer were suggested to prevent one's being struck by lightning. But after Benjamin Franklin classified it as "electricity," a measure of control over it was achieved by the invention of the lightning rod. Certain physical disorders were formerly classified as "demonic possession," and this suggested that we "drive the demons out" by whatever spells or incantations we could think of. The results were uncertain. But when those disorders were classified as "bacillus infections," courses of action were suggested that led to more predictable results. Science seeks only the *most generally useful* systems of classification; these it regards for the time being, until more useful classifications are invented, as "true."

CHAPTER 12

The Two-Valued Orientation

And the admired art of disputing hath added much to the natural imperfection of languages. . . . this is unavoidably to be so where men's parts and learning are estimated by their skill in disputing. And if reputation and reward shall attend these conquests . . . 'tis no wonder if the wit of man so employed should perplex, involve and subtilize the signification of sounds, so as never to want something to say in opposing or defending any question—the victory being adjudged not to him who had truth on his side, but the last word in the dispute.   JOHN LOCKE

People with college educations, the student said, know more, and hence are better judges of people. But aren't you assuming, I asked, that a college education gives not only what we usually call "knowledge" but also what we usually call "shrewdness" or "wisdom"? Oh, he said, you mean that there isn't any use in going to college!   FRANCIS P. CHISHOLM

Once we have cast another group in the role of the enemy, we know that they are to be distrusted—that they are evil incarnate. We then twist all their communications to fit our belief.   JEROME D. FRANK

Iₙ THE EXPRESSION "We must listen to both sides of every question," there is an assumption, frequently unexamined, that every question has two sides—and only two sides. We tend to think in opposites, to feel that what is not good must be bad and that what is not bad must be good. When children are taught English history, for example, the first thing they want to know about every ruler is whether he was a "good king" or a "bad king." Much popular political thought, like the plots of television westerns, views the world as divided into "good guys" and "bad guys"—those who believe in "one-hundred-per-cent Americanism" as opposed to those who harbor "un-American ideas." The same tendency is clearly discernible in those who do not believe in the existence of "neutral" nations; any nation that was not fully committed to "our side" in the Soviet-American cold war was believed to be on the Soviet side. This penchant to divide the world into two opposing forces—"right" versus "wrong," "good" versus "evil"—and to ignore or deny the existence of any middle ground, may be termed the *two-valued orientation*.

The Two-Valued Orientation and Combat

In terms of a single desire, there are only two values, roughly speaking: things that gratify or things that frustrate that desire. If we are starving, there are only two kinds of things in the world so far as we are concerned at the moment: edible things and inedible things. If we are in danger, there are the things that we fear and the things that may help and protect us. At such basic levels of existence, in our absorption in self-defense or food-seeking, there are, in terms of those limited desires, only two categories possible. Life at such levels can be folded neatly down the middle, with all good on one side, all bad on the other, and *everything is accounted for*, because things that are irrelevant to our interests escape our notice altogether.

In a situation of actual physical combat, the two-valued orientation is inevitable—and necessary. Total absorption in the fight reduces reality for the time being into two, and only two, objects of concern—oneself and the enemy. This narrowed view of the world is accompanied by accelerated heartbeat and circulation, increased muscular tension, and the release by the adrenal glands of hormones into the blood to contract the arteries and thus slow down the flow of blood in case of injury. This ability to direct and mobilize one's entire mental and physical resources in the face of physical danger—which the physiologist Walter B. Cannon described as the "fight or flight" mechanism—has been necessary to survival through most of the long history of the human race, and probably remains so.

However, for the symbol-using class of life at a high level of cultural development, fighting and fleeing—the primitive outlets for fear, hatred, and anger—are not available. Although we may sometimes get angry enough at our rivals and enemies to *want* to strike them down, or even to kill them, we have to content ourselves most of the time with verbal assault: calling them names, criticizing them, reporting them to the boss, writing letters of complaint or accusation, outmaneuvering them in social or business competition, or instituting lawsuits against them. Words are not blows; name-calling breaks no bones, and even a smashing insult results in no loss of blood. However, some individuals—especially those who are quick to lose their tempers and slow to regain them—are in an almost constant state of overstimulation, as if under the influence of a higher-than-necessary concentration of adrenal hormones in their systems. For such people, the two-valued orientation is a way of life.

The Two-Valued Orientation in Politics

Under a two-party political system such as we have in the United States, there is abundant occasion for uttering two-valued pronouncements. I have often listened to political speeches carried by sound trucks in crowded Chicago streets and I have been impressed with the thoroughness with which the Republicans (or Democrats) have been castigated and the Democrats (or Republicans) praised. Not a shadow of praise or even of extenuation is offered to the opposing party. When I once asked a candidate for state representative why this was so, I was told, "Among our folks, it don't pay to be subtle."

Fortunately, most voters regard this two-valuedness of political debate as "part of the game," especially around election time, so that it does not appear to have uniformly harmful consequences; overstatements on either side are at least partially canceled out by overstatements on the other. Nevertheless, there remains a portion of the electorate—*and this portion is by no means confined to the uneducated*—who take the two-valued orientation seriously. These are the people (and the newspapers) who speak of their opponents as if they were enemies of the nation rather than fellow citizens with differing views as to what is good for the nation.

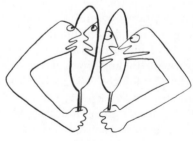

Argument

On the whole, however, a two-valued orientation in politics is difficult to maintain in a two-party system of government. The parties have to cooperate with each other between elections and therefore have to assume that members of the opposition are something short of fiends in human form. The public, too, in a two-party system, sees that the dire predictions of Republicans regarding the probable results of Democratic rule, and the equally dire predictions of the Democrats regarding Republican rule, are never more than partially fulfilled. Furthermore, criticism of the administration is not only possible, it is energetically encouraged by the opposition. Hence the majority of people can never quite be convinced that one party is wholly good and the other wholly bad.

But when a nation's traditions (or its lack of traditions) permit a political party to feel that it is *so good for the country that no other party has any right to exist*—and such a party gets control—there is immediate silencing of opposition. In such a case, the party declares its philosophy to be the official philosophy of the nation and its interests to be the interests of the people as a whole. "Whoever is an enemy of the National Socialist party," as the Nazis said, "is an enemy of Germany." Even if you loved Germany greatly, but didn't agree with the National Socialists as to what was good for Germany, you were liquidated. *Under the one-party system, the two-valued orientation, in its most primitive form, becomes the official national outlook.*

Because the Nazis carried the two-valued orientation to extremes never before reached by a political party—extremes of ridiculousness as well as extremes of barbarity—it is worthwhile recalling, in the context of semantic study, some of the techniques they used. First of all, the two-valued assumption was explicitly stated over and over again:

Discussion of matters affecting our existence and that of the nation must cease altogether. Anyone who dares to question the rightness of the National Socialist outlook will be branded as a traitor.

HERR SAUCKEL, **Nazi Governor of Thuringia, June 20, 1933**

Everyone in Germany is a National Socialist—the few outside the party are either lunatics or idiots.   ADOLF HITLER, **Klagenfurt, Austria, April 4, 1938**

Everyone not using the greeting "Heil Hitler," or using it only occasionally and unwillingly, shows he is an opponent of the Fuehrer or a pathetic turncoat. . . . The German people's only greeting is "Heil Hitler." Whoever does not use it must recognize that he will be regarded as outside the community of the German nation.   LABOR FRONT CHIEFS IN SAXONY, **December 5, 1937**

National Socialists say: legality is that which does the German people good; illegality is that which harms the German people.

DR. FRICK, **Minister of the Interior**

Anyone or anything that stood in the way of Hitler's wishes was "Jewish," "degenerate," "corrupt," "democratic," "internationalist," and, as a crowning insult, "non-Aryan." On the other hand, everything that Hitler chose to call "Aryan" was by definition noble, virtuous, heroic, and altogether glorious. Courage, self-discipline, honor, beauty, health, and joy were "Aryan." Whatever he called upon people to do, he told them to do "to fulfill their Aryan heritage."

An incredible number of areas were examined in terms of this two-valued orientation: art, books, people, calisthenics, mathematics, physics, dogs, cats, architecture, morals, cookery, religion. If Hitler approved, it was "Aryan"; if he disapproved, it was "non-Aryan" or "Jewish-dominated."

We request that every hen lay 130 to 140 eggs a year. The increase can not be achieved by the bastard hens (non-Aryan) which now populate German farm yards. Slaughter these undesirables and replace them. . . .

NAZI PARTY NEWS AGENCY, April 3, 1937

The rabbit, it is certain, is no German animal, if only for its painful timidity. It is an immigrant who enjoys a guest's privilege. As for the lion, one sees in him indisputably German fundamental characteristics. Thus one could call him a German abroad.   GENERAL LUDENDORFF in *Am Quell Deutscher Kraft*

Proper breathing is a means of acquiring heroic national mentality. The art of breathing was formerly characteristic of true Aryanism and known to all Aryan leaders. . . . Let the people again practice the old Aryan wisdom.

BERLIN *Weltpolitische Rundschau*

Cows or cattle which were bought from Jews directly or indirectly may not be bred with the community bull.

MAYOR OF KOENIGSDORF, BAVARIA
Tegernseerzeitung, Nazi Party organ October 1, 1935

There is no place for Heinrich Heine in any collection of works of German poets. . . . When we reject Heine, it is not because we consider every line he wrote bad. The decisive factor is that this man was a Jew. Therefore, there is no place for him in German literature.   *Schwarze Korps*

Because the Japanese were, before and during World War II, on friendly terms with Hitler's Germany, they were classified as "Aryans." At one point in the war, when Germany was hoping for Mexico as an ally, the German ambassador in Mexico City announced that Mexicans were members of the Nordic race who had emigrated by way of the Bering Strait and come south! But the greatest error in classification that the Nazis made was when they labeled certain theories in physics as "non-Aryan," and deprived the originator of those theories, Albert Einstein, of his property, position, and citizenship. Hitler could hardly have guessed then that those same theories would have military consequences beyond his wildest dreams.

The connection between the two-valued orientation and combat is clearly apparent in the history of Nazism. From the moment Hitler achieved power, he told the German people that they were surrounded by enemies. Long before World War II started, the German people were called upon to act *as if* a war were already in progress. Everyone, including women and children, was pressed into "war" service of one kind or another. In order to keep the combative sense from fizzling out for want of tangible enemies before the start of actual warfare, the people were kept fighting at home against alleged enemies within the gates: principally the Jews, but also anyone else whom the Nazis happened to dislike.

Education, too, was made to serve the purposes of war and to create a warlike spirit:

There is no such thing as knowledge for its own sake. Science can only be the soldierly training of our minds for service to the nation. The university must be a battleground for the organization of the intellect. Heil Adolf Hitler and his eternal Reich!   **Rector of Jena University**

The task of universities is not to teach objective science, but the militant, the warlike, the heroic.   DR. DRIECK, **Headmaster, Mannheim public schools**[1]

The official National Socialist orientation never permitted a relaxation of the two-valued conviction that nothing is too good for the "good," and nothing is too bad for the "bad," and *that there is no middle ground.* "Whoever is not for us is against us!" This is the cry of intolerance armed with certainty.

Man's Inhumanity to Man

The cruelties of the Nazi treatment of Jews and other "enemies"—the wholesale executions, the gas chambers, the "scientific" experiments in torture, starvation, and vivisection performed on political prisoners—have often taxed the credulity of the outside world. Stories of Nazi prison camps and death chambers are still regarded in some quarters as wartime anti-Nazi fabrications.

To the student of two-valued orientations, however, these stories are all too credible. If good is "absolutely good" and evil is "absolutely evil," the logic of a primitive, two-valued orientation demands that "evil" be

---

[1] The National Socialist pronouncements quoted in this chapter are from a collection of such utterances by Adolf Hitler and his associates, compiled by Clara Leiser and published under the title *Lunacy Becomes Us* (1939).

exterminated by every means available. Murdering Jews becomes, under this orientation, a moral duty—to be carried out systematically and conscientiously. Judging from the evidence produced at the Nuremberg trials as well as at the Eichmann trial, this appears to be how the task was regarded. Nazi prison guards and executioners carried out their ghastly tasks, not in rage or in fiendish glee, but simply as matters of duty. So completely had the abstraction "Jew" blotted out all other perceptions, that killing Jews became almost a matter of course. Aldous Huxley has said that it is the function of propaganda to enable people to do in cold blood things that they could otherwise do only in the heat of passion. Two-valued propaganda, seriously believed, has precisely this effect.

The Marxist Two-Valued Orientation

The orientation of Russian communist spokesmen is also notoriously two-valued, the world being divided, in their view, into "peace-loving, progressive, scientific, materialist socialists," like themselves, and "warmongering, bourgeois, reactionary, idealist, imperialistic capitalists," like us—or anyone else who disagrees with their views. Because the communists are extremely concerned with ideology, there is no talk of "blood," "instinct," and "soul" as there was in Nazi Germany, and much talk about "historical necessity," "the class struggle," "objective reality," and "the nature of capitalist exploitation and colonialism." Nazi Germany offers classic examples of the two-valued orientation in rabble-rousing and popular oratory. Russian communism offers the best examples of the two-valued orientation among social theorists, philosophers, and intellectuals.

Lenin molded the theories of Karl Marx into a political weapon, and the combative fervor of the revolutionist has remained an important ingredient of communist oratory and orientation ever since. Lenin had, as Anatol Rapoport has explained, "an intense compulsion to view each difference of opinion as irreconcilable":

If someone whom he considered to be in the enemy camp expressed any view acceptable to him, he took great pains to prove that the opponent was either guilty of inconsistency or was muddle-headed, or else (a favorite explanation) was masking his real nature. If someone in his own camp expressed a view unacceptable to him, he again either accused him of muddle-headedness or argued that eventually this view would drive his erring colleague to the complete acceptance of the enemy position. As Lenin wrote, "Enmesh a single claw and the bird is caught. . . . You cannot eliminate one basic assumption, one substantial part of this philosophy of Marxism (it is as if it were a block of steel) without abandoning objective truth, without falling into the arms of bourgeois-reactionary falsehood."[2]

[2]Anatol Rapoport, "Death of Communication with Russia?" *ETC.*, VIII (1950), p. 89.

In short, you either agree completely with Lenin (and those who are running the party in his name) or you are an outcast.

There is a curious preoccupation with labeling in Marxist polemics—a need to characterize the ideological position of an individual or a school of thought with an epithet. In analyzing an author's outlook, a philosophical tendency, or a scientific theory, the Marxist critic first of all has to decide "what it is." Is it "idealism" or "materialism"? Is it "agnosticism," "bourgeois charlatanism," "empirio-criticism," "fideism," "formalism," "immanentism," or "revisionism"? Is it "Trotskyism," "Kautskyism," "Machism," "Kantianism," or "Berkeleianism"? Is it "Michurinism," or "Weismannism"? Some of these "-isms" are "good," some "bad."

When Marxist polemicists decide that something deserves one of the "bad" labels, they let go with both barrels. Thus, B. Bykhovsky, writing in 1947 on "Semantic Philosophy," found it to be "nothing but . . . a neo-nominalism" which is trying to bring back to life a discredited "subjective idealism." Then comes the blast:

The semantic fad in Anglo-American philosophy is one of the manifestations of the decomposition and decay which characterize the idealist philosophy of the imperialist epoch. . . . The grimaces of the Semantic obscurantists, that is, the Walpurgis Night, is celebrated in the darkness which pervades the spiritual life of the modern bourgeoisie. . . . Like all the currents of modern idealist philosophy, semantic idealism is a spiritual weapon of imperialism in its struggle against the progressive ideas of our time. Poisoning the consciousness of the intellectuals with the poison of skepticism, nihilism, and agnosticism, scientific, moral, political, the semanticists are the most vicious enemies of progressive ideas.[3]

The two-valued character of Soviet orientations is ironically illustrated by the career of Stalin. Long idolized as a great leader, the epitome of strength and wisdom and communist virtue (a "good guy"), he was accused after his death of numberless crimes, among them that of building up a "cult of personality" for the sake of power and self-aggrandizement. Towns and streets which had been named after him were renamed, and his body was removed from enshrinement and hauled away to be buried in obscurity (a "bad guy"). Apparently, official ideology could find no middle ground for him at some point between "great hero" and "great villain."

The official ideology has remained as two-valued as ever. The following account of an interview with a Soviet professor of philosophy is given by Maurice Hindus, who studied the development of the Soviet Union over many years:

[3] B. Bykhovsky, "The Morass of Modern Bourgeois Philosophy" (trans. Anatol Rapoport), *ETC.*, VI (1948), pp. 13–18. The article appeared originally in the *Bolshevik: A Theoretical Political Journal* (Moscow), August 30, 1947.

"Suppose," I asked, "a student questions the validity of dialectical materialism?"

[Dialectical materialism, to oversimplify, is the Marxist theory, derived from Karl Marx and Friederich Engels, that holds that changes in nature and society take place through a struggle of opposites, which transforms them into something new.]

"You must remember," the professor replied, "that throughout his five years in the university our student takes courses in dialectical materialism and related subjects. Besides, the study of all our courses is permeated with this philosophy. The student cannot possibly question its validity."

"Suppose he disagrees with the professor's position that there is no truth other than what the dialectical materialism he studies reveals to him? In America, students are free to disagree with their professors."

"Then we reason with the student. On the conclusion of a lecture we have from ten to fifteen minutes of questions and the student is free to bring up whatever arguments come to his mind. The professor takes up the arguments one by one and proves them false. . . . "

"Einstein," I said, "was one of the greatest scientists of all time, and so far as I know he never accepted the philosophy of dialectical materialism."

"We have translated the book Einstein wrote with Enfield [Infeld]. We study the book because the authors are great scientists. But we reject their idealistic doctrines."

"Suppose the student sees merit in these doctrines?"

"We argue him out of it."

"But suppose he remains unconvinced?"

"Impossible. We have the question period and we hold seminars and in the end we defeat our ideological enemies."

"But if the student persists in contradicting the professor?"

"It doesn't happen. It cannot happen. Our arguments are incontrovertible."

"And if it were to happen?"

This time the professor replied solemnly: "Then the student would place himself outside our Soviet society."[4]

At this writing, it seems that a few cracks may have appeared in the rigidity of official Soviet thinking. Under Mikhail Gorbachev's policy of *glasnost*, which has been translated variously as "openness" or "publicity," tentative voices in politics, history, literature, and the arts have been allowed to be heard. These voices question further the official accounts of the history of the Stalin years and the centralized role of the state in the economy. But the two-valued orientation dies hard. As yet, the Soviets have allowed no criticism of Lenin to surface. However, in 1988, when thirteen of the 1,500 members of the Supreme Soviet voted "nyet" on a bill for the first time in modern Soviet history, the event was reported as news on the front pages of newspapers around the world.

[4] Maurice Hindus, *House Without a Roof* (1961).

Two-Valued Logic

The term "two-valued orientation" was originated by Alfred Korzybski, whose main concern was with the orientations that determine health or disorder in people's semantic reactions. Although he described the two-valued orientation as characteristic of a primitive or emotionally disturbed outlook, he was not attacking two-valued *logic*. Ordinary logic, like that used in arithmetic, is strictly two-valued. Within the framework of ordinary arithmetic, two plus two equals four. This is the "right" answer, and all other answers are "wrong." Many demonstrations in geometry are based on what is called "indirect proof": in order to prove a statement, you take its opposite and assume it to be "true" until you find in the course of further calculation that it leads to a flat contradiction; such a contradiction proves it to be "false," whereupon the original statement is regarded as "true." This too is an application of two-valued logic. Korzybski had no quarrel with arithmetic or geometry, and neither do I.

Logic is a set of rules governing consistency *in the use of a language.* When we are being "logical," our statements are consistent *with each other;* they may be accurate "maps" of real "territories" or they may not, but the question whether they are or are not is outside the province of logic. Logic is language about language, not language about things or events. The fact that two quarts of marbles plus two quarts of milk do not add up to four quarts of the mixture does not affect the "truth" of the statement, "Two plus two equals four," because all that this statement says is that "four" is the *name* of "the sum two and two." Of such a statement as "Two plus two equals four," a two-valued question may be asked: "Is it true or false?"—meaning, "Is it or is it not consistent with the rest of our system? If we accept it, shall we be able to talk consistently without eventually contradicting ourselves?" As a set of rules for establishing discourse, a two-valued logic is one of the possible instruments for creating order out of linguistic chaos. It is indispensable, of course, to most of mathematics.

In some areas of discourse and within some special groups of people, it is possible, so to speak, to "police" the language so that it comes to have some of the clarity and freedom from ambiguity enjoyed by mathematics. In such cases, people may agree to call certain animals "cats," certain forms of government "democracy," and a certain gas "helium." They would also have clear agreements as to what *not* to call "cats," "democracy," or "helium." The two-valued rule of traditional (Aristotelian) logic, "A thing is either a cat or not a cat," and the Aristotelian "law of identity," "A cat is a cat," make a great deal of sense when we understand them as *devices for creating and maintaining order in one's vocabulary.* They may be translated, "We must, in order to understand one another, make up our minds whether we are going to call Tabby a 'cat' or 'not a cat.' *And once we have entered into an agreement as to what to call him, let's stick to it.*"

Such agreements do not, of course, completely solve the problem of what things to call by what names, nor do they guarantee the certainty of statements logically deduced. In other words, definitions, as stated in Chapter 9, say nothing about things, but only describe (and often prescribe) people's linguistic habits. Even with the strictest of agreements, therefore, as to what to call "cats" and what not to call "cats," whatever we may logically deduce about cats may turn out, on extensional examination of Tabby, Cinders, or Fluff, not to be true.

Cats are creatures that meow.
Tabby, Cinders, and Fluff are cats.
Therefore Tabby, Cinders, and Fluff meow.

But what if Fluff has a sore throat and cannot meow? The *intensional* cat (the cat by definition, whatever our definition may be, "creatures that meow" or *any* other) is NOT the *extensional* cat (Fluff, April 16, 2 P.M.). Each cat is different from every other cat; each cat also, like Bessie the Cow, is a process, undergoing constant change. Therefore, the only way to guarantee the "truth" of logically deduced statements and to arrive at agreements through logic alone is to talk about cats-by-definition, and not about actual cats at all. The nice thing about cats-by-definition is that, come hell or high water, they always meow (although, to be sure, they only meow-by-definition).

This principle is well understood in mathematics. The mathematical "point" (which "has position but occupies no space") and the mathematical "circle" (which is a "closed figure in which all points are equidistant from the center") exist only as *definitions;* actual points occupy *some* space, and actual circles are never *exactly* circular. Hence, in Einstein's words, "As far as the laws of mathematics refer to reality, they are not certain; and as far as they are certain, they do not refer to reality." Therefore, even in an area such as chemistry, in which the vocabulary is quite strictly "policed," statements logically deduced still *have to be checked* against extensional observation. This is another reason why the rule for extensional orientation—cat_1 is not cat_2—is extremely important. No matter how carefully we have defined the word "cat," and no matter how logically we have reasoned, actual cats still have to be examined.

The belief that logic will substantially reduce misunderstanding is widely and uncritically held, although, as a matter of common experience, we all know that people who pride themselves on their logic are usually, of all the people we know, the hardest to get along with. Logic can lead to agreement only when, as in mathematics or the sciences, there are pre-existing, hard-and-fast agreements as to what words stand for. But among our friends, business associates, and casual acquaintances—some of them Catholic and some Protestant, some of them no-nonsense scientists and some mystics, some sports fans and some interested in nothing but money—only the vaguest of linguistic agreements exist. In ordinary conversation, therefore, we have to learn people's vocabularies in the course of talking with them—which is what all sensible and tactful people do, without even being aware of the process.

On the whole, therefore, except in mathematics and other areas where clear-cut linguistic agreements either exist or can be brought into existence, the assiduous study and practice of traditional, two-valued logic is not recommended. Even in mathematics, two-valued logic is only one of many possible systems of logic. The logic of probability, on the basis of which insurance companies quote premiums, bookmakers quote odds, and physicists predict the behavior of neutrons, may be regarded as an infinite-valued logic. The habitual reliance on two-valued logic *in everyday life* quickly leads to a two-valued orientation—and we have already seen what *that* leads to.

One factor that contributes to difficulties in thinking clearly stems from the nature of language. A word generally has meaning in relation to its opposite; you need to have "rich people" in order for "poor people" to mean anything. In the same way, happy implies sad, wise implies foolish, and so on. As the Swiss linguist Ferdinand de Saussure explained, "Concepts . . . are . . . defined negatively by their relations with other terms of the system. Their most precise characteristic is in being what others are not." That is, words (and myths and many other things) have meaning because they relate to other words through opposition. What happens, unfortunately, is that many people *do not recognize that the patterns we pick up from our use of language do not apply to the real world.*

Korzybski was rarely concerned with the specific *content* of people's beliefs—whether people are religious or unreligious, liberal or conservative. He was concerned, rather, with how people hold their beliefs and convictions: whether with a two-valued orientation ("I am right and everybody else is wrong") or a multi-valued orientation ("I don't know—let's see"). Korzybski saw the two-valued orientation as an *internalization* of the laws of Aristotelian logic, which say that:

A is A (law of identity);
Everything is either A or not-A (law of the excluded middle);
Nothing is both A and not-A (law of noncontradiction).

These "laws of logic" frequently mislead us. Aristotelian logic suggests that if something is "good," it must be "all good" (identity); that which is "not good" must be "bad" (exclusion); and that nothing can be "good" and "bad" at the same time (contradiction). In real life, however, good and bad are usually mixed, and it is seldom possible to impose such simplistic categories upon experience. The difficulty with Aristotle's "laws of logic" is that while they seem to be sensible, in fact they are inadequate to deal with reality, forcing us to press it into narrow confines.

For example, a football game may be "good" (exciting) and "bad" (your team loses). A book may be "good" (full of useful information) and "bad" (difficult). Aristotle forces one to make oversimplified, all-inclusive generalizations. Korzybski regarded his own "non-Aristotelian" system as an internalization of modern, multi-valued and infinite-valued logics. He called it general semantics, a *"non-Aristotelian system."* This has led some people to believe that Korzybski was fighting Aristotle. He was not. He was fighting *un*sanity, whether individual or national. As for Aristotle, he must have been one of the sanest men of his time; but anyone whose knowledge and thinking are limited to a two-valued Aristotelian framework can hardly behave sanely in *our* time.

Defeating One's Own Ends

Action resulting from two-valued orientations notoriously fails to achieve its objectives. The mobs that tried to force dissenting pacifist or religious groups to kiss the flag during World War I did not advance the cause of national defense; they weakened it by creating burning resentments. Southern lynch mobs did not solve the racial problem; they made matters worse. Among the things that harden "hardened criminals" is the way they are treated by a two-valued society and a two-valued criminal justice system. In short, the two-valued orientation increases combativeness but sharply diminishes the ability to evaluate the world accurately. When guided by it for any purpose other than fighting, we almost always achieve results *opposite* from those intended.

Nevertheless, some orators and editorial writers employ the crude, unqualified two-valued orientation with extraordinary frequency, although allegedly in the interests of peace, prosperity, good government, and other laudable aims. Do such writers and speakers use this primitive approach because they know no better? Or are they so contemptuous of their audiences that they feel that it doesn't pay to be subtle? Another possibility is that they are sincere; they cannot help having two-valued reactions when certain hated subjects come into their minds. And still another explanation, less pleasant to think about but in many instances highly probable, is that the two-valued furor is a means of diverting public attention from urgent and practical issues. By making enough of an uproar about "reciting the Pledge of Allegiance," "returning prayer to public schools," or "who's to blame for the mess in Central America," one can keep people from noticing what is going on in legislative lobbies "crowded," as Winston Churchill once said, "with the touts of protected industries."

CHAPTER 13

The Multi-Valued Orientation

Faith in reason is not only a faith in our own reason but also—and even more—in that of others. Thus a rationalist, even if he believes himself to be intellectually superior to others, will reject all claims to authority since he is aware that, if his intelligence is superior to that of others (which is hard for him to judge), it is so only in so far as he is capable of learning from criticism as well as from his own and other people's mistakes, and that one can learn in this sense only if one takes others and their arguments seriously. Rationalism is therefore bound up with the idea that the other fellow has a right to be heard, and to defend his arguments.

KARL R. POPPER

A *Matter of Degree*

Except in quarrels and violent controversies when our emotions tend to lead us astray, the language of everyday life shows what may be termed a multi-valued orientation. We have *scales* of judgment. Instead of "good" and "bad," we have "very bad," "bad," "not bad," "fair," "good," "very good"; we also have mixed judgments: in some respects "good" and in others "bad." Instead of "sane" and "insane," we have "quite sane," "sane enough," "mildly neurotic," "sane on most subjects," "neurotic," "extremely neurotic," and "psychotic." The greater the number of distinctions, the greater becomes the number of courses of action suggested to us. This means that we become increasingly capable of reacting *appropriately* to the many complex situations life presents. Physicians do not lump all people together into the two classes of the "healthy" and the "ill." They distinguish an indefinite number of conditions that may be described as "illness" and have an indefinite number of treatments or combinations of treatments for them.

The two-valued orientation is an orientation based ultimately, as we have seen, on a single interest. But human beings have many interests: they want to eat, to sleep, to have friends, to publish books, to sell real estate, to build bridges, to listen to music, to maintain peace, to conquer disease. Some of these desires are stronger than others, and life presents a perpetual problem of weighing one set of desires against others and making choices: "I like having the money, but I think I would like having that car even better." "I don't like to stand in line for tickets, but I do want to see that show." "I'd like to fire the strikers, but I think it's more important to obey the labor board."

For weighing the various and complicated desires that civilization gives rise to, a finely graduated scale of values is necessary, as well as foresight, lest in satisfying one desire we frustrate even more important ones. *The ability to see things in terms of more than two values may be referred to as a multi-valued orientation.*

The *Multi-Valued Orientation and Democracy*

The multi-valued orientation shows itself, of course, in almost all intelligent or even moderately intelligent public discussion. The editors of responsible papers, such as The *New York Times, Chicago Tribune, San Francisco Chronicle, St. Louis Post-Dispatch, Los Angeles Times*—to name only a few—and the writers for reputable magazines, such as The *New Republic, Harper's, Atlantic Monthly,* The *National Review,* or *Commonweal,* almost invariably avoid the unqualified two-valued orientation.

They may condemn communism, but they try to see what makes communists act as they do. They may denounce the actions of a foreign power, but they weigh the extent to which American actions may have provoked the foreign power into behaving as it did. They may attack a political administration, but they do not forget its positive achievements. It does not matter whether it is from fair-mindedness or timidity that some writers avoid speaking in terms of angels and devils, pure "good" and pure "evil." The important thing is that they do avoid it, and in so doing, they keep open the possibility of adjusting differences, reconciling conflicting interests, and arriving at just estimates. There are people who object to this "shilly-shallying" and insist upon an "outright yes or no." They are the Gordian-knot cutters; they may undo the knot, but they ruin the rope.

Indeed, many features of the democratic process presuppose the multi-valued orientation. Even that most ancient of judicial procedures, the trial by jury, restricted to the conclusions "guilty" and "not guilty," is not as two-valued as it looks, since in the very selection of the charge to be brought against the defendant a choice is made among many possibilities, and also, in the jury's verdict as well as in the judge's sentence, guilt is often modified by recognition of "extenuating circumstances." Modern administrative tribunals and boards of mediation, not tied down by the necessity of arriving at clear verdicts of "guilty" and "not guilty," and empowered to issue "consent decrees" and to close agreements between litigants, are even more multi-valued than the trial by jury and therefore, for some purposes, considerably more efficient.

To take another example, very few bills ever pass a democratic parliamentary body in exactly the form in which they were proposed. Opposing parties argue back and forth, make bargains and compromises with each other, and by this process tend to arrive at decisions that are more nearly adjusted to the needs of everyone in the community than the original proposals. The more fully developed a democracy, the more flexible its orientations, and the more fully does it reconcile the conflicting desires of its people.

Even more multi-valued is the language of science. Instead of saying "hot" and "cold," we designate the temperature in degrees *on a fixed and agreed-upon* scale: $-20°F$, $37°C$, and so on. Instead of saying "strong" and "weak," we designate strength in horsepower or watts; instead of "fast" and "slow," we designate speed in miles per hour or feet per second. Instead of being limited to two answers or even to several, we have access to an infinite number when we use these numerical methods. The language of science, therefore, can be said to offer an *infinite-valued orientation.* Having at its command the means to adjust action in an infinite number of ways, according to the exact situation at hand, science travels rapidly and gets things done.

The Pitfalls of Debate

In spite of all that has been said to recommend multi-valued and infinite-valued orientation, it must not be overlooked that in the *expression of feelings*, the two-valued orientation is almost unavoidable. There is a profound emotional truth in the two-valued orientation that accounts for its adoption in strong expressions of feeling, especially those that call for sympathy, pity, or help in a struggle. "Fight racism!" "Down with slums and up with better housing!" "Throw out the crooks! Vote the Reform ticket!" "Say no to drugs!" The more spirited the expression, the more sharply will things be dichotomized into the "good" and the "bad."

Where there are expressions of feeling and therefore affective elements in speaking and writing, the two-valued orientation almost always appears. It is hardly possible to express strong feelings or to arouse the interest of an apathetic listener without conveying to some extent this sense of conflict. Anyone who is trying to promote a cause, therefore, shows the two-valued orientation somewhere in the course of speaking or writing. It will be found, however, that the two-valued orientation is *qualified* in all conscientious attempts at presenting what is believed to be truth—qualified sometimes, in the ways explained above, by pointing out what can be said against the "good" and what can be said for the "bad"—qualified at other times by the introduction, elsewhere in the text, of a multi-valued approach to the problems.

The two-valued orientation, in short, can be compared to a paddle, which performs the functions, in primitive methods of navigation, both of starter and steering apparatus. In civilized life, the two-valued orientation may be the starter, since it arouses interest with its affective power, but the multi-valued or infinite-valued orientation is the steering apparatus that directs us to our destination.

Although we like to think of ourselves as rational beings, there are few among us who do not exhibit the two-valued orientation when we are stirred up by controversy. In the course of a debate, if *one* of the debaters has a two-valued orientation which leads him to feel that the Democrats, for example, are "entirely good" and the Republicans "entirely bad," he unconsciously forces his opponent into the position of maintaining that the Democrats are "entirely bad" and the Republicans "entirely good." If we argue with such a person at all, there is hardly any way to escape being put into a position that is as extreme on one side as his is on the other. This fact was well stated by Oliver Wendell Holmes in his *Autocrat of the Breakfast-Table,* in which he speaks of the "hydrostatic paradox of controversy":

"You know that, if you had a bent tube, one arm of which was of the size of a pipestem, and the other big enough to hold the ocean, water would stand at the same height in one as in the other. Controversy equalizes fools and wise men in the same way—*and the fools know it.*"

Disputes in which this "equalization" is likely to occur are, of course, a waste of time. The *reductio ad absurdum* of this kind of discussion is often to be found in the high school and college debate as still practiced in some localities. Since both the affirmative and negative can do little other than exaggerate their own claims and belittle the claims of the opposition, the net intellectual result of such encounters is usually negligible— unless teachers consciously guide the discussions in the direction of multi-valuedness, and draw attention to the processes of abstraction underlying the question under debate.

Parliaments and congresses, it will be observed, do not try to conduct much of their serious discussion on the floor. Speeches are made principally for the constituents back home and not for the other legislators. The main work of government is done in the committee room, where the traditional atmosphere of debate is absent. Freed from the necessity of standing resolutely on affirmative and negative positions, legislators in committee are able to investigate facts, thrash out problems, and arrive at workable conclusions that represent positions between the possible extremes. It would seem that, in training students to become citizens in a democracy, practice in being members of and testifying before committees of inquiry would be more suitable than debating after the fashion of medieval scholars for victory.

In the course of everyday conversation, most of us need to watch for the two-valued orientation in ourselves. In a competitive society, conversation is often a battleground in disguise on which we are constantly (and unconsciously) trying to win victories—showing up the other fellow's errors, exposing his lack of information, confronting him (and all others present) with the superiority of our own erudition and logic. This habit of jousting for status is so deeply ingrained in most of us (especially in professional and university circles) that every meeting of intellectuals and every literary cocktail party is likely to include, as part of the entertainment, some sort of verbal dogfight among those present. Most people in such circles are so accustomed to this jousting that they rarely take offense at the remarks of their opponents. Nevertheless, they waste in argument a good deal of time that might more profitably be spent exchanging information and views. An unconscious assumption, convenient for the purposes of those who are looking for occasions to argue and therefore underlying most of this kind of conversation, is that statements are either "true" or "false."

An important way to get the most out of conversation (and out of other forms of communication) is the following *systematic* application of the multi-valued orientation. Instead of assuming a statement to be "true" or "false," one should assume that it has a *truth value* between 0 and 100 percent. For example, let us say that we are sympathetic to organized labor, and someone says to us, "Labor unions are rackets." Our immediate temptation is to say, "They are not"—and the battle would be on. But what is the truth value of the statement? It is clearly neither 0 percent ("No unions are rackets") nor 100 percent ("All unions are rackets"). Let us then silently grant a *tentative* truth-value of 1 percent ("One union out of 100 is a racket") and say, "Tell me more." If there is no more basis for the remark than the vague memory of something somebody once wrote in a newspaper column, the assertion will fizzle out shortly, so that we need not be bothered anymore. But if the person does have experience with even *one* instance of union racketeering, he is talking about something quite real to him, although he may be vastly overgeneralizing his experience. If we listen sympathetically to his experience, the following are some of the things that may happen:

1. We may learn something we never knew before. We may, without giving up our pro-union sympathies, at least modify them so that they rest upon a clearer recognition of the shortcomings of unions as well as of their advantages.

2. He may moderate his statement with such an admission as, "Of course, I haven't had experience with many unions." Again, if he tries to describe as extensionally as possible his experience with a labor union, he may find that some term other than "racketeering" more accurately fits the facts. In these and other ways, then, he may modify his remarks and make them increasingly acceptable as he proceeds.

3. By inviting him to communicate to us, we establish lines of communication with him. This enables us to say things to him later that he may then be disposed to listen to.

4. Both may profit from the conversation.

To attempt to converse in this way is to make all our social contacts occasions for what we have earlier called "the pooling of knowledge." We can, if we are able to listen as well as to speak, become better informed and wiser as we grow older instead of being stuck, like some people, with the same little bundle of prejudices at sixty-five that we had at twenty-five.

Statements made in everyday conversation, even if based on slipshod inferences and hasty over-generalizations, can usually be found to have some modest degree of truth value. To find the needle of meaning in the haystacks of nonsense that the other fellow is talking is to learn something, even from the apparently prejudiced and uninformed. And if the other fellow is equally patient about looking for the needle of meaning in *our* haystacks of nonsense, he may learn something from us. Ultimately, all civilized life depends upon the willingness on the part of all of us to learn as well as to teach. To delay one's reactions and to be able to say "Tell me more," and then *to listen before reacting*—these are practical applications of some of the theoretical principles with which this book has been concerned. No statements, not even our own, say all about anything; inferences—for example, that the man who made the nasty remarks about unions is a "labor-hating reactionary"—need to be checked before we react to them; a multi-valued orientation is necessary to democratic discussion and to human cooperation.

The Open and Closed Mind

Important insights into the two-valued orientation are to be found in *The Open and Closed Mind* by Milton Rokeach of Michigan State University. First, Rokeach says, let us divide a communicative event into two elements, the *speaker* and the *statement.* To put matters as simply as possible, the listener may either accept or reject (like or dislike) the speaker; he may likewise accept or reject (agree or disagree with) the statement. Then the following are the possible ways for the listener to react to the communication:

1. accept the speaker and accept the statement;

2. accept the speaker but reject the statement;

3. reject the speaker but accept the statement;

4. reject the speaker and reject the statement.

A person with what Rokeach calls a "closed mind" is able to have only reactions (1) and (4), either accepting the speaker *and* the statement, or rejecting the speaker *and* the statement. The person with the "open mind," however, is able to have, in addition to reactions (1) and (4), the more complex reactions (2) and (3): of accepting the speaker but rejecting the statement, or rejecting the speaker but accepting the statement.

The person with the closed mind is apparently one who finds life threatening. If either the speaker or the statement is unacceptable to him, he rejects *both*. As the reader will recall, according to Anatol Rapoport's account of Lenin's evaluations, this is exactly the orientation Lenin habitually exhibited: an individual on his side who said anything unacceptable to him was shown to be either muddleheaded or "unconsciously" on the enemy side; anyone on the "enemy" side who said anything acceptable to him was also declared to be either muddleheaded or "masking his true

Snap judgment killing a budding thought

nature." In short, the closed mind is definitely two-valued in its orientation: you have to like *everything* about the speaker or *nothing.*

Psychologically, Rokeach says, all human beings are engaged simultaneously in two tasks: (1) they seek to know more about the world, and (2)
they wish to protect themselves from the world—especially from information that might prove upsetting. As the need for defense against disturbing
information gets stronger, curiosity about the world gets weaker. ("A person will be open to information *insofar as possible,* and will reject it, screen
it out, or alter it *insofar as necessary.*")

Rokeach refers to the things you believe in as your "belief system," and
to the things you don't believe in as your "disbelief system." (For example,
if you are a Catholic, Catholicism is your "belief system," and your "disbelief system" would be atheism, Protestantism, Judaism, Buddhism, and so
on.) If you are a reasonably secure and well-organized individual, you enjoy your own belief system, but you are also open to information about
your disbelief system. (You are able, although Catholic, to take in information about Protestantism, Judaism, Buddhism, and so on, and to *see the
differences* among the various bodies of ideas that you *do not* believe in.)
To be open to information about the disbelief system, says Rokeach, *is to
have an open mind.*

However, if you are chronically insecure or anxious or frightened, you
cling desperately to your belief system, and you are too busy defending
yourself against real or imagined threats to take in information about the
disbelief system. That is, if "communism" and "socialism" are both part
of your disbelief system, *the more frightened you are, the less you are able
to distinguish between them.*

The term "socialism" is used in a variety of ways in a number of contexts. There is the Russian kind of state-controlled economy organized under the banner of the Union of Soviet *Socialist* Republics. There is "democratic socialism" (like Sweden's) with "socialistic" measures (health,
welfare, unemployment benefits, and such) instituted through democratic,
parliamentary procedures. There are also "socialistic" measures imposed

by armed dictatorships with the help of informers and secret police (for example, the collectivization of farms in Russia and China). Then there are all the measures *called* "socialistic" by their opponents: prepaid medical care, income tax, Social Security, Aid to Families with Dependent Children, or whatever. The frightened individual's reaction to all of these different measures is to see them as alike: "One is just as bad as the other— they are all socialism, which means that they are all communism." Other disturbing areas are also seen as "communism": the fluoridation of the public water supply, abstract art, or the demand of blacks for equal rights. According to Rokeach, *this inability to see the differences among the various things you do not believe in characterizes the closed mind.*

With such a view, the individual with the closed mind looks around at the world through frightened eyes and sees "communism" making progress everywhere. (He does not observe communist setbacks.) From here it takes only a short inferential step to conclude that all these "communists" are secretly united in a vast conspiracy. Further inferences are made to explain why this "conspiracy" is so "successful." Furthermore, it is believed, our own government has been penetrated by "communists," their "dupes," and "sympathizers." Therefore, it is argued, the most urgent task is to expose and drive from office all the "communists" now occupying high places in our society—especially in government and education. "The greatest dangers to America are internal!"

CHAPTER 14

Art and Tension

But my position is this: that if we try to discover what the poem is doing for the poet, we may discover a set of generalizations as to what poems do for everybody.

KENNETH BURKE

A well-chosen anthology [of verse] is a complete dispensary of medicine for the more common mental disorders, and may be used as much for prevention as cure.

ROBERT GRAVES

Animals KNOW their environment by direct experience only; human beings crystallize their knowledge and their feelings in phonetic symbolic representations; by written symbols, they accumulate knowledge and pass it on to further generations. Animals feed themselves where they find food, but human beings, coordinating their efforts by linguistic means, feed themselves abundantly and with food prepared by a hundred hands and brought great distances. Animals exercise but limited control over each other, but human beings, again by employing symbols, establish laws and ethical systems, which are linguistic means of imposing order and predictability upon human conduct. Acquiring knowledge, securing food, establishing social order—these activities make sense to the biologist because they contribute to survival. For human beings, each of these activities involves a symbolic dimension—a dimension of which lower animals have no inkling.

Let us attempt to state the functions of literature in scientifically verifiable terms—in other words, in terms of biological "survival value." Granted that this is a difficult task in the present state of psychological knowledge, it is nonetheless necessary that we try to do so, since most explanations of the necessity or value of literature (or the other arts) take the form of purr-words—which are really no explanations at all. For example, Wordsworth speaks of poetry as "the breath and finer spirit of all knowledge"; Coleridge speaks of it as "the best words in the best order." The explanations of literature given by many teachers and critics follow a similar purr-word pattern, usually reducible to "You should read great literature because it is very, very great." If we are to give a scientific account of the functions of literature, we shall have to do better than that.

Having included under the term "literature" all the affective uses of language, we are helped in our inquiry by recent psychological and psychiatric investigations, as well as by the insights of critics and students of literature. These sources indicate that, from the point of view of the utterer, one of the most important functions of the utterance is the relieving of *tensions*. We have all known the relief that comes from uttering a long and resounding series of impolite vocables under the stress of great irritation. The same releasing of psychological tensions—Aristotle called it *catharsis*—appears to be effected at all levels of affective utterance, if we are to believe what writers themselves have said about the creative process. The novel, the drama, the poem, like the oath or the expletive, arise at least in part out of internal necessity when the organism experiences a serious tension, whether resulting from joy, grief, disturbance, or frustration. And as a result of the utterances made, the tension is, to a greater or lesser degree—perhaps only momentarily—mitigated.

A frustrated or unhappy animal can do relatively little about its tensions. A human being, however, with an extra dimension (the world of symbols) to move around in, not only undergoes experience, but also *symbolizes his experience to himself.* Our states of tension—especially the unhappy tensions—*become tolerable* as we manage *to state what is wrong—to get it said*—whether to a sympathetic friend, or on paper to a hypothetical sympathetic reader, or even to oneself.[1] If our symbolizations are adequate and sufficiently skillful, our tensions are brought *symbolically under control.* To achieve this control, we may employ what Kenneth Burke has called "symbolic strategies"—that is, ways of reclassifying our experiences so that they are "encompassed" and easier to bear. Whether by processes of "pouring out our hearts" or by "symbolic strategies" or by other means, we may employ symbolizations as mechanisms of relief when the pressures of a situation become intolerable.

As we all know, language is social, and, for every speaker, there may be hearers. An utterance that relieves a tension for the speaker can relieve a similar tension, should one happen to exist, in the hearer. And because human experience remains fairly constant, this process is possible even when speaker and hearer are separated by centuries or by different cultures. The symbolic manipulation by which John Donne, in one of his Holy Sonnets, "encompassed" his feelings of guilt enables us too, at another time and under other circumstances, to encompass our feelings of guilt about, in all probability, a different set of sins.

William Ernest Henley confronted the fact of his chronic invalidism—he had been ill since childhood and had spent long periods of his life in hospitals—by stating, in his well-known poem "Invictus," his refusal to be defeated:

> Out of the night that covers me,
> Black as the pit from pole to pole,
> I thank whatever gods may be
> For my unconquerable soul.
>
> In the fell clutch of circumstance
> I have not winced nor cried aloud,
> Under the bludgeonings of chance
> My head is bloody, but unbowed.
>
> Beyond this place of wrath and tears
> Looms but the horror of the shade,

---

[1] An indication of the importance of "getting it said" is given in the research of Charles W. Slack of the Harvard Psychological Clinic. Dr. Slack "hired," at modest hourly wages, unemployed young men hanging around street corners in Cambridge. He asked them to be "research consultants" to help inquire into the question of "how guys foul up." Their task was to talk into tape-recorders about themselves and their problems. A dramatic improvement in behavior was shown by almost all who took part in the project: they got jobs and held them; the number of arrests among them dropped by half.

And yet the menace of the years
Finds, and shall find me, unafraid.

It matters not how strait the gate,
How charged with punishments the scroll,
I am the master of my fate:
I am the captain of my soul.

How, at a different time and under different circumstances, other people can use Henley's utterance to take arms against a different sea of troubles is shown by the fact that this poem has been one of the favorite poems of American blacks and is sometimes recited or sung chorally by their organizations. Indeed, the entire poem takes on different meanings depending on what a reader, putting himself into the role of the speaker of the poem, projects into the words "the night that covers me."[2]

Poetry has often been spoken of as an aid to sanity. Kenneth Burke calls it "equipment for living." It would appear that we can take these statements seriously and work out their implications in many directions. What are, for example, some of the kinds of symbolic manipulation by which we attempt to equip ourselves in the face of the constant succession of difficulties and tensions, great and small, that confront us day by day? Of course, the stimulus of social tension is not necessary for all literature, but unquestionably it is often a significant spur to creation.

Some "Symbolic Strategies"

First of all, of course, there is what is called literary "escape"—a tremendous source of literature, poetry, drama, comic strips, and other forms of affective communication. Edgar Rice Burroughs, confined to a sickbed, symbolically traipsed through the jungle, in the person of Tarzan, in a series of breath-taking and triumphant adventures—and by means of this symbolic compensation made his sickbed endurable. At the same time he provided diversion that may have helped make life endurable for millions of readers. One may not think much of the Tarzan stories; still, one must admit that in order to derive what relief they offer from pain or boredom,

---

[2] Anyone saying, as I do, that a poem may mean different things to different people, may seem to invite the charge that such a relativistic position makes it impossible "to distinguish between right and wrong readings of a poem." It is perhaps necessary, therefore, to clarify what is asserted here: saying that a poem may have different meanings for different people is *not* the same as saying that a poem can mean anything at all.

Incidentally, another example of a poem acquiring a changed meaning in a changed context is provided by the Freedom Riders of the civil rights movement who "sat in" and refused to budge from segregated premises. They responded to threats with the old hymn, "We shall not be, we shall not be moved," endowing the words with a meaning not found when sung in church.

it takes, both in the telling and in the reading of such stories, the symbolic process, and hence a thoroughly human nervous system.

Let us take another example of symbolic strategy. When a disgruntled employee calls his employer a "half-pint Hitler," is he not using a "strategy" that, by means of introducing his employer (a petty tyrant) into a perspective which includes Hitler (a great tyrant), symbolically reduces his employer to what Burke calls manageable proportions? And did not Dante, unable to punish his enemies as he wished them to be punished, likewise symbolically put them in their places in the most uncomfortable quarters in Hell? There is a world of difference between the completeness and adequacy of such a simple epithet as "half-pint Hitler" and Dante's way of disposing of his enemies—and Dante accomplished many more things in his "Inferno" besides symbolically punishing his enemies—but are they not both symbolic manipulations by means of which the utterers derive a measure of relief or relaxation of psychological tensions?

Let us take another example. Upton Sinclair was deeply disturbed by the Chicago stockyards as he saw them in 1906. He could have tried to forget them; he could have buried himself in reading or writing about other things, such as idyllic lands long ago and far away or entirely nonexistent—as do the readers and writers of escape literature. He could have tried, by a different symbolic manipulation, to show that present evil was part of greater good "in God's omniscient plan." This has been the strategy of many religions as well as many authors. Still another possibility would have been actually to reform conditions at the stockyards so that he could contemplate them with equanimity—but he would have had to be an important official in a packing company or in the government to initiate a change in conditions. What he did, therefore, was to *socialize his discontent*—pass it on to others—on the very good theory that if enough people felt angry or disgusted with the situation, they could collectively change the stockyards in such a way that one could adjust oneself to them. Sinclair's novel *The Jungle* (1906) upset so many people that it led to a federal investigation of the meat industry and to the enactment of legislation controlling some of its practices.

As is now well known, when tensions are experienced constantly and permitted to accumulate, they may lead to more or less serious psychological maladjustment. Adjustment, as modern psychology sees the process, is no static condition arising from neither knowing nor caring what is wrong with the world. It is a dynamic, day-to-day, moment-to-moment process, and it involves changing the environment to suit one's personality as much as it involves adapting one's feelings to existing conditions. The greater resources one has for achieving and maintaining adjustment, the more successful the process will be. Literature appears to be one of the available resources.

Both the production and enjoyment of literature, then, being human symbolic devices employed in the day-to-day process of equipping our-selves for living, appear to be extensions of our adjustment mechanism be-yond those provided for us by that part of our biological equipment which we have in common with lower animals. If a man were to spend years of his life trying to discover the chemical constituency of salt water without bothering to find out what has already been said on the subject in any elementary chemistry book, we should say that he was making very imper-fect use of the resources available to us. Similarly, can it not be said that people, worrying themselves sick over their individual frustrations, con-stantly suffering from petty irritations and hypertensions, are making ex-tremely imperfect use of the available human resources of adjustment when they fail to strengthen and quiet themselves through contact with literature, music, painting, and the other arts?

What all this boils down to, then, is that poetry (along with the other arts), whether good or bad and at whatever level of crudity or refinement, exists to fulfill a necessary biological function for a symbol-using class of life, that of *helping us to maintain psychological health and equilibrium.*

Equipment For Living

Psychiatrists recognize no distinct classes of the "sane" and the "insane." Sanity is a matter of degree, and "sane" people are all capable of becoming more sane, or less, according to the experiences they encounter and the strength and flexibility of the internal equipment with which they meet them. Even as one's physical health has to be maintained by food and exercise, it would appear that one's psychological health too has to be maintained in the very course of living by "nourishment" at the level of affective symbols: literature that introduces us to new sources of delight; literature that makes us feel that we are not alone in our misery; literature that shows us our own problems in a new light; literature that suggests new possibilities to us and opens new areas of possible experience; litera-ture that offers us a variety of "symbolic strategies" by means of which we can "encompass" our situations.

But there are certain kinds of literature, like certain kinds of processed food, that look very much like nourishment but contain none of the essen-tial vitamin ingredients, so that great quantities can be consumed without affecting one's spiritual undernourishment. (One could mean by "essential vitamin ingredients" in this context, "maps" of actual "territories" of hu-man experience, directives that are both realistic and helpful, and so on.) Certain kinds of popular writing claim to throw light on given problems in life—stories with such titles as "Money Hungry: Too Much is Never Enough"—but, like patent medicines, these offer apparent soothing to sur-face symptoms and ignore underlying causes. Other kinds of fiction, like drugs and liquor, offer escape from pain and again leave causes untouched, so that the more of them you take the more you need. Fantasy-living—which is one of the important characteristics of schizophrenia—can be aggravated by the consumption of too much of this narcotic literature. Still other kinds of fiction, movies, television programs, and the like often give a false, prettified picture of the world—a world that can be adjusted to *without effort*. But readers who adjust themselves to this unreal world become progressively less adjusted to the world as it is. Such "adjustment to unreality" must lead to an enormous amount of disappointment and heartbreak among the young and unsophisticated when they discover that the world is not as it was depicted in romantic tales.

On the other hand, it will not do to apply too crudely the principle of literature as an aid to sanity. Some might be tempted to say that, if literature is an instrument for maintaining sanity, the writings of many not-too-sane geniuses will have to be thrown out as unhealthy. It would seem, on the contrary, that the symbolic strategies devised by extremely tortured people like Feodor Dostoyevski or Donne or Percy Bysshe Shelley for the encompassing of their situations are valuable in the extreme. They mixed themselves powerful medicines against their ills, and their medicines not only help us to encompass whatever similar tortures we may be suffering from, but may serve also as antitoxins for future sufferings.

Furthermore, when a work of literature is said to be "permanent," "lasting," or "great," does it not mean that the symbolic strategy by which the author encompassed his disturbance (achieved his equilibrium) works for other people troubled by other disturbances at other times and places? Is it possible, for example, to read Sinclair's strategic handling of the Chicago stockyards without awareness that it applies more or less adequately to other people's disturbances about factory conditions in Turin, or Manchester, or Kobe, or Seoul? And if it applies especially well to, say, Detroit, does not the Detroiter regard Sinclair's book as having lasting value? And if, under changing conditions, there are no longer social situations which arouse similar tensions, or if the strategies seem no longer appropriate, do we not consider the author to be "dated," if not "dead"?[3] But if an author has adequately dealt with tensions that people in different times and under

---

[3] *The Jungle is* quite dated in most respects, although still powerful in some. Working people in the United States (and in many other parts of the world as well) are simply not treated as badly as they are in this novel, partly because of unionization, of course, and also partly because of advances in technology and a more highly developed public conscience. But ever since its publication in 1906, it has been widely read by working classes all over the world: few American books have been translated into so many languages.

The symbolic strategies of works of great literary art, unlike those of *The Jungle*, are usually too complex and subtle for such a rough analysis as has been attempted here. *The Jungle* has been chosen for discussion because books like this, which are far from being great masterpieces and yet give a great deal of profoundly felt insight into segments of human experience, are especially helpful in the understanding of the theories of literature proposed in this chapter. The strategies, being not too subtle, can be clearly seen and described.

different conditions appear to experience, do we not call those writings "universal" and "undying"?

The relationship between literature and life is a subject about which little is known scientifically at the present time. Nevertheless, in an unorganized way, we all feel that we know something about that relationship, since we have all felt the effects of some kind of literature at some time in our lives. Most of us have felt, even if we have not been able to prove, that harmful consequences can arise from the consumption of such literary fare as is offered in many movies, in popular magazines, and in television programs. But the imperfection of our scientific knowledge is revealed by the fact that, when there is widespread argument as to whether or not violence on television should be banned, equally imposing authorities on both sides are able to "prove" their cases; some say that television stimulates children's imaginations in unhealthy ways and offers inappropriate models of behavior, while others say that crimes of violence are committed by disturbed youths who would have committed them anyway, and that television shows, by offering to normal children a symbolic release of their aggressive tendencies, actually help to calm them down. This question remains a vexing one because the number of complex influences on human behavior is so great that experimental verification of the extent of any one influence is nearly impossible.

Because no one yet has answers to such questions, it would seem to be extremely desirable for students of literature and of psychology to work together. If they do, perhaps they will some day be able to state, in the interests of everyday sanity, what kinds of literature contribute to maturity and what kinds help to keep us permanently infantile and immature in our evaluations.

Art as Order

At least one other important element enters into our pleasure both in the writing and reading of literature—but about this there is still less available scientific knowledge. It pertains to what are called the artistic or esthetic values of a work of the imagination.

In Chapter 8, we spoke of the relationships, in a novel for example, of the incidents and characters to each other—that is, the meaningful arrangement of experiences that makes a novel different from a jumbled narrative. Before we speak of a narrative as a "novel" and therefore as a "work of art," we must be satisfied that, regardless of whether or not we could "live the story" through imaginative identification with the characters, the incidents are arranged in some kind of *order*. Even when we don't happen to like the story, if we find a complex, but discernible and interesting, order to the incidents in a novel, we are able to say, "It certainly is beautifully put together." Indeed, sometimes the internal order and neat relationships of the parts to each other in a novel may be so impressive that we enjoy it in spite of a lack of sympathy with the kinds of incidents or people portrayed. Why is order interesting almost of itself?

I would suggest that if an answer is to be found to this question, it will have to be found in terms of human symbolic processes and the fact that symbols of symbols, symbols of symbols of symbols, and so on, can be man-ufactured indefinitely by the human nervous system. This fact, already explained in Chapter 2 (and further in Chapter 9), can be given a special application that may enable us to understand the functions of literature.

Animals, as we have remarked, live in the extensional world—they have no symbolic world to speak of. There would seem to be no more "order" in an animal's existence than the order of physical events as they impinge on its life. Man, however, both *lives* (at the extensional level) and *talks about his life to himself* (at the symbolic level, either with words or, in the case of painters and musicians and dancers, with nonverbal sym-bols). A human being is not satisfied simply to know his way around exten-sionally; he can hardly help talking to himself about what he has seen and felt and done.

The data of experience, when talked about, are full of contradictions. Mrs. Robinson loves her children, but ruins them through misdirected love; the illiterate peasants of a Chinese village show greater social and personal wisdom than the educated people of great cities; people say crime doesn't pay, but in some cases it pays extremely well; a young man who is by temperament a scholar and a poet feels compelled to commit a political murder; a faithful wife of twenty years deserts her husband for no appar-ent reason; a ne'er-do-well acts courageously in a dangerous situation— these and a thousand other contradictions confront us in the course of our lives. Unordered, and bearing no relationship to each other, our statements about experience are not only disconnected, but they are difficult to under-stand or to use.

Insofar as we are aware of these contradictions, this disorder among our statements is itself a source of tension. Such contradictions provide us with no guide to action; hence they leave us in a state of indecision and bewilderment that is not resolved until we have, *by talking to ourselves about our talking* (symbolizing our symbols), "fitted things together," so that things don't seem to be "meaningless" anymore. Religion, philosophy, science, and art are equally, and through different methods, ways of re-solving the tensions produced by the contradictory data of experience: by talking about our talking, then talking about our talking about our talking, and so on, until some kind of *order* has been established among the data.

Talking about things, talking about talking, talking about talking about talking, and so on, represent what we have called talking at different *levels of abstraction*. The imposition of order upon our pictures of the world is, it appears, what we mean by "understanding." When we say that a scientist "understands" something, does it not mean that he or she has ordered his or her observations at the objective, descriptive, and higher inferential levels of abstraction into a workable system in which all levels are related to other levels in a few powerful generalizations? When a great religious leader or philosopher is said to "understand" life, does it not mean that he or she has also ordered his or her observations into a set of attitudes, often crystallized into exceedingly general and powerful directives? And when a novelist is said to "understand" the life of any segment of humanity (or humanity as a whole), has he or she not also ordered his or her observations at many different levels of abstraction—the particular and concrete, the general, and the more general?

The novelist, however, presents that order not in a scientific, ethical, or philosophical system of highly abstract generalizations, but in a set of symbolic experiences at the descriptive level of affective reports, involving the reader's feelings through the mechanism of identification. And these symbolic experiences, in the work of any competent novelist, are woven together to frame a consistent set of attitudes, whether of scorn, or compassion, or admiration of courage, or sympathy with the downtrodden, or a sense of futility, depending on the author's outlook.

Some of the ways of organizing a set of experiences for literary purposes are purely mechanical and external: these are the "rules" governing the proper construction of the novel, the play, the short story, the sonnet, and so on. But more important are the ways of organization suggested by the materials of the literary work—the experiences which the writer wishes to organize. When the materials of a story do not fit into the conventional pattern of a novel, the novelist may create a new organization altogether, more suited to the presentation of his experiences than the conventional patterns. In such a case, critics speak of the materials as "creating their own form." In such a case, too, the order may seem like disorder at first— one thinks of Laurence Sterne's *Tristram Shandy* and James Joyce's *Ulysses*—because the principles of organization, being new, have to be discovered in the course of reading. The reason a poem, novel, or play assumes the shape it ultimately does is the concern of the technical literary critic. The critic studies the interplay of external and internal demands which has finally shaped the materials into a work of art.

To symbolize one's experiences adequately and then to order them into a coherent whole constitute an integrative act. The great novelist, dramatist, or poet is one who has successfully integrated and given coherence to vast areas of human experience. Literary greatness requires, therefore, great extensional awareness of the range of human experience as well as great powers of ordering that experience meaningfully. This is why the discipline of the creative artist is endless: there is always more to learn, both about human experience (which is the material to be ordered) and about the techniques of the craft (which are the means of ordering).

From the point of view of the reader, the fact that language is social is again of central importance. The ordering of experiences and attitudes accomplished linguistically by the writer produces some ordering of the reader's own experiences and attitudes. The reader becomes, as a result of this ordering, somewhat more "in order" as well. That's what art is for.

CHAPTER 15

Poetry and Advertising

I've snuff and tobaccy and excellent jacky;
I've scissors and watches and knives;
I've ribbons and laces to set off the faces
Of pretty young sweethearts and wives.

W. S. GILBERT

The advertisement is one of the most interesting and difficult of modern literary
forms.

ALDOUS HUXLEY

The Poet's Function

ONE DOES NOT often mention poetry and advertising in the same breath. Poetry is universally conceded to be the loftiest of the verbal arts. Advertising, on the other hand, is not even an autonomous art; it is but the handmaiden of commerce. Its name carries connotations, often well deserved, of half-truth, deception, and outright fraud; of appeals to vanity, fear, snobbery, and false pride; of radio and television programs hideous with wheedling voices.

There are many more contrasts. The best poetry seems to be fully appreciated only by the few and to be beyond the comprehension of the many. The best advertising, however, is thought about, laughed over, and acted upon by multitudes. Poetry is, in the general apprehension, something special, to be studied in schools, to be enjoyed by cultivated people who have time for that sort of thing, to be read on solemn or momentous occasions. Advertising is part of everyday life.

Nevertheless, poetry and advertising have much in common. To begin with, they both make extensive use of rhyme and rhythm ("What's the word? Thunderbird!"). They both use words chosen for their affective and connotative values rather than for their denotative content. ("Take a puff . . . it's springtime! Gray rocks and the fresh green leaves of springtime reflected in a mountain pool. . . . Where else can you find air so refreshing? And where can you find a smoke as refreshing as Salem's?")

William Empson, the English critic, said in his *Seven Types of Ambiguity* that the best poems are ambiguous; they are richest when they have two or three or more levels of meaning at once. Advertising, too, although on a much more primitive level, deliberately exploits ambiguities and plays on words: a vodka is advertised with the slogan, "Leaves you breathless"; an automobile is described as "Hot, Handsome, a Honey to Handle"; an unbridled stallion ravishes a woman's bedroom, followed by the words "Colt 45. It works every time."

But the most important respect in which poetry and advertising resemble each other is that they both strive to give meaning to the data of everyday experience; they both strive to make the objects of experience symbolic of something beyond themselves. Speaking of the untutored, "wild and rude" Peter Bell in the poem of that name, William Wordsworth said:

> A primrose by the river's brim,
> A yellow primrose was to him.
> And it was nothing more.

The poet, not content to let a yellow primrose remain merely a yellow primrose, strives to invest it with meanings. In the poet's eye, the primrose comes to symbolize many things: the joy of early spring, his love of his darling Lucy, the benevolence of God, the transitoriness of life, or other things.

Similarly, an advertising writer cannot permit a bar of soap to remain a bar of soap and "nothing more." Whatever the object for sale is, the copywriter, like the poet, must invest it with significance so that it becomes symbolic of something beyond itself—symbolic of domestic happiness (like Van Camp's pork and beans), of aristocratic elegance (like Joy perfume), of rugged masculinity (like Marlboros), or of solid, traditional American virtues (like Chevrolet). From toothpaste to tires, convertibles to colas, the task of the copywriter is *the poeticizing of consumer goods.*

Art and Life

All literary and dramatic enjoyment involves, to some degree, as stated in Chapter 8, the reader's imaginative identification with the roles portrayed in the story or play, and her projection of herself into the situations described. The same principles hold for poetry and advertising, of course. In reading poetry, we identify ourselves with the characters the poet creates, or with the poet himself. Advertisers also invite us to identify ourselves with the roles they portray. "Put yourself in this picture!" says the advertiser, showing radiant groups of young people drinking Seven-Up; families wide-eyed with joy as they try out their new Suzuki Samurai or sit down to their dinner of fried chicken made with new, improved Mazola; aristocratic gentlemen and sportsmen wearing Armani shirts; and the lovely young woman who, having found a toothpaste that cleans her breath while it cleans her teeth, is now a happy bride.

The identification that great poets invite us to make requires of the reader both close attention and imaginative strenuousness; it is not everyone who can empathize with Lucifer in Milton's *Paradise Lost* or with "The Ancient Mariner" of Coleridge. The identifications that advertisers invite us to make are easy and pleasant: most of us would *like* to be as handsome and well-dressed and joyous and radiant as the people in the advertisements. Looking at the four-color picture of the serene mother

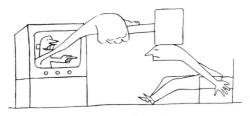

Hard sell

holding her box of Downy, surrounded by spotless children and piles of fluffy towels, the harassed housewife is expected to dream herself into the picture and say, "That's for me!" According to the advertisements, happiness is always within reach.

In spite of this marked contrast in the demands which poetry and advertising make upon their audiences, both have the common function of entering into our imaginations and shaping those idealizations of ourselves that determine, in large measure, our conduct. "Life," said Oscar Wilde, "is an imitation of art." Insofar as both poetry and advertising exact this tribute of imitation, they are both, in a real sense, "creative." Outsiders to the advertising business are often surprised and sometimes amused to learn that the art and copy departments of advertising agencies are known as "creative departments" and their head is known as "creative director." The more you think about it, the more appropriate the term becomes—whether or not you approve of what is created.

Let us call this use of verbal magic (or verbal skulduggery) for the purpose of giving an imaginative, symbolic, or ideal dimension to life, and all that is in it, *poetry.* If we speak separately of what we ordinarily call poetry and advertising, let us speak of the latter as *sponsored poetry*, and of the former as *unsponsored poetry.*

Using our terms in this way, we see that our age is by no means deficient in poetry, if we include under that term the poetry of consumer goods. We have more access to poetry (or perhaps we should say that poetry has more access to us) than people have had at any other time in history. It is not possible to listen to most radio or television stations for ten minutes without running into a panegyric for a beer, a spray deodorant, or a chewing gum. Most American large-circulation magazines are so full of sponsored poetry about breakfast foods, hams, electric appliances, clothing, liquor, and automobiles, and this poetry is so lavishly illustrated by the most expensive processes of color reproduction and printing in order to attract attention, that reading the articles and stories is like trying to do your algebra homework in Times Square on New Year's Eve.

The Laureate's Task

To say that poetry is sponsored, however, is not to say that it is necessarily bad. Poets have been sponsored in times past, although the conditions of their sponsorship were different. The court poet, or poet laureate, is a typical example of the sponsored poet of a previous age. Such a poet, a paid retainer in the court of a monarch, or nobleman, had the task of saying, in odes and epics on suitable occasions, how great and powerful was the ruler who employed him, and how happy the people were under that ruler's benign and just government. Good poet laureates rose above the level of personal flattery of the kings they worked for, and sometimes gave expression to the highest ideals of their times and of their nation. Virgil was poet laureate to the Emperor Augustus. When Virgil wrote *The Aeneid*, according to the *Encyclopedia Britannica* (11th edition), "The problem before him was to compose a work of art on a large scale, which should represent a great action of the heroic age, and should at the same time embody the most vital ideas and sentiments of the hour—which in substance should glorify Rome and the present ruler of Rome." In brief, Virgil had a sponsor and was working under assignment. Nevertheless, because of the character of Virgil as a poet and as a man, and because of his genuine dedication to his task, the fulfillment of his assignment turned out to be a very great poem indeed—many would say the greatest poem of his age.

Another example of a poet laureate is Alfred, Lord Tennyson, who held that post under Queen Victoria. In 1852, Tennyson was called upon to write a poem on the occasion of the burial of the Duke of Wellington in Westminster Abbey. His task was to express the sentiments of his queen and his nation at the death of a national hero. These opening lines from his "Ode on the Death of the Duke of Wellington" (a poem of over 500 lines) show unmistakably that sponsored art can also be art of a very impressive kind, certainly worthy of attentive study in a course in English literature:

> Bury the Great Duke
> With the empire's lamentation,
> Let us bury the Great Duke
> To the noise of the mourning of a mighty nation,
> Mourning when their leaders fall,
> Warriors carry the warrior's pall,
> And sorrow darkens hamlet and hall.
>
> Where shall we lay the man whom we deplore?
> Here, in streaming London's central roar.
> Let the sound of those he wrought for,
> And the feet of those he fought for,
> Echo round his bones for evermore.
>
> Lead out the pageant: sad and slow,
> As fits an universal woe,
> Let the long long procession go,
> And let the sorrowing crowd about it grow,
> And let the mournful martial music blow;
> The last great Englishman is low.

It is a curious fact that American advertising has occasionally shown itself capable of performing a poet laureate's function—that of giving expression to a nation's ideals and sentiments on an important public occasion. In 1950, the tomb of the Unknown Soldier of World War II was dedicated in Washington, and at that time the following advertisement appeared in the newspapers of Boston and in national magazines:

He Is the Stranger Who Is My Brother

This is the story of a man I never knew, and yet I know all about him. He is dead now, and he lies in a tomb of polished marble whose splendor would surprise him. And people come from everywhere to stand here with their heads bowed, their eyes serious, their hearts filled with mourning for this man they never knew.

Because he wore a uniform when he died, they call him the Unknown Soldier. I think he was a good soldier, though fighting was never his business. He was a man of peace, I'm sure, though he never told me.

He was born on a farm in the Dakotas . . . or was it a miner's cottage in Pennsylvania, a tenement in the Bronx, a ranch house in Texas, a duplex apartment on Park Avenue? I can't be sure, as I stand here with my hat in my hand, reverent at the grave of this man I never knew.

Was he a poet, bookkeeper, truck driver, surgeon, lumberjack, errand boy, student? Was he telling a joke, or cursing his sergeant, or writing to his family, when the missile came?

I don't know. For when they picked this man, from among all our nameless dead, he was lying quiet in a closed coffin, and known only to God.

But I do know that he is deserving of honor and respect. For, whoever he may be, I feel sure he must have believed, as I do, in the equality of men, the promise of men, the duty of men to live justly with each other and with themselves.

And that is why I stand here with my hat in my hand, reverent at the grave of the stranger who is my brother, my father, my son, my countryman, my friend.

John Hancock Mutual Life Insurance Company
Boston, Massachusetts

A comparison of this advertisement with Tennyson's "Ode" is instructive. Both express a nation's mourning. Both express, too, something of the spirit of the nations that produced them: Tennyson's poem reflects the pomp and military pride of the British Empire of the mid-nineteenth century; the insurance company advertisement is phrased in the simple, colloquial accents of the democratic America of the mid-twentieth century. The advertisement, necessarily addressed to a wider public than the poem, makes freer use of clichés; the reader trained in literary appreciation would find its language commonplace. Nevertheless, the writer of this advertisement performed on this occasion a laureate's task for a nation that had no poet laureate.

The Problems of the Unsponsored Poet

Let us turn from sponsored poetry to unsponsored poetry—the kind poets write not to satisfy any external demand, but to satisfy themselves. For decades, there has been much wringing of the hands at the sad state of modern poetry. Robert Hillyer, a poet himself, in an article on "Modern Poetry vs. the Common Reader" in the *Saturday Review*, speaks of the poets of today as being in a "welter of confusion and frustration." He is distressed by their obscurity of language—"the flight from clarity," as he calls it. He is certain that both the unintelligibility and the tone of despair characteristic of much modern verse are due to the moral defects of the poets themselves. "Their confusion," he writes, "is a sign of artistic effeminacy and egotism."

It is true that many modern poets, from T. S. Eliot to Ezra Pound to Wallace Stevens to Delmore Schwartz to Robert Lowell to Sylvia Plath, are not easy to understand on first reading, or even on second or third reading. But Mr. Hillyer is mistaken, it seems to me, in blaming the difficulties of modern poetry on the moral shortcomings of poets. He fails to take into account the context in which the unsponsored poet has to write today.

The unsponsored poet of today works in a semantic environment in which almost all the poetry that ordinary people hear and read is the sponsored poetry of consumer goods. Poetic language is used so constantly and relentlessly for the purposes of salesmanship that it has become almost impossible to say anything with enthusiasm or joy or conviction without running into the danger of sounding as if you were selling something. John Keats could write:

> To one who has been long in city pent
> 'Tis very sweet to look into the fair
> And open face of heaven,—to breathe in prayer
> Full in the smile of the blue firmament. . . .

Today, anyone writing like this would immediately be suspected of working for the Hawaii Visitors' Bureau or for a steamship line promoting Mediterranean cruises.

Robert Herrick could write without self-consciousness about the beauty of a woman:

> Whenas in silks my Julia goes,
> Then, then, methinks, how sweetly flows
> The liquefaction of her clothes

And so could William Wordsworth:

> She was a phantom of delight
> When first she gleamed upon my sight;
> A lovely apparition sent
> To be a moment's ornament;
> Her eyes as stars of twilight fair

Today, such lines remind us inevitably of the promises of advertising copy. Herrick's Julia is a testimonial to the effects of wearing Vanity Faire lingerie and Hanes hosiery, while Wordsworth's unnamed beauty obviously exemplifies the results of using Clairol and L'Oreal eye shadow. Indeed, anyone who is moved to express thankfulness for the freedoms we enjoy in America will soon begin to sound like an advertisement of the Investor-Owned Electric Light and Power Companies on the necessity of keeping the government out of the utilities business.

The Symbols We Live By

Advertising is a symbol-manipulating occupation. The symbols of fashion and elegance are used to glamorize clothing and cosmetics. The symbols of youthful gaiety sell soft drinks and candy bars. The symbols of adventure, sexuality, and sportsmanship are used to promote cigarettes and liquor. The symbols of love and delight in one's new baby have been completely appropriated by the sellers of prepared baby foods, canned milk, and disposable diapers. Advertising is a tremendous creator and devourer of symbols. Even the symbols of patriotism are used for the purposes of salesmanship. There are advertisers who assure us that "It's *American* to want something better," while a beer called "Lucky Lager" has advertised with the slogan, "It's *Lucky* if you live in America." Not even the symbols of religion are off limits—Christmas and Easter are so strenuously exploited commercially that they almost lose their religious significance. And there are other examples of the commercial use of religious symbols: a Midwestern flour company, for example, once organized the women's auxiliaries of churches into listener clubs for a quasi-religious program it was sponsoring. The women were urged to save box-tops from the company's cake flour in order to earn furniture and equipment for their churches—with the results that these churches were converted in effect into promotional outlets for that company's cake flour.

The problems of the unsponsored poet in an environment dominated by advertising are therefore difficult. Poets, too, must work with the symbols that exist in the culture, and they must create new ones as well. Almost all the symbols of daily living—especially those symbols that have any connotations of happiness and joy—have been appropriated by the advertisers. If unsponsored poets seem to concern themselves too much with negative moods, such as disillusionment, despair, or cynicism, part of the reason may well be that the positive moods have come to smell too much of salesmanship. Also, the verse of unsponsored poets is often difficult to understand and full of obscure symbolism. For at least a generation there have been no poets—not even Robert Frost or Carl Sandburg—who could communicate with as large a portion of the literate public as Tennyson and

Longfellow did in their time. One reason for the obscurity of modern poets may again be that the familiar symbols of courtship, home, mother, nature, and love of country have been so completely appropriated for commercial purposes as to appear unusable to the unsponsored poet. They are practically driven to use obscure symbols out of the Upanishads or Zen Buddhism in their search for something the advertisers have not already used.

Some poets, more aware of the world around them than others, have known very clearly who their chief rivals are in the business of manufacturing dreams—and, therefore, patterns of living. e. e. cummings, in his famous "Poem, or Beauty Hurts Mr. Vinal" which remains quite timely, equates advertising with bad poetry. In the 1950s, the so-called beat poets made something of a cult of rejecting the consumer-advertising culture. A "square," in beat culture and its descendant hippie culture of the '60s and early '70s, means a person who believes the advertisements, and who is therefore caught in the rat race of late-model cars, wall-to-wall carpeting, installment payments, conformity, and constant financial anxiety. To be "hip" is, among other things, to have ceased believing the ads. "I can do *without* things," cries a newly liberated young lady of Venice, California, quoted by Lawrence Lipton in *The Holy Barbarians*. "God!—do you know what a relief that is?"

Such reaction against advertising and consumer culture may have been short-lived: In the '80s, an apparent wave of materialism and fascination with purchased symbols of success seems to have engulfed much of the American public, including many people who participated in the counterculture of a few years earlier.

Symbols For Our Times

"Poets," said Shelley, "are the unacknowledged legislators of the world." Poets, by creating new ways of feeling and perceiving, help to create the new ways of thinking that bring us to terms with a changing world. Every age finds its appropriate symbols. In medieval times, religious images symbolized what people believed in and lived by: God, the angels, and the saints. In Renaissance times, the prevailing image was that of the human body, which was used in endless ways to symbolize the ideas of an age of humanism.

With what symbols shall the poet bring us to terms with the realities of our own times? In the past few decades, whole new areas of thought and exploration have been opened up by the sciences—by electronics, by astrophysics, by microbiology, by the study of nucleoproteins and their role in genetics, by radioactive tracer studies, and by nuclear physics. Instant communications bring us unsettling news from parts of the world that we had never thought about before. Astronauts shoot through space, so that the limits of the planet we live on are no longer the limits of our exploration. We can, and do, describe these new developments in the language of science, but how are we to take these new and urgent realities into our hearts as well as our minds, unless poets give us new images with which to experience them?

CHAPTER 16

The Dime in the Juke Box

The habit of common and continuous speech is a symptom of mental deficiency.

WALTER BAGEHOT

The tongue is the most mobile structure of the human body.

WENDELL JOHNSON

MANY A PRACTICAL-MINDED LECTURER and clergyman has no doubt discovered the principle that when someone in the audience asks a question he cannot answer, the thing to do is to make an appropriate *sounding* set of noises, and few people will notice that the question has not been answered. Words are used sometimes intentionally, often unintentionally, as smoke screens for ignorance and the absence of ideas.

At one time, when the then governor of Wisconsin forced the resignation of the then president of the state university, the merits and demerits of the case were heatedly debated in newspapers throughout the state. I was an extension lecturer for the University of Wisconsin at the time and often encountered acquaintances and strangers who asked, "Say, doc, what's going on down there in Madison? It's all politics, isn't it?" I never found out what anybody meant by "it's all politics," but in order to save trouble I usually answered, "Yes, I suppose it is." Thereupon the questioner would look pleased with himself and say, "That's what I thought!" In short, "politics" was the appropriate-sounding word in this context. The question at the heart of the controversy—namely, whether the governor had *abused his political powers* or had *carried out his political duty*—was never asked and never answered.

Intensional Orientation

In previous chapters, we have analyzed particular kinds of misevaluation. These can now be summed up under one term: *intensional orientation*— the habit of guiding ourselves by *words alone*, rather than by the facts to which words should guide us. We all tend to assume, when professors, writers, politicians, or other apparently responsible individuals open their mouths, that they are saying something meaningful. When we open our own mouths, we are even more likely to make that assumption. As Wendell Johnson says, "Every man is his most enchanted listener." The result of such indiscriminate lumping together of sense and nonsense is that "maps" pile up, independent of "territory." And, in the course of a lifetime, we

An idea drowns in a sea of words.

may pile up entire systems of meaningless noises, placidly unaware that they bear no relationship to reality whatever.

Intensional orientation may be regarded as a general term covering the multitude of more specific errors already pointed out:

1. The unawareness of contexts

2. The tendency toward automatic reactions

3. The confusion of levels of abstraction (confusing what is inside one's head with what is outside)

4. The consciousness of similarities, but not of differences

5. The habit of being content to explain words by means of definitions—that is, more words

When we are intensionally oriented, "capitalists," "bureaucrats," and "labor bosses" *are* what we *say* they are. People in communist countries *must* be unhappy because they are ruled by communists. (The intensional communist meanwhile believes that people in capitalist countries must be unhappy because they are ruled by "imperialist warmongers.") Atheists *must* be immoral because if people do not fear God they have "no reason to behave themselves." Politicians must be untrustworthy because all they do is "play politics."

Oververbalization

Let us take a term, such as "churchgoer," which denotes churchgoer₁, churchgoer₂, churchgoer₃ . . . , who attend divine services with moderate regularity. Note that the *denotation* says nothing about the churchgoers' character. It simply says that they go to church. The intensional meanings or *connotations* of the term, however, are quite a different matter. "Churchgoer" suggests "good Christian"; "good Christian" suggests fidelity to spouse and home, kindness to children, honesty in business, sobriety of living habits, and a whole range of admirable qualities. These suggestions further *suggest*, by two-valued orientation, that nonchurchgoers are likely not to have these qualities.

If our intensional orientations are serious, therefore, we can manufacture verbally a whole system of values—a whole system for the classification of mankind into sheep and goats—out of the connotations, informative and affective, of the term "churchgoer." That is to say, once the term is given, we can, by proceeding from connotation to connotation, keep going indefinitely. A map is independent of territory, so that we can keep on adding imaginary mountains and rivers after we have drawn in all the mountains and rivers that actually exist in the territory. Once we get

started, we can spin out whole essays, sermons, books, and even philosophical systems on the basis of the word "churchgoer"—without paying a par-
ticle of further attention to churchgoer$_1$, churchgoer$_2$, churchgoer$_3$. . . .

There is no way of stopping this process by which free associations, one
word "implying" another, can be made to go on and on. That is why, of
course, there are so many people in the world whom one calls windbags.
That is why many orators, newspaper columnists, commencement-day
speakers, politicians, and high-school elocutionists can speak at a moment's
notice on any subject whatever. Indeed, a great many of the "personality
development" and "dynamic salesmanship" courses offered commercially,
and some English and speech courses in our schools, are merely training in
this very technique—how to keep on talking when one hasn't a thing to
say.

The kind of associative "thinking" we have been discussing, which is
the product of intensional orientation, is called *circular* because, since all
the possible conclusions are contained in the connotations of the word
to start with, we are bound, no matter how hard or how long we "think,"
to come back to our starting point. Indeed, we can hardly be said ever to
leave our starting point. Of course, as soon as we are face-to-face with a
fact, we are compelled to shut up, or start over again somewhere else. That
is why it is so rude in certain kinds of meetings and conversations to bring
up any facts. They spoil everybody's good time.

Now let us say that while churchgoers$_{1,\ 2,\ 3}$, etc. prove to be the fine
people that we (intensionally) expect them to be, churchgoer$_{17}$ is discovered
to be unfaithful to his wife and dishonest in his trusteeship of other people's
money. Some people find such a case completely bewildering: how *can* a
man be a churchgoer and such a rascal at the same time? Unable to separate the intensional from the extensional "churchgoer," such people are
forced to one of three conclusions, all absurd:

1. "This is an exceptional case"—meaning, "I'm not changing my mind about
   churchgoers, who are *always* good people no matter how many exceptions you
   can find."

Hypnotic effect of one's own words

2. "He isn't *really* that bad. He *can't* be!"—that is, denying the facts in order to escape the necessity of accounting for them.

3. "You can't believe *anything* anymore. I'll never trust another churchgoer as long as I live."

An unfounded complacency, which can so easily be followed by "disillusionment," is perhaps the most serious consequence of intensional orientation. And, as we have seen, we all have intensional orientation regarding some subjects. In the 1930s, the federal government, confronted by mass unemployment, created the Works Progress Administration (WPA), an agency that hired men and women and thought up public projects for them to work on. These WPA jobs were described scornfully by opponents of the administration as "made work," to be distinguished from "real work" such as private industry was at that time failing to provide. It became a matter of pious faith on the part of these critics of the administration to believe that "WPA workers don't ever *really* work." The capacity for verbal autointoxication being as great as it is in some people, many of the believers in this faith were able to drive daily past gangs of WPA workers sweating over the construction of roads and bridges and still to declare quite honestly, "I've never yet seen a WPA worker do any work!"

Another instance of this same self-induced blindness (also known as "tunnel vision") used to be found in widespread attitudes toward "women drivers." Many men encountered hundreds of cars daily driven expertly by women; yet they would declare, again quite honestly, "I never saw a woman yet who could *really* drive a car." By *definition*, driving was regarded to be a "man's job"; women were said to be "timid," "nervous," "easily frightened," and therefore they "couldn't drive." If such men happened to know women who had driven successfully for years, they would maintain that those women had "just been lucky," or that "they don't drive like women." (As is well known, the statistics of insurance companies indicate that women as a group have better safety records than men.)

The important fact to be noticed about such attitudes toward "churchgoers," "WPA workers," and "women drivers" is that we should never have made such mistakes nor so blinded ourselves if we had never heard anything about these groups beforehand. Such attitudes are not the product of ignorance; genuine ignorance doesn't have attitudes. They are the result of false knowledge—false knowledge that robs us of whatever good sense we were born with. As we have already seen, part of this false knowledge we make up for ourselves, with our confusions of levels of abstraction and other evaluative errors described in earlier chapters. However, a great deal of it is *manufactured* simply through our universal habit of *talking too much*.

Many people, indeed, move in a perpetual vicious circle. Because of intensional orientation, they are oververbalized; by oververbalization, they strengthen their intensional orientation. Such people burst into speech as automatically as juke boxes; a dime in the slot, and they're off. With habits of this kind, it is possible for us to *talk ourselves into un-sane attitudes*, not only toward "women drivers," "Jews," "capitalists," "bankers," "liberals," and "labor unions," but also toward our personal problems: "mother," "relatives," "money," "popularity," "success," "failure"—and, most of all, toward "love" and "sex."

Advertising and Intensional Orientation

Among the forces in our present culture contributing to intensional orientation, advertising must be counted as one of the most important. The fundamental purpose of advertising—the announcing of products, prices, new inventions, or special sales—is not to be quarreled with; such announcements deliver needed information, which we are glad to get. But in national advertising directed to the consumer, the techniques of persuasion are rarely informative. As stated in the previous chapter on "Poetry and Advertising," the main endeavor is to "poeticize" or glamorize the objects to be sold by giving them brand names and investing those names with all sorts of desirable affective connotations suggestive of health, wealth, popularity with the other sex, social prominence, domestic bliss, fashion, and elegance. The process is one of creating intensional orientations toward brand names:

If you want love interest to thrive, then try this dainty way. . . . For this way is glamorous! It's feminine! It's alluring!. . . . Instinctively, you prefer the costly perfume of Verona Soap. . . . It's a fragrance men love. Massage each tiny ripple of your body daily with this delicate, cleansing lather. . . . Thrill as your senses are kissed by Verona's exquisite perfume. Be radiant.

Advertisers further promote intensional habits of mind by playing on words: the "extras" of skill and strength that enable champions to win games are equated with the "extras" of quality that a certain brand of cigarettes is claimed to have; the "protective blending" of colors that harmonizes wild animals with their environment and makes them invisible to their enemies is equated with the "protective blending" of whiskeys.

There is another subtle way in which advertising promotes intensional habits: through the practice of making slogans out of commonplace facts, advertisers make the facts appear to be unique to particular products. Rosser Reeves of the Ted Bates and Company advertising agency has cited with admiration a number of phenomenally successful campaigns using this technique—the parenthetical comments are his own: "OUR BOTTLES ARE WASHED WITH LIVE STEAM" ("His client protested that every other brewery did the same"); "IT'S TOASTED" ("So, indeed, is every other cigarette"); "GETS RID OF FILM ON TEETH" ("So, indeed, does every other toothpaste"); "STOPS HALITOSIS" ("Dozens of mouthwashes stop halitosis"); "STOPS B.O." ("All soaps stop body odor").[1] The skill that advertisers and propagandists often display in this kind of slanting reminds us of William Blake's famous warning:

> A truth that's told with bad intent
> Beats all the lies you can invent.

When advertising by verbal hypnotism succeeds in producing these intensional orientations, the act of washing with Verona Soap becomes, in our minds, a thrilling prospect indeed. Brushing our teeth with Colgate toothpaste becomes a dramatic and timely warding-off of terrible personal calamities, like getting fired or losing one's girlfriend. The smoking of Marlboros becomes an assertion of masculinity (instead of an invitation to lung cancer)—making one a rugged, outdoor, he-man type, like a cowboy or a paratrooper—even though in actuality one may be simply a clerk at a necktie counter. The taking of unnecessary (and even dangerous) laxatives becomes "following the advice of a world-renowned Viennese specialist." We are sold daydreams with every bottle of mouthwash and delusions of grandeur with every package of breakfast food.

Advertising, then, has become in large part the art of overcoming us with pleasurable affective connotations. When the consumer demands, as a step toward being guided by facts rather than by affective connotations of brand names, that certain products be required by law to have informative labels and verifiable government grading, manufacturers and their advertisers raise a hue and cry about "government interference with business."[2] This is the sort of argument presented against grade-labeling *in spite of the fact that businesses, both retail and wholesale, rely extensively on grading according to federally established standards when they do their own purchasing.*

In other words, many advertisers prefer that we be governed by automatic reactions to brand names rather than by thoughtful consideration of the facts about their products. An important reason for this preference lies

---

[1] Rosser Reeves, *Reality in Advertising* (1961), pp. 55–57.

[2] For example, a pamphlet called "Your Bread and Butter: A Salesman's Handbook on the Subject of Brand Names," prepared by "Brand Names Research Foundation" (no address given), undertakes to explain "What's Behind All the Smoke" of the consumer movement's demand for grade-labeling of consumer goods. Most of the members of organizations in the consumer movement, the pamphlet says, are "honestly concerned with solving the perennial problems of common sense buying," but a "vocal minority" of "self-appointed champions of the consumer" are the "spokesmen." These people, it is explained, "want to standardize most consumer goods, to eliminate advertising and competing brands, to see government controls extended over production, distribution and profits. They believe in a planned economy, with a government brain trust doing all the planning."

in the mechanics of present-day retail distribution. Most of the buying of groceries, for example, is done at supermarkets, where the consumer must make choices among huge and dazzling displays of packaged merchandise, with no clerk to explain the advantages of one choice over another. There-fore, to use the terminology of the trade, the buyer must be "presold" *be-fore* arriving at the market—and this is done by getting the consumer to remember, through tireless reiteration in radio and television commercials, a brand name, and by investing that name with nothing but pleasant con-notations. Anyone who has spent time around children who watch a lot of television knows how effective television advertising is at making brand names and logos instantly recognizable and desirable.

Thoughtful purchasing is the last thing many merchandisers want. Once the customer is hooked on a brand name, all sorts of tricks can be played on him or her. A widespread practice is to reduce the contents of a package without reducing its size or price; many items traditionally bought in one-pound and half-pound packages now are offered in such sizes as 15 oz., 14 1/2 oz., 7 oz., and 6 3/4 oz. These figures are often printed in tiny letters on the package in places where they are least likely to be seen. For the unwary, the costs of "brand loyalty" can be high.

Within recent years, the advertising of brand names has climbed to a higher level of abstraction. In addition to the advertising of specific prod-ucts by their brand names, there has been a wave of *advertising of advertis-ing.* As the pamphlet of the Brand Names Research Foundation urges, "So it's up to you as a salesman for a brand name to keep pushing not only YOUR BRAND, but brands in general. *Get on the Brand Wagon!*" A whis-key advertisement says: "AMERICA IS NAMES. . . . Seattle, Chicago, Kansas

The slogan

City . . . Elm Street, North Main, Times Square . . . Wrigley, Kellogg, Squibb, Ipana . . . Heinz, Calvert . . . Goodrich . . . Chevrolet. Names [the American has] always known . . . names of things he's bought and used . . . believed in . . . Yes, America is names. *Good* names. Familiar names that inspire confidence . . . For America *is* names . . . *good* names for good things to have. . . . "

High-fashion magazine ads often contain an alluring or suggestive picture with no printed information other than the name of a brand of jeans or perfume. This sort of advertising of advertising has become increasingly common. The assumption is dinned into us that, if a brand name even *sounds* familiar, the product it stands for must be good. ("The best in the land if you buy by brand.") *A graver example of systematic public miseducation can hardly be imagined. Intensional orientation is elevated to a guiding principle in the life of the consumer.* (Generic brands—for which consumers purportedly pay less because of reduced advertising costs—offer a small ray of sanity in this dismal situation.)

Sometimes it seems as if the conflict between the aims of the advertiser and those of the educator is irreconcilable. A teacher of home economics who says, "Buy wisely," is advising careful and reflective purchasing in the light of one's real needs and of accurate information about the product. An advertiser who says, "Buy wisely," often means, "Buy our brand, regardless of your special situation or special needs, because DUZ DOES EVERYTHING!" The teacher's job is to encourage intellectual and moral self-discipline. The job of the advertiser often seems to be to encourage thoughtlessness ("impulse buying") and self-indulgence, even at the cost of lifelong bondage to finance companies.

However, I am far from certain that the conflict between the aims of the advertiser and the educator is inevitable. It is inevitable *if* advertising cannot perform its functions except through the promotion of mistaken reactions to words and other symbols. Because advertising is both so powerful and so widespread, it influences more than our choice of products; it also influences our patterns of evaluation. It can either increase or decrease the degree of sanity with which people respond to words. Thus, if advertising is informative, witty, educational, and imaginative, it can perform its necessary commercial function and contribute to our pleasure in life without making us slaves to the tyranny of affective words.

If, however, products are sold largely by manipulating affective connotations—"*emollient-rich* Night of Olay," "*enriched flavor* Merit cigarettes," "contains *RD-119*,"—the influence of advertising is to deepen the already grave intensional orientations widely prevalent in the public. The schizophrenic is one who attributes a greater reality to words, fantasies, daydreams, and "private worlds" than to the actual world. Surely it is possible for advertising to perform its functions without aggravating our all-too-prevalent verbomania! Or is it?

Higher Education, Learned Jargon, and Babuism

Education of the wrong kind also contributes tremendously to our intensional orientations. Some people look upon education largely as a matter of acquiring a learned vocabulary (including terms like "intensional orientation") *without* a corresponding concern (and sometimes with no concern at all) for *what the vocabulary stands for.*

In the course of getting an education, students have to read many difficult books. Some of these books, the student may feel, are much more difficult to read than they need to be, because of the addiction of many scholars to extremely difficult terminology. Students, like other people, often ask why all books cannot be written more simply.

There are of course two answers to this question. The first is that some books are difficult because the ideas they deal with are difficult. An advanced work in chemistry or economics is difficult to one who knows no chemistry or economics for the simple reason that such a work presupposes on the part of the reader a background of previous study.

But there is another reason why books may be difficult. A learned vocabulary has two functions: first, it has the *communicative function* of giving expression to ideas—including important, difficult, or recondite ideas; secondly, it has a *social function* of conferring prestige upon its users and arousing respect and awe among those who do not understand it. ("Gosh, he must be smart. I can't understand a word he says!") It can be stated as a general rule that *whenever the social function of a learned vocabulary becomes more important to its users than its communicative function, communication suffers and jargon proliferates.* (The word "jargon" is used here, as it is defined in *Webster's Third New International Dictionary,* to mean "pretentious or unnecessarily obscure and esoteric terminology.")

This rule may be illustrated by a passage from an issue of the *American Journal of Sociology:*

In any formal organization, the goals as reflected in the system of functional differentiation result in a distinctive pattern of role differentiation. In turn, role differentiation, whether viewed hierarchically or horizontally, leads to what Mannheim called "perspectivistic thinking," namely, incumbency in a particular status induces a corresponding set of perceptions, attitudes and values. In an organization, as in society as a whole, status occupants tend to develop a commitment to subunit goals and tasks—a commitment that may be dysfunctional from the viewpoint of the total organizational goals. In other words, "perspectivistic thinking" may interfere with the coordination of effort toward the accomplishment of total organizational goals thus generating organizational pressures to insure adequate levels of performance.

In this passage, the author is merely saying (1) that in any formal organization, different people have different tasks; (2) that people sometimes get engrossed in their own special tasks to a degree that interferes with the goals of the organization as a whole; and therefore (3) that the organization has to put pressure on them to get the overall job done. What is clear from this passage (the *only* thing that is clear) is that the author's concern with professional standing as a sociologist has almost completely submerged any concern with communicating ideas. Thus, students are compelled in their studies to read, in addition to material that is intrinsically difficult, material that is made unnecessarily difficult by jargon.

The foregoing sociological passage, however, has at least the merit of possessing a discoverable meaning. There are some readings a college student encounters for which even this much cannot be said with certainty. For example:

The being that exists is man. Man alone exists. Rocks are, but they do not exist. Trees are, but they do not exist. Horses are, but they do not exist. Angels are, but they do not exist. God is, but he does not exist. The proposition "man alone exists" does not mean by any means that man alone is a real being while all other beings are unreal and mere appearances or human ideas. The proposition "man exists" means: man is that being whose Being is distinguished by the open-standing standing-in in the unconcealedness of Being, from Being, in Being. The existential nature of man is the reason why man can represent beings as such, and why he can be conscious of them. All consciousness presupposes ecstatically understood existence as the *essentia* of man—*essentia* meaning that as which man is present insofar as he is man. But consciousness does not itself create the openness of beings, nor is it consciousness that makes it possible for man to stand open for beings. Whither and whence and in what free dimension could the intentionality of consciousness move, if instancy were not the essence of man in the first instance?[3]

These are only samples of the many kinds of abstract prose that the student—especially the college and university student—encounters in daily studies. Sometimes the professor, who presumably understands the readings assigned, lectures at equally high levels of abstraction, so that the student is never quite sure, from the beginning of the course to the end, what it is all about. What is the effect upon students of readings and lectures of this kind? Obviously, the student is left with the impression that simplicity

Brief, as in legal brief

---

[3] Martin Heidegger, "The Way Back into the Ground of Metaphysics," in *Existentialism from Dostoyevsky to Sartre*, translated and edited by Walter Kaufmann (1957), pp. 214–15.

and clarity of style will get one nowhere in intellectual life, and that even a simple idea (or no idea at all) will gain academic respectability if it is phrased in a sufficiently abstract and incomprehensible vocabulary.

The British in India used to have a derogatory term for the pretentious and often comically inappropriate English used by poorly trained Indian clerks and civil servants; they called it "babu English."[4] The term is admittedly offensive, and I use it only because it contains an idea for which there is no other term. Abandoning its original application, then, let us use "babu English," or "babuism," as a general term to mean *discourse in which the speaker or writer throws around learned words he does not understand in order to create a favorable impression*. Babuism probably has existed and will continue to exist in every culture in which there is a learned class of magicians, shamans, priests, teachers, lawyers, and other professional verbalizers with big vocabularies. Babuism results whenever people who are not learned try to confer upon themselves by purely verbal means the social advantages of being *considered* learned.

Elsewhere in this volume, much has been said of the common tendency to confuse symbols with the things they stand for. The student may do the same: confuse symbols of learning (such as an abstract and difficult vocabulary) with learning itself. A student who, unable to understand the reading material and feeling responsible for the failure to understand, may conscientiously go over assignments repeatedly to achieve familiarity with the *vocabulary* of the course—a vocabulary that cannot help becoming a "babu English," since the student still does not know what it is all about. A verbally clever student will be able to parrot enough of this vocabulary in a final paper to make it sound extremely plausible. The teacher reading the paper will also not be too sure what it is all about, but will recognize the vocabulary as familiar and so will give it a passing grade. Thus the student, by learning to speak and write several kinds of babu—literary babu, psychological babu, educational babu, philosophical babu, the babu of art criticism, and so forth—will eventually get a bachelor's degree. Perhaps he or she will go on to graduate school and get a Ph.D. and proceed to teach it to others.

Thus does intensional orientation, like Ol' Man River, keep a-rollin' along.

CHAPTER 17

The Empty Eye

Now that TV's content has been determined and homogenized by the commercial impetus that once merely underlay the spectacle, and now that TV's basic purpose is to keep you watching, the images all point back toward that now-imperceptible managerial intention. And because TV is, on the whole, devised by and for the same class and generation, it constitutes a vehicle of collective self-allurement and self-solace, so that the spectacle has all the eerie resonance of a great bad dream. TV's images, furthermore, are all the richer in unconscious meanings for the increased sophistication of the visual technology that represents them. Calculated always to jolt the nerves of the half-attentive, the spectacle is less and less elaborately scripted and plotted, while more and more reliant on stark pictures and a lightning pace (along with infectious music), and on words as blunt as pictures. Such is the imperative behind all the ads and newscasts, game shows and cartoons, and nearly all the talk shows, dramas, and sitcoms, so that TV's "concentrated volume of appeal" actually gives more and more away the more it tries to rush and dazzle us beyond understanding what it's all about.

MARK CRISPIN MILLER

Mᴏᴅᴇʀɴ ꜱᴏᴄɪᴇᴛʏ inundates its citizens not only with a Niagara of words, but also, these days, with a torrent of pictures. Television spews out both words and pictures in dizzying quantity and variety: movies, talk shows, cartoons, dramatic programs, comedies, variety shows, children's shows, sporting events, news programs, political advertisements, and incessant commercial messages. What began with a few channels in each city has become, in many areas, a smorgasbord of a dozen channels or more, in two or three languages, some offering nonstop news, others nonstop sports, even some with nonstop advertising. Since the 1950s, this new combination of visual and verbal information, with its immediacy and affective power as well as its hypnotizing banality, has become an integral part of our lives. About 98 percent of American homes have a television, with its empty eye staring out on the inhabitants more than seven hours a day.

Distinctions between types of programming that once were clear have become blurred. News programs, entertainment programs, and commercials have become more alike as competition for the public's attention has become more intense. Many commercials consist of vignettes, told in a kind of visual shorthand that creates dramatic suspense, which is released when characters buy or consume the product being advertised.

Dramatic programs like "Dynasty" and "Miami Vice" resemble long ads for high-fashion clothing, fancy cars, and expensive real estate. Many game shows appear to be little more than an excuse to display new products, with contestants competing breathlessly to acquire them. Political campaigns stage events that are covered by news organizations; then the campaigns recycle the news footage into political ads. Then, news organizations file reports about those political ads.

Close on the heels of "happy talk" news—an attempt to make news more entertaining—comes "infotainment," consisting of shows dressed up in a news-program format that are little more than segments from forthcoming movies and interviews with actors and singers. "Reality television" also uses the news format for crime stories and gossip once the exclusive province of supermarket tabloids.

"Seeing is Believing"

What does television tell its viewers about the world? Beyond the data explicitly offered—"Toyota-thon year-end sales extravaganza, through Sunday only"—"a severe storm headed our way, details at 11:00"—what are television's characteristics themselves contributing to the way we think about the world?

Not so long ago, some people believed that if a piece of information were printed in a book, it must be "true." Such an attitude still prevails

Television suckling its young

with respect to television because, as everyone "knows," "seeing is believing." I actually overheard one shopper in a store telling another about a product, "Sure, it works. Haven't you seen it on TV?" Television's ability to suggest that we are actually experiencing the events depicted, or at least seeing them accurately, is the source of its greatest power. Television dramatic shows, like movies and theatrical productions, depend on viewers' suspending their disbelief and identifying with characters portrayed, without saying, "Wait a minute—people can't really beam themselves through space," or "That isn't really the court of Henry VIII; it's a studio soundstage somewhere in Southern California." Although most people understand that there are differences between fictional television, advertising, and nonfiction or "news" programs, it is worthwhile examining just how each conveys its representations of reality, so we can understand how—and whether—to "believe" what we "see."

The power of television news to capture the public's attention became apparent in the 1960s. In 1963, the nation was gripped by horror and grief at the assassination of President Kennedy; the event and its aftermath kept the nation riveted to television screens for days. Other major events, though reported in newspapers and magazines as well, were likewise widely and instantaneously experienced on television. Several incidents occurred in 1968 alone: the first expedition to set foot on the moon, the assassination of Senator Robert F. Kennedy, the riots at the Democratic National Convention, and North Vietnam's Tet offensive—television coverage of which brought into American homes bloody images from a war that previously had seemed quite remote.

Each of these events, seen over several days by a huge section of the

American public, became part of a shared set of experiences, all seen through the eye of television. Since then, television has become the primary source of news information for a large section of the American public, with newspapers, magazines, and radio assuming supplemental roles.[1]

The World Through a Keyhole

The television picture is an abstraction. Like most man-made images— drawings, paintings, and photographs—it is an array of bright and dark areas that the human eye assembles into an "image." The process of abstraction is present at many steps in the production of a television image. The television camera translates light waves into electronic impulses for subsequent transmission and reproduction, reducing light reflected by the complex reality of the world to an electronic code. Even more importantly, the camera—and its operator—also abstracts by *selecting which part of the world it will record and which part it will ignore.*

In the context of fictional or dramatic programs, again, most people are aware of this abstraction process. Just as, in live theater, there are "backstage" areas that no one in the audience is expected to see, there are likewise "off-camera" areas on every television soundstage. Anyone who has ever seen a television program or movie being filmed "on location" has been struck by the huge and intrusive amount of paraphernalia needed— cameras, lights, sound booms, makeup, and props—and how different the reality looks from the version that appears on the screen.

Even in news footage and other images that we tend to accept as "real," this distinction between on- and off-camera also exists. An unwritten rule of both newspaper and television news photography is that the camera never shows evidence of its own presence—no photographers, technicians, or other cameras, and only selected reporters, are to be depicted. This rule is generally observed even though the presence of cameras and reporters may be exerting a major effect on the events being photographed. As an example, public officials and reporters who work together regularly at a state capitol or a city hall may banter with each other before a press conference, but assume an entirely different demeanor when the lights come on and the cameras start rolling. To a person present at a public hearing, cameras and lights may physically dominate the entire proceeding, but the televised report may exhibit little direct evidence of the presence of such apparatus.

The narrow vision of the television camera also makes spaces and

[1] According to *TV Basics 87–88* from the Television Bureau of Advertising, 66 percent of adults say television is their primary source of news; 55 percent say television is the most believable, and 80 percent say television is more influential than newspapers, radio, or magazines.

groups of people seem much larger. After seeing one of the most familiar television rooms in America, the studio where "The Tonight Show" is filmed, visitors often say, "It's so small." On "the tube," the studio seems boundless and the crowd huge because the camera seldom shows the space as a whole. Many people who stage demonstrations and political rallies know this fact. When the cameras arrive, chanting becomes louder and more unified, and organizers often try to get their people to crowd together in front of the lens to wave, cheer, or jeer so that they will appear to be a much bigger group than they are. During the 1960s and '70s, some television and newspaper editors became so aware of this phenomenon and the extent to which it was exploited by various groups that they issued guidelines to their reporters and photographers on ways to avoid being manipulated into "creating" news where there might otherwise be none.

The very presence or absence of the camera also affects television's definition of news. Many foreign governments limit or censor the information and pictures that reporters may issue from their countries, knowing that television news organizations—and many newspapers—will not report events of which they do not have pictures or firsthand accounts. South Africa has curtailed the activities of both foreign and domestic journalists in reporting the struggle against apartheid, and accounts of events there have consequently become less vivid. Even though the Israeli military censors some reports and film from that country, Israel is by contrast a relatively open society. Because reporters have been free to film incidents involving rebellious Palestinian Arabs in the Occupied Territories, their reports may have given viewers abroad a distorted impression of civil unrest throughout the country. Yet many other countries in the Middle East, Africa, and elsewhere that could be considered more oppressive than Israel are either closed to Western journalists or ignored by the television networks. News footage of famine in Ethiopia and of the 1988 earthquake in Soviet Armenia resulted in massive and spontaneous outpourings of Western aid, which in turn became the subject of news accounts, while other disasters, such as flooding in Bangladesh and a severe earthquake in Colombia, engendered no such wave of public sympathy, partly because they were so remote that they were not easily televised.

Yet another level of abstraction occurs in the editing of news footage— an hour-long interview in which an economist or political thinker explains his or her viewpoint is reduced to a series of 20-second snippets; a twenty-minute political speech is reduced to a ten-second "sound bite" for the evening news; a complicated piece of legislation that took years of discussion and compromise to draft is referred to as "the welfare reform bill" and summarized in less than a minute over film of a presidential bill-signing ceremony. Such abbreviation occurs in print reporting as well, but television newscasts generally offer even less detail and background information than print accounts.

"Into America's Living Room"

What television news loses in depth and specificity by comparison to printed reports, it often gains in brevity and emotional immediacy. Because television seems to bring war, riot, famine, or murder directly "into America's living room," it has tremendous emotional impact. That impact has been heightened by the lifting of visual taboos.

Before the Vietnam War, it was rare for any American news medium to show pictures of dead bodies or severely wounded American soldiers. In earlier wars, when the public learned about the destruction of war through news accounts, it was often at a much higher level of abstraction—accounts of "engagements," "pitched battles," "breakthroughs," "advances," and occasionally "sacrifices." All that changed with graphic, bloody images from the television coverage of the Vietnam War.[2] Newspapers, to a lesser degree, went along. Now almost every week the news brings grisly footage of poison-gas victims, starving children, or the bloated bodies of drowned humans and animals floating in floodwaters in some disaster-torn part of the world. These pictures may shock us, anger us, or even sicken us, but they seldom fail to move us.

Television's power to stimulate intense emotion, as well as its power of abstraction by way of selective editing, join with the limited time available for providing context to create a view of the world that is dominated by singular, violent events. We are often shown these events in stark highlight, to the exclusion of other news. Thus, the seizing of a single airplane by terrorists monopolizes the networks as they follow the plane from airport to airport. Newscasts alternate breathless reports from correspondents on the ground, who report whatever tidbits of information are available, with countless repetitions of a single frightening image, like that of the body of a murdered hostage being thrown from the cockpit of the plane onto the pavement.

Terrorists know that a small band of maniacs commandeering a well-chosen target, preferably an American airliner, can monopolize not only the attention of Western governments but that of most of the Western public through the mesmerizing lens of television. By such means, they not only gain worldwide attention for what would otherwise often be minor causes, such as the freeing of other accused terrorists, but they elevate their splinter movements to the status of nations by forcing the major powers of the world to negotiate with them. The question of whether television coverage exacerbates terrorism is widely discussed, often *on* television, without much concrete action taken to reduce such manipulation of the medium by terrorists.

[2] Changes since 1950 in television coverage of wars, the Cold War, and relations with the Soviet bloc are discussed in detail by J. Fred MacDonald in *Television and the Red Menace: The Video Road to Vietnam* (1985).

"Film at 11:00"

If pictures give television its power, excessive reliance on them constitutes its weakness. Television news focuses on things it can easily symbolize visually, at the expense of things that are harder to depict. A few homeless people or a family being evicted can be televised to depict the larger problems of housing shortages and homelessness, but it's hard to televise houses not being built, rents increasing, or employment declining. It's easy to televise motorists in a gasoline line but hard to televise a national strategy for lessening dependence on imported oil. The visual aspect of television, adept at specifics, has trouble climbing back up the abstraction ladder to levels of greater generality and applicability.

In covering crime and urban violence, the preference of television news editors and producers for dramatic pictures focuses attention on footage of crime scenes, corpses covered with blankets, and the reactions of frightened neighbors, at the expense of detailed accounts of what police are doing to catch the perpetrators, discussions of what social and economic conditions cause crime, analysis of the effectiveness of correctional institutions, or reports of what response government officials are taking to meet the problem. Such more abstract accounts usually do not make good pictures, so, by and large, they—and many other actions of local, state, and federal government—play but a small part on television newscasts.

Television reporting has one other major distinction from print coverage. Printed reports are generally much easier to verify. With the written account in hand, it is possible to refresh one's memory as to exactly what was said and what was not and then to check the report by calling the people mentioned, consulting official records, or obtaining minutes of official proceedings. Compared to printed accounts, television reports may be equally accurate, but unless a recording is made they are harder to remember and verify, since the average viewer has no permanent record of what was said.

What often lingers from television news, then, is an impression, sometimes an unconscious one, of emotional tone. Thus, pictures can make a stronger impression than the words that accompany them.

"Go For The Gusto"

Perhaps the most powerful aspect of television lies in its power to sell products. Even when it purports to be entertaining us, television is showing us the "good life" and the products it consists of—fast cars, stylish clothes, beautiful furnishings, modern kitchen conveniences. It also uses every device of the poet and every tool of the cinematographer to sell us those products.

In most modern television commercials, the words are of secondary

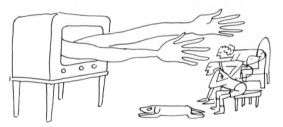

The commercial

importance to the pictures. Watch with the sound off and observe the mi-nute plots develop, told in pictures that sometimes last less than a second. Television ads are the Persian miniature paintings of cinematography. No-where is the content of images more carefully controlled, the appearance of reality more closely manicured. Every frame of film is made to serve the purpose of the ad.

Romance and sexual adventure, it is suggested, can be found when "the night belongs to Michelob." In this elaborately orchestrated beer commer-cial, a man waits impatiently at a nightclub while a young woman hurries to finish dressing, hails a cab, and finally arrives to consummate their ren-dezvous—entering the nightclub as Frank Sinatra sings, "The Way You Look Tonight." Payoff? The evening will be a success because they drink the right beer.

Another couple's evening in the urban fast lane ends with the lovers in a convertible parked by the river in the moonlight. The car? "The heart-beat of America, today's Chevrolet." In another commercial, we are re-minded that romantic conquest, the kind leading to matrimony, "takes time"—the kind of time told by Citizen watches. This image-dominated ad never reveals its sponsor until the last moment, which is preceded by a series of images of dancing, courtship, and nuzzling between a handsome man and a striking woman. You're being sold the story, and about the time you decide you'd like this romantic ideal to happen to you, you're offered the product as an implied means to make it come true.

The implicit assumption of television advertising—that everyone wants and can have fine cars, good food, and the best services—has had some unforeseen consequences. In 1962, at a lunch counter in a little town in South Carolina, a group of four black high-school students requested ser-vice and were refused. They decided to stay until they were served; this was the first "sit-in." When news spread that such a sit-in was happening, other young blacks from all over the South began to sit in at other lunch counters. The great social revolution of the black civil-rights movement of the 1960s was on.

Why was it 1962 rather than any other year when these young people decided to sit in at this drugstore in South Carolina? Louis Lomax, who describes the incident in *The Negro Revolt*, explains that these young people were not particularly well educated; they were just simple ordinary high-school kids. Why did they do what their parents had not done before on such a grand scale? Their parents and generations before them had tolerated the white drugstore where blacks were not served. They had tolerated segregation in the use of Jim Crow bus stations, Jim Crow lunch counters, Jim Crow water fountains, and Jim Crow restrooms. All over the South, the older generation had "known better" than to protest. Why did these young people resist? I think one reason was that they—then sixteen, seventeen, or eighteen years old—were the first generation to have spent their entire childhood being baby-sat by a television screen. That was the difference between the generations.

In other words, television is an amazingly powerful instrument of social change. What does television say? It says again and again: these are the good things we have in our culture. Come and enjoy them. Come and enjoy them. It never says: Stay away if you happen to be black. It never says: Stay away if you don't have any money. It just assumes that you have money; it just assumes everyone should enjoy the good things that the culture has to offer: hamburgers and Cokes at lunch counters, fine cars, nice clothes—everything in the world that is pleasant to own or consume. And so these high-school kids were simply accepting television's invitation. Hadn't the television, politely and urgently, again and again, several times a day for years and years and years, urged them to enjoy the fruits of the culture?

The same forces of change unleashed by television on American society thirty years ago are now being turned loose in developing nations across the world. Especially since the development of the satellite relay and the "Earth station" antenna, television has recognized no geographic or national boundaries. People in Latin America, Africa, Eastern Europe, and Asia, whose ancestors were isolated for centuries from other ways of life, are suddenly being allowed to see that not all the world lives in the same conditions as their own. Ideas, information, and especially images of "how the other half lives" are making their way into parts of the world previously tightly closed. The full consequences of this sudden, rapid flow of information have yet to be seen.

Whatever strange ideas people may get about American society by watching "Dallas," they see a world of glittering material wealth that makes our own everyday reality—and almost certainly theirs as well— seem drab by comparison. Several years ago, on a visit to a Caribbean island, my son Alan spent several hours traveling by Jeep trail over a mountain pass to reach a remote beach. As he arrived at the only development within miles, a small bar open to the breeze and thatched with pond fronds, he was astounded to see the only three people in this idyllic spot huddled around a small television set that blared, "Cindy Johnson, COME ON DOWN! You're the next contestant on "The Price is Right'!"

What, Me Work?

Television, said Marshall McLuhan, values personal fulfillment very highly. That is the hidden message he saw in romances and romantic comedies, in which everyone involved struggles with obstacles in order to achieve love and sexual happiness. The indulgence of personal idiosyncrasies is also the leitmotif of "warmhearted" situation comedies from "M*A*S*H" through "Three's Company," "L.A. Law," and "Night Court." Every character, no matter how offbeat, unappealing, or downright deviant, eventually gets a sympathetic moment that leaves the audience with a "warm, fuzzy" feeling and the idea that no one is beyond the pale of human kindness. It's a lovely thought, but, in reality, acceptance by one's peers is usually won only at the cost of some consideration for their feelings as well.

Television's advocacy of individual gratification through romance and consumption of material goods is not balanced by advocacy of thrift or of work. As we observed in Chapter 9, it is hard to photograph "work." In television dramas and comedies alike, the workplace is just another setting for the same activities that go on elsewhere. The simulated law office, newsroom, police station, or hospital may be rife with intrigue, romance, flirtation, deception, or hilarity, but it is seldom clear what the people there are getting paid for. Yet they all have such nice cars, such lovely clothes, such interesting lives.

Combined with hour after hour of commercials offering instant gratification through purchasing and instant well-being through consumption, dramatic television's depiction of life adds up to a continuous display of conspicuous consumption without visible means of support. Is it any wonder that, among the first generations of television-raised Americans, there have arisen groups—from young urban professionals to inner-city drug dealers—displaying a fascination with symbols of material wealth, in the form of German luxury cars, gold jewelry, and expensive watches?

After the Bad Guys

Television dramas have always been built around the two-valued orientation. For years, bad guys in westerns literally wore black hats; when that became too simple-minded for some audiences, producers developed "adult westerns" in which the good guys wore black hats and went off in the end with women rather than with horses. As the public grew sated with cowboys, the search began for new characters and settings, but on television, there will always be villains. Crooks served as villains for a couple of decades' worth of police and detective shows, and they were very convenient: always wicked, never displaying any attractive qualities. Generic crooks have given way in recent years to drug dealers and international terrorists—some of whom seem almost glamorous.

Other kinds of villains have also cropped up, often surrounded by trappings of power and material wealth—at least, until they get caught. Politicians are either portrayed as buffoons in comedies, or, in dramas, as completely venal, self-interested, or adulterous. Most businessmen in television dramas will do anything for a profit—lie, cheat, steal, kill. Worse yet is "big business," a faceless institution against whose grasping designs for development (always a threatening prospect) ordinary people must band together. When all other sources of villains fail, scriptwriters turn to the Central Intelligence Agency for bogeymen totally lacking in scruple. Television writers, producers, and advertisers seem to think we need simple, two-valued explications of the problems of modern life. Rare is the television drama about conflict between *two* "good" forces or between *two* "evil" ones. Rarer still is a drama in which it's hard to tell which is which. The black hats may not be visible, but they're still there.

The Casting of the President

Perhaps no other area of American life has been more changed by television than electoral politics, especially at the statewide and national levels. Once, the two major political parties were an indispensable part of the political system. They have been weakened by many things—population movement, the growth of suburbia, the decay of central cities and of manufacturing industries, a slowing of the growth of labor unions, and an increasing emphasis throughout society on individual fulfillment rather than group action. Television has abetted the decline of political parties and gained influence as a result of it. Personality now outweighs party membership for an increasing number of voters who "vote for the candidate, not the party."

Television's political impact became clear in the first televised debate of the 1960 presidential campaign, when, to radio listeners judging by traditional debating terms, Vice President Richard M. Nixon was judged to have beaten Senator John F. Kennedy. Television viewers came away with a much more negative impression of Nixon, who wore an ill-fitting shirt and refused to use makeup, appearing with a "five o'clock shadow" that made him seem less than appealing. Kennedy was rested and deeply tanned from campaigning in California, as Fawn M. Brodie says in her biography, *Richard Nixon: The Shaping of His Character:*

Those who missed the television and heard Kennedy only on radio thought Nixon had clearly bested his opponent. But many television viewers who saw the Nixon pallor, the trickle of sweat pouring down his chin, the struggle to overcome his discomfiture . . . remembered very little else.

The debate was seen by political analysts as helping swing the election to Kennedy, and political managers ever since have believed that the non-verbal and visual impression a candidate makes on television is as important or more important than the things the candidate says.

The shift from print to television as the public's preferred source of news has caused many of the changes in electoral politics. An illustrative example of the two different kinds of reporting is provided by Michael J. Robinson and Margaret Sheehan in their article "Traditional Ink vs. Modern Video Versions of Campaign '80."[3] Robinson and Sheehan contrast accounts by Helen Thomas of United Press International and Lesley Stahl of CBS News, both describing the same visit to Philadelphia by then-President Jimmy Carter in September 1980. First UPI:

> After three days on the campaign trail, President Carter is clearly convinced that the once divided Democratic Party is now closing ranks behind his candidacy. . . .
>
> Carter said in an interview on WPVI-TV that . . . he has seen "a remarkable coalescing of unity within the Democratic Party."
>
> In the interview at a black Baptist Church, Carter mentioned that Sen. Edward Kennedy, D-Mass., his rival in the primaries, had telephoned to express his hope that the Democratic Party "will be united" in November. . . .
>
> Former Kennedy supporters . . . are falling into line. They include Philadelphia Mayor William Green, who never left Carter's side during his visit to drum up votes, particularly among ethnic groups and blacks.
>
> Also Wednesday, Carter won endorsements from three powerful unions that had endorsed other candidates in the primaries. . . .
>
> In his speech from the pulpit to an enthusiastic gathering in Zion Baptist Church . . . Carter warned that a Democratic Party divided as it was in 1968 could lead to a Republican victory in November.
>
> During the day, he toured the Italian market, shaking every hand in sight, and had a corned beef and cabbage lunch at an Irish restaurant. . . .

The CBS story was introduced by sub-anchor Charles Kuralt:

KURALT: You remember that great old photograph of Calvin Coolidge wearing a war bonnet. Campaigning politicians need to identify themselves with every segment of the population: the old, the young, and the ethnic. It's a tradition. And as Lesley Stahl reports, President Carter stayed busy today—following tradition.

[3] William C. Adams, ed., *Television Coverage of the 1980 Presidential Campaign* (1983), Ablex Publishing Corp., Norwood, N.J.

STAHL: What did President Carter do today in Philadelphia? He *posed*, with as many different types of symbols as he could *possibly* find. There was a picture at the day care center. And one during the game of bocce ball with the senior citizens. Click, another picture with a group of teenagers. And then he performed the ultimate media event—a walk through the Italian market.

The point of all this, *obviously*, to get on the local news broadcasts and in the morning newspapers. It appeared the president's intention was not to say anything controversial. . . . Simply the intention was to be seen, as he was, and it was photographed, even right before his corned beef and cabbage lunch at an Irish restaurant with the popular mayor, Bill Green.

There were more symbols at the Zion (black) Baptist Church. . . .

Over the past three days the president's campaign has followed a formula—travel into a must-win state, spending only a short time there but ensuring several days of media coverage. . . .

And today the president got a bonus, since the Philadelphia TV markets extend into neighboring New Jersey—another must-win state.

As Robinson and Sheehan point out, the UPI print account focuses on the candidate and what he said, as well as on the role in politics of other elected officials, unions, churches, and ethnic groups. Listening to the words of the CBS piece, a viewer accustomed to television can easily imagine the accompanying pictures of the president walking in the Italian market, eating corned beef with the mayor, speaking to a black church group. The very *words* of Stahl's account emphasize the importance of images over traditional forms of political organization.

Strictly speaking, to characterize President Carter's activities as "posing" is an inference, rather than a report, but Robinson and Sheehan quote a Carter press aide who later said the Stahl piece "made me cringe . . . she was absolutely right about the photo opportunities." Robinson and Sheehan said, "What keeps this piece from being labeled subjective is that no political observers, including the Carter people, think Stahl was wrong in her analysis."

Although Carter's opponent, Ronald Reagan, has been the politician best noted for taking advantage of "photo opportunities" as a campaign technique, and although the 1988 campaign between George Bush and Michael Dukakis was likewise dominated by such events by both parties, this example shows that the idea has been established for some time. Planning political events to take maximum advantage of free television exposure means it no longer matters much what the candidate said to the people at the black church, the Italian market, or the corned-beef luncheon. Nor does it matter what they said to him. What campaign managers hope is that people watching television will see the candidate seeming to interact with people with whom the viewer can identify. The organizational work of traditional politics—reaching voters individually and in small groups through speeches, personal contacts, and written accounts of statements and positions by the candidate—has been almost completely replaced by efforts to place the candidate in front of television cameras.

While television photographers still generally avoid actually depicting their own presence at political events, commentary like Stahl's has become more common. Many television—and some print—reporters are now including in their stories discussions of how events are covered and of candidates' efforts to take advantage of television news. Notice how the UPI reporter, Helen Thomas, generally gave credence to the events and words she perceived: President Carter says the party is closing ranks, and Thomas duly reports that he says so. In contrast, the effect of Stahl's posture—telling listeners not only what the candidate did but how he was trying to present himself—casts a shadow of disapproval and more than a hint of cynicism over her words.

The use of news cameras to create images desired by the campaign was brought to new heights in the 1988 presidential campaign. Here are two of the more fatuous examples: George Bush visited a factory where flags are made, and Michael Dukakis took a ride in a tank, wearing a helmet and sticking his head out the top to be photographed. Their respective campaigns hoped that news photos would show that Bush was a patriot—because he appeared in front of a lot of flags—and that Dukakis favored a strong defense—because after all, there he was on a tank.

Even though television reporters widely reported the fact that such "events" were intended to manipulate television cameras into serving the purposes of the campaign organizations that planned them, the pictures were nevertheless broadcast, thus fulfilling the campaigns' practical objectives. Later, news footage of the tank ride was used by the Dukakis campaign in a political ad. The Bush camp, thinking Dukakis looked silly in the helmet, recycled the identical footage for its own *anti*-Dukakis ad.

As television coverage achieves greater importance in wooing voters, Stahl's insider's viewpoint describes the modern political process as many, if not most, participants see it, while Thomas's piece almost seems to be written about a monochrome world that no longer exists.

Brain Surgery—The Video

If people increasingly rely on television for information, does this new form of communication threaten to supplant the written word? We can now buy videotaped instruction in auto mechanics, computer operation, home repair, foreign languages, music, art, and religion. Movie versions of many major works of literature are available on video recordings. What kind of world will this produce? Can the principles and practice of nuclear physics, electrical engineering, computer design, astronomy, business management, architecture, or neurosurgery be conveyed in moving pictures and

Educational TV

spoken words as well as they can be through the printed word? If not, will society develop two kinds of literacy, print and video, separate and unequal?

Television excels in teaching some things—skills involving movement, such as dance or carpentry, and ideas dependent on images from faraway places. In combining eloquent words with well-chosen pictures, as in Robert MacNeil's series "The Story of English," the medium of television can cast new light on distant history. By example, it can challenge our habitual attitudes. The appearance of a mentally retarded man as a regular, sympathetic character on the series "L.A. Law" allows us to see new ways of reacting enacted in everyday settings, rather than merely preached.

But these few bright moments on the small screen are the exception. If humanity had used writing in the same limited way we use television, we would have created for ourselves little more than tabloid newspapers and comic books.

CHAPTER 18

Rats And Men

Reactors that produce, say, five million kilowatts of electricity are too large to be accepted by our present economic and political units. The scale of the new energy source determined by the logic of economics and of the inherent nature of the technology is larger than the scale determined by our traditionally fragmented political and economic structures. But it is not only nuclear energy in its peaceful aspects that makes our divided world obsolete. As John von Neumann pointed out some ten years ago, the H-bomb and the ICBM also make geographic boundaries obsolete. The imperative toward unification resulting from the intrinsic massiveness of modern technology is not confined to nuclear energy. Our communications systems, our transportation systems, the possibility of using superconducting cable for transmission of electricity, all these and many other new technologies point strongly to the mismatch between the size of our political or economic units and the size of our technologies. I think all of us who are involved in these new technologies can only hope that before they destroy us, our political instruments will accommodate to the logic of massiveness, and that the major fruit of the new technologies will be a unified and peaceful world.　　　　ALVIN M. WEINBERG

"Insoluble" Problems

PROFESSOR N. R. F. MAIER of the University of Michigan performed a series of interesting experiments in which "neurosis" is induced in rats. The rats are first trained to jump off the edge of a platform at one of two doors. If the rat jumps to the right, the door holds fast, and it bumps its nose and falls into a net; if it jumps to the left, the door opens, and the rat finds a dish of food. When the rats are well trained to this reaction, the situation is changed. The food is put behind the other door, so that in order to get their reward they now have to jump to the right instead of to the left. (Other changes, such as marking the two doors in different ways, may also be introduced by the experimenter.) If the rat fails to figure out the new system, so that each time it jumps it never knows whether it is going to get food or bump its nose, it finally gives up and refuses to jump at all. At this stage, Dr. Maier says, "Many rats prefer to starve rather than make a choice."

Next, the rats are forced to make a choice, being driven to it by blasts of air or an electric shock. "Animals which are induced to respond in the insoluble problem situation," says Dr. Maier, "settle down to a specific reaction (such as jumping *solely* at the left-hand door) which they continue to execute regardless of consequences. . . . The response chosen under these conditions becomes fixated. . . . Once the fixation appears, the animal is incapable of learning an adaptive response in this situation." When a reaction to the left-hand door is thus fixated, *the right-hand door may be left open so that the food is plainly visible.* Yet the rat, when pushed, *continues to jump to the left*, becoming more panicky each time. When the experimenter persists in forcing the rat to make choices, it may go into convulsions, racing around wildly, injuring its claws, bumping into objects, then going into a state of violent trembling, until it falls into a coma. In this passive state, it refuses to eat, refuses to take any interest in anything: it can be rolled up into a ball or suspended in the air by its tail—the rat has ceased to care what happens to it. It has had a "nervous breakdown."[1]

It is the "insolubility" of the rat's problem that leads to its nervous breakdown, and, as Dr. Maier shows in his studies of disturbed children and adults, rats and human beings seem to go through pretty much the same stages. First, they are trained to make a given choice habitually when confronted by a given problem; secondly, they get a terrible shock when they find that the conditions have changed and that the choice doesn't produce the expected results; third, whether through shock, anxiety, or frustration, they may fixate on the original choice and continue to make

---

[1] Norman R. F. Maier, *Frustration: The Study of Behavior Without a Goal* (1949). See especially Chapter 2, "Experimental Evidence of Abnormal Behavior Reactions," and Chapter 6, "Comparison of Motivational and Frustration-Induced Behavior Problems in Children."

that choice regardless of consequences; fourth, they sullenly refuse to act at all; fifth, when by external compulsion they are forced to make a choice, they again make the one they were originally trained to make—and again get a bump on the nose; finally, even *with the goal visible in front of them*, to be attained simply by making a different choice, they go crazy out of frustration. They tear around wildly; they sulk in corners and refuse to eat; bitter, cynical, disillusioned, they cease to care what happens to them.

Is this an exaggerated picture? It hardly seems so. The pattern recurs throughout human life, from the small tragedies of the home to the world-shaking tragedies among nations. Parents, in order to instill a sense of responsibility, may nag their child to keep his or her room clean. If the room stays messy, the parents nag some more. The child becomes more resentful and less neat—so the parents nag even more. Governed, like the rat, by a fixed reaction to the problem of the child's messy room, the parents can meet it only in one way. The longer they continue, the worse it gets, until they are all nervous wrecks.

Again, whites in a northern city, deploring the illiteracy and high crime rate among blacks, segregate them, persecute them (it is well documented that the police are often tougher on black suspects than on whites), flee the city rather than improve the public schools, and deny blacks opportunities for employment and advancement. The denial of opportunity perpetuates illiteracy and the high crime rate, which in turn perpetuate the segregation, persecution, and denial of opportunity. The search for a way to break up this vicious cycle taxes the best minds among those interested in orderly social change: city council members, educators, urban planners, and members of civil-rights organizations, as well as those in state and federal government.

To cite another example, students trying to express themselves in writing may write poorly. In order to improve their writing, says the English teacher, I must teach them the fundamentals of grammar, spelling, and punctuation. By thus placing excessive emphasis on grammar and mechanics while ignoring the students' ideas, the teacher quickly destroys student interest in writing. That interest destroyed, the students write even more poorly. Thereupon, the teacher redoubles the dose of grammar and mechanics. The students become increasingly bored and rebellious. Such students fill the ranks of "remedial English" classes in high school and college.

Again, a nation, believing that the only way to secure peace and dignity is through armed strength, may embark on a huge armaments program. The program arouses the fears of neighboring nations, so that they too increase their armaments to match those of the first nation. Anxiety and tension increase. Our neighbors are arming themselves, the first nation declares, and it is clear that we shall continue to feel anxious about our national security so long as we are not adequately prepared for all emergencies; we must therefore *double* our armaments. This naturally makes the neighboring nations even more anxious, so that they too double their armaments. Anxiety and tension increase even more. It is clear, the first nation declares, that our mistake has been to underestimate our defense needs. This time we must be sure to be sufficiently armed to preserve peace. We must triple our armaments. . . .

Of course, these instances are oversimplified, but it is often because of vicious cycles of this kind that we are unable to get at or do anything about the conditions that lead to disaster. The pattern is frequently recognizable; the goal may be in sight, attainable by a mere change in methods. Nevertheless, governed by fixed reactions, the rat "cannot" get food, the parents "cannot" cure the child's faults. Minorities will "have to wait" two or three generations "until the time is ripe" for social change, and we "cannot afford" to stop devising and manufacturing weapons so deadly that they cannot be used without destroying civilization itself.

There is, however, an important difference between the insolubility of the rat's problems and the insolubility of human problems. Dr. Maier's rats were driven to their nervous breakdowns by problems more complicated than would naturally occur in a rat's environment. But human breakdowns are ordinarily caused by problems that human beings themselves have created: problems of religious and ethical belief; problems of money and credit and mortgages and trust funds and stock-market fluctuations; problems of man-made custom and etiquette and social organization and law.

Rats can hardly be blamed for not being able to solve problems set for them by Dr. Maier; there are limits to a rat's powers of abstraction. But there are no clear limits to the potential human capacity to abstract and organize and make use of abstractions. Hence, if human beings find problems insoluble because of fixed reactions—if they are frustrated because they can respond in only one way, regardless of context or circumstances, to certain symbolically defined situations—they are functioning at less than full human capacity. They can be said, in Korzybski's suggestive phrase, to be "copying animals" in their reactions. Wendell Johnson summarized this idea aptly when he said, "To a mouse, cheese is cheese; that's why mousetraps work." How do these fixations occur in human beings?

Cultural Lag

A basic reason for such "insoluble" problems in society is what might be called "institutional inertia." An "institution," as the word is used in sociology, is "an organized pattern of group behavior, well-established and accepted as a fundamental part of a culture" (*American College Dictionary*). Human beings are so constituted that they inevitably organize their energies and activities into patterns of behavior that are more or less uniform throughout a social group. People who are identified with institutions therefore have their own way of looking at things: people in a communist (or capitalist) society accept and perpetuate communist (or capitalist) habits of economic behavior; the soldier looks at the world through a soldier's eyes and abstracts from it what a soldier has been trained to abstract; the banker and the union official and the stockbroker similarly abstract in accordance with their special training. And through long habituation to a professional or institutional way of looking at the world, each tends to believe that his abstractions of reality—his maps of the territory—*are* reality: defense *is* defense; deficit *is* deficit; a strikebreaker *is* a strikebreaker; a blue chip *is* a blue chip.

Hence we have the peculiar fact that, once people become accustomed to institutions, they eventually get to feeling that their particular institutions represent the *only right and proper* way of doing things. The institution of human slavery, like the caste system in India, was claimed by its defenders to be "divinely ordained," and attacks upon the institution were regarded as attacks upon natural law, reason, and the will of God. Those who had contrary institutions, on the other hand, regarded their system of free labor as "divinely ordained," and slavery as contrary to natural law, reason, and the will of God. In a similar way, today, those who believe in corporate capitalist enterprise regard their way of organizing the distribution of goods as the *only proper way;* while communists adhere to their way with the same passionate conviction. This loyalty to one's own institutions is understandable: almost everyone in any culture feels that its institutions are the very foundations of reasonable living. A challenge to those institutions is almost inevitably felt to be a threat to *all* orderly existence.

Consequently, social institutions tend to change slowly, and—most important—they tend to continue to exist long after the necessity for their existence has disappeared, and sometimes even when their continued existence becomes a nuisance and a danger. This is not to say, of course, that *all* contemporary institutions are obsolete. Many institutions are changing rapidly enough to keep up with changes in conditions. Many, however, are not. The continued existence of obsolete institutional habits and forms (like the systems of county government in many states of the Union, geographically arranged to suit the needs of a horse-drawn population) is called by sociologists "cultural lag." In everyday language, "cultural lag" is summed up in a peculiarly appropriate expression, "horse-and-buggy" ways.

The Fear of Change

The pressing problems of our world are then problems of cultural lag—problems arising from trying to organize a jet-propelled, supersonic, electronic, and nuclear world with horse-and-buggy institutions. The rate of technological advancement for almost two hundred years now has been greater than the rate of the change of our social institutions and their accompanying loyalties and ideologies; and the disparity between the two rates is increasing rather than decreasing. Consequently, in every contemporary culture that has felt the impact of technology, people are questioning the appropriateness of nineteenth-century (eighteenth-century, medieval, or Stone Age) institutions to twentieth-century conditions. They are progressively more alarmed at the dangers arising from old-fashioned nationalism in a world that has become, technologically and economically, one world; they are increasingly anxious over the possibility of attaining a sane world economic order with the instruments of nineteenth-century capitalism or of nineteenth-century socialism. Wherever technologies are producing changes not adequately matched by changes in social institutions, there are people under strain and tension.

Some, of course, meet these strains and tensions in the only sensible way possible: they strive to change or abandon outmoded institutions and to bring into being new institutions or newer forms of old institutions. Changes in educational practice, in governmental organization, in the responsibilities of trades unions, in the structure of corporations, in the techniques of librarianship, in the marketing of agricultural commodities, and so on, go on all the time because extensional people are constantly striving to bring institutions into closer relationship with reality. The European Economic Community is a triumphant example in Europe of what can be done by extensionally minded people when they are really determined to modify ancient social institutions and practices in favor of a more workable economic order. In 1992, the EEC is scheduled to eliminate most internal economic barriers to create a continent-wide open market. This plan is even more astounding in light of the fact that, within living memory, Europe has been torn by two major wars rooted partly in nationalism and in economic conflict.

Even within relatively short time spans, institutional change must be continued or the rapid pace of our changing world will outstrip it. Until recently, an especially successful example of institutional adaptation has been the Federal Deposit Insurance Corporation. Prior to 1934, bank failures resulted in the partial or total loss of the savings of depositors; panics, once started, were almost impossible to control. Since the setting up of FDIC, however, panics have disappeared. For decades, bank failures were extremely rare, and even when they occurred, individual depositors did not lose their money. Even with the recent crisis in the savings and loan industry, American people now take the stability of their banks for granted, with a serenity that could hardly have been imagined before 1934. Yet that crisis shows that even successful institutional innovations such as the FDIC need to change to keep pace with the society around them.

On seeing the need for changes, however, some people agitate for cures that, on examination, appear to be no better than the ailment; still others agitate for changes that cannot possibly be brought about. In some of the most important areas of human life—especially in our ideas about international relations and in the closely related problem of an equitable world economic order—areas in which our failure to find solutions threatens the future of civilization itself—we are, all over the world, in a state of cultural lag.

What causes this cultural lag? In the case of many groups, the cause is obviously ignorance. Some people manifestly don't know the score, so far as the realities of the modern world are concerned. Their "maps" represent "territories" that have long since passed out of existence. In other cases, the lag is due to fixed economic or political interests. Many individuals enjoy power and prestige within the framework of outmoded institutions— and with institutional inertia to support them, it is not hard for them to believe that their familiar institutions are beautiful and wonderful things. Indeed, there is little doubt that the desire of the wealthy and powerful to keep their wealth and power is a major reason for cultural lag in any society. Threatened with social change, they often act in such narrowly shortsighted and selfish ways that, like the Bourbons, they seem willing to destroy both the civilization they live in and themselves in grim, pigheaded attempts to hang on to their prerogatives.

But wealth and power are not in themselves guarantees either of social irresponsibility or of stupidity, and the existence of a powerful wealthy class in a culture is not in itself a guarantee that there will be cultural lag. At least some of the rich and powerful have known how to yield gracefully to institutional adjustments—sometimes they have even helped to introduce them—and by so doing they have maintained their favored position and have saved both society and themselves from the disasters that attend complete social disruption. When this happens, cultural lag is kept small enough to be manageable. In some Latin American countries today, there is a touch-and-go race going on between social reform and revolution, the outcome depending largely on the willingness of the privileged class to accept and adjust to change.

But even when the rich and powerful are shortsighted and irresponsible, they must have support among those who are neither rich nor powerful in order to be able to hold back necessary institutional adjustments. To comprehend cultural lag, then, we must account not only for the shortsightedness of the powerful, but also for the shortsightedness of the ordinary citizens who support policies that are contrary to their own interests. In addition to institutional inertia (which is a tremendous force for keeping people busy doing things they should have stopped doing long ago), it appears that fear is another major force influencing both rulers and the ruled in the direction of institutional rigidity. Perhaps the ultimate strength of cultural lag comes from those persons, in all walks of life, whom change has made afraid.

The Revision of Group Habits

Whether the cultural lag arises from inertia, from shortsighted selfishness, from fear of change, or from a combination of these and other reasons, it is clear that the solution of social problems is basically a matter of adapting institutional habits to new conditions.

Perhaps the most dramatic thing about human behavior is how many problems that are "insoluble" for institutional reasons are promptly solved the moment a war breaks out. War is an institution the demands of which, at least in modern culture, take precedence over almost all other demands. Before World War II, it would have been "impossible" to send the slum children of London to the country for the sake of their health. But when the air raids on London began, the evacuation of all the children took place over a weekend. Institutionally minded economists, before the war, demonstrated time and again that it was "impossible" for either Germany or Japan to fight without an adequate gold supply. Nevertheless, Germany and Japan put up quite a fight in spite of the predictions of extremely reputable editorialists and economists. One of the lessons of war is that institutions, while powerful and long-lasting, are often not insuperably rigid *if the emergency is great enough.*

The problem, then, the world over, is to learn that the emergency is serious enough—in international affairs, in race relations, in the world population explosion, in preserving the natural environment, and in many other areas—to require modifying or abandoning some of our institutions. And the problem for us as citizens, once we understand the emergency, is how we can contrive ways of adjusting our thinking and acting so that institutional adjustments may be made both realistically and rapidly, with a minimum of human suffering and a maximum of general benefit.

The Extensional Approach

Every widely debated public issue—changes in the methods of distributing medical care, ideas for improving the welfare system, proposals for unifying the armed services under a single command, proposals to set up new ways of settling disputes between nations—is, then, a discussion of institutional adaptation. If we persist in discussing our social problems in terms of "justice" versus "injustice," "natural law, reason, and the will of God" versus "the forces of anarchy and chaos," or "the right to life" versus "the right of choice," reactions of fear and anger become general on both sides—and fear and anger paralyze the mind and make intelligent decision-making impossible. The escape from this two-valued debate lies in thinking about social problems as problems of institutional adaptation. Once we begin to do so, our questions with respect to hotly debated social issues automatically begin to become more extensional. We cease to ask whether a proposed institutional change is "right" or "wrong," "progressive" or "reactionary." We begin to ask instead, "What will be the results? Who would benefit, and by how much? Who would be harmed, and to what degree? What safeguards does the proposal contain to prevent further harm? Are people actually ready for such a measure? What will be the effect on prices, on the labor supply, on public health, on the environment? And who says so, on the basis of what kind of research and what kind of expert knowledge?" From extensional answers to such extensionally directed questions, decisions begin to flow. The decisions that flow from extensional information are neither "left-wing" nor "right-wing." They are simply some sensible things to do under the circumstances.

Here, let us say, is a proposed municipal ordinance to permit trucks to pass over Oak Street bridge. Backing the measure are the trucklines, which will save much time and money if the measure is passed. If our discussion of the proposal is reasonably extensional, our questions about it will be of the following kind: "Will the bridge structure stand the additional load? What will be the effect on traffic flow on Oak Street and streets approaching it? Is there danger of an increase in street accidents? Will the beauty of the city be adversely affected? What will be the effect on residences or businesses on and near Oak Street?" When such questions have been answered by persons of known ability in making accurate predictions in their several fields of knowledge, all citizens will have the materials with which to reach a conclusion according to their individual interests and values, whether they are concerned with the safety of children walking to school, with the beauty of the city, with trucking profits, with the effect on tax rate, or whatever. Their decisions, made against a background of responsibly made predictions, will have some kind of reasonable relationship to their individual desires.

Let us further suppose, however, that the measure is advantageous to practically no one in town *except* the trucklines. Then, if the trucklines want the measure passed, they may try to *prevent* the public from discussing the issue extensionally. The technique (familiar in the discussion of legislation affecting railroads, insurance, housing, medical care, and so on) is immediately to move the discussion to higher levels of abstraction and to talk about "unreasonable restraints on business," and the need to protect "free enterprise" and "the American way" against harassment by "politicians," "officeholders," and "petty bureaucrats." By systematic confusion of levels of abstraction, the "freedom" of trucklines to operate over Oak Street bridge is made to appear one with the freedoms fought and bled for at Valley Forge.

The tragedy is not only that many of us are innocent enough to be deceived by systematic confusion in levels of abstraction in the news; a deeper tragedy is that, in many communities, newspapers and television provide us with almost no extensional materials for discussion. Partly because many newspapers and television newscasts have largely given up their news function in favor of entertainment, and partly because the sensational, two-valued utterances of extreme partisans make livelier stories than the testimony of extensionally minded experts, news accounts in some communities are scanty sources of information on important public issues.

The tenor of discussion (and therefore of public opinion) being what it is, what are the chances for institutional adaptation with respect to some of our most pressing problems? The replacement of maladjustments by new maladjustments and the continuation of old maladjustments under new names may be as near as we can get to correcting cultural lag.

The End of The Road

When, as the results of protracted debate of a futile kind, years pass without the successful accomplishment of institutional adjustments, cultural lag widens. As social dislocations grow more serious, fear and confusion spread. As fear and confusion spread, societies, like individuals, grow increasingly disturbed at their failure to solve their problems. Lacking the knowledge or the confidence to try new patterns of behavior and at the same time panicky with the knowledge that their traditional methods no longer work, societies often appear to behave, to a greater or lesser degree, like Dr. Maier's rats, who, presented with an insoluble problem, revert to a fixed response regardless of the circumstances and cease to adapt or learn new responses. Thus do societies, as they have so often done in the past and continue to do today, fixate on *one* solution to their most pressing problem: the *only* way to appease the angry gods is to throw *still more* babies to the crocodiles; the *only* way to protect the social order is to detect and hunt down *still more* witches; the *only* way to prevent moral decay is to insist on *stricter* obedience to religious law; the *only* way to ensure prosperity is to reduce federal expenditures; and the *only* way to ensure peace is to have *still greater* armaments. (The last two beliefs are, of course, held simultaneously.)

Such mental blockages—patterns of repetitious behavior—prevent us from meeting our "insoluble" problems with the only approach that can ever help us solve them: the extensional approach—for we cannot distribute goods, feed people, or establish cooperation with our neighbors by intensional definitions and high-level abstractions. What is done in the extensional world must be done by extensional means, no matter who does it. If we as citizens of a democracy are going to carry our share in the important decisions about the things that concern us so greatly, such as the problems of peace and a just world economic order, we must prepare ourselves to do so by coming down out of the clouds of high-level abstractions and learning to consider the problems of the world, whether at local, state, national, or international levels, as extensionally as we now consider the problems of getting food, clothing, and shelter.

If, however, we cling to our fixations and our intensional orientations, and the belligerent, two-valued sense of "I am right and you are wrong" that they produce, we have little before us but a fate similar to that of Dr. Maier's rat. We shall remain pathologically incapable of changing our behavior, and there will be nothing for us to do but, like the rat, to try the same wrong solutions over and over again. After prolonged repetition of such futile conduct, would it be remarkable if we found ourselves finally in a condition of political "nervous breakdown"—sick of trying, disillusioned with the processes of democracy, and willing to permit dictators to dangle us upside down by our tails?

The Scientific Attitude

The most striking characteristic of science has been its continued success in the solving of "insoluble" problems. It was once considered "impossible" to devise means of traveling over twenty miles an hour, but now we have attained speeds of more than 24,000 miles an hour. It was "impossible" for humans to fly—people "proved" it again and again—but now we fly across oceans as a matter of everyday routine. I was told repeatedly during the course of my education that the release of atomic energy was merely a *theoretical* possibility—of course, they would never actually *do* it. Scientists may almost be called the professional accomplishers of the "impossible." They do this because, as scientists, they are extensionally oriented. They may be, and often are, intensionally oriented toward what they call "nonscientific" subjects; therefore, the physical scientist talking about social or political problems or about love and marriage may be no more sensible than the rest of us.

As we have seen, scientists have special ways of talking about the phenomena they deal with, special "maps" to describe the "territories" with which they are concerned. On the basis of these maps, they make predictions; when things turn out as predicted, they regard their maps as "true." If, however, things do not turn out as predicted, they *discard* their maps and make new ones; that is, they act on *new sets of hypotheses* that suggest *new courses of action.*[2] Again they check their map with the territory. If the new one does not check, they cheerfully discard it and make still more hypotheses, until they find some that *work.* These they regard as "true," but "true" *only for the time being.* When, later on, they find new situa-

---

[2] Alfred North Whitehead, in *Science and the Modern World*, says that it is not unusual for a scientist to *rejoice* upon being proven wrong, that all human progress has depended on "new questions" rather than on "new answers" to the "old questions."

tions in which the "working" hypotheses no longer work, they are again ready to discard them, to reexamine the extensional world, and to make still more new maps that again suggest new courses of action.

When scientists work with a minimum of interference from financial or political influences—when, that is, they are free to pool their knowledge with their co-workers all over the world and to check the accuracy of one another's maps by observations independently made and freely exchanged, without regard to whether their hypotheses fit preconceived expectations—they make rapid progress. Highly multivalued and extensional in their orientations, they are troubled less than others by fixed dogmas and nonsense questions. In a way that is paradoxical in terms of traditional orientations but quite understandable in terms of the new, the conversations and writings of scientists are full of admissions of ignorance and declarations of partial knowledge. Expressions like the following appear with impressive frequency in the conversation of nuclear physicists with whom the writer has been acquainted: "According to Henderson's last paper— although there may be still later findings not yet published. . . . " "No one knows exactly what happens, but our guess is that it's something like this. . . . " "What I tell you is probably wrong, but it's the only plausible theory we've been able to construct. . . . " It has been said that knowledge is power, but *effective knowledge is that which includes knowledge of the limitations of one's knowledge.*

The last thing a scientist would do is cling to a map because it was inherited from his grandfather or because it was used by George Washington or Abraham Lincoln. By intensional orientation, "If it was good enough for Washington and Lincoln, it's good enough for me." By extensional orientation, we *don't know until we have checked.*

The Left-Hand Door Again

Notice the differences between the technological, scientific attitudes that we have toward some things and the intensional attitudes we have toward others. When we are having a car repaired, we think in terms of mechanisms. We do not ask: "Is the remedy you suggest consistent with the principles of thermodynamics? What would Faraday or Newton have done under similar circumstances? Are you sure that the remedy you suggest does not represent a degenerative, defeatist tendency in the technological traditions of our nation? What would happen if we did this to *every* car? What has Aristotle to say on this?" These are non-sense questions. We only ask, "What will be the *results*?"

But a different thing happens when we are trying to repair society. Few people have a sense of societies as mechanisms—as collections of ongoing institutions. Accustomed to thinking of social problems in terms of simple moral indignation, we denounce the wickedness of labor unions (or of capitalists), we denounce the zeal of conservatives (or the fervor of liberals), we denounce Russia (or, if we are Russians, we denounce "American imperialism"). In so doing, we miss entirely the basic requirement of "mapping" social problems, namely, the initial task of describing the *established patterns of group behavior* (that is, the institutions) that constitute a society and contribute to its social problems. Indignant at the "wickedness" of those with whom we disagree, we do not ask of a proposed institutional change what the results will be. We are usually more interested in "punishing the wicked" than in determining results. And suggested social remedies are almost always discussed in the light of questions to which verifiable answers cannot be given: "Are your proposals consistent with sound economic policy? Do they accord with the principles of true liberalism (or true conservatism)? What would Alexander Hamilton, Thomas Jefferson, or Abraham Lincoln have said? Would it be a step in the direction of communism or fascism? What would happen if everybody followed your scheme? Why don't you read Aristotle?" And we spend so much time discussing non-sense questions that often we never get around to finding out exactly what the results of proposed actions would be.

During the course of our weary struggles with such non-sense questions, someone or other is sure to come along with a campaign to tell us, "Let's get *back* to normalcy. . . . Let's stick to the good *old-fashioned, tried-and-true* principles. . . . Let's *return* to *sound* economics and *sound* finance, to *basics*. . . . America must get *back* to this. . . . America must get *back* to that. . . . " Most such appeals are, of course, merely invitations to take another jump at the left-hand door—in other words, *invitations to continue driving ourselves crazy.* In our confusion, we accept those invitations—with the same old results.

CHAPTER 19

Towards Order
Within and Without

But I say unto you, that every idle word that men shall speak, they shall give account thereof in the day of judgment. For by thy words thou shalt be justified, and by thy words thou shalt be condemned. MATTHEW 12:36–37

Rules For Extensional Orientation

Just as a mechanic carries around a pair of pliers and a screwdriver for use in an emergency—just as we all carry around in our heads tables of multiplication for daily use—so can we all carry in our heads convenient rules for extensional orientation. These rules need not be complicated; a short, rough-and-ready set of formulas will do. Their principal function will be to prevent us from going round in circles of intensional thinking, to prevent automatic reactions, to prevent us from trying to answer unanswerable questions, to prevent us from repeating old mistakes endlessly. They will *not* magically show us what better solutions are possible, but they will *start us looking* for courses of action that are better than the old ones. The following rules, then, are a brief summary of the parts of the book that directly apply to problems of evaluation. (Memorizing these guidelines will prove valuable.)

1. A map is NOT the territory it stands for; words are NOT things.
   A map does not represent ALL of a territory; words never say ALL about anything.
   Maps of maps, maps of maps of maps, and so on, can be made indefinitely, with or without relationship to a territory. (Chapters 2 and 9.)

2. The meanings of words are NOT in the words; they are in us. (Chapters 2 and 10.)

3. Contexts determine meaning (Chapter 4):

   I like fish. (*Cooked, edible fish.*)
   He caught a fish. (*Live fish.*)
   You poor fish! (*Not fish at all.*)
   To fish for compliments. (*To seek.*)

4. Beware of the word "is," which, when not used simply as an auxiliary verb ("he is coming"), can crystallize misevaluations:

   The grass *is* green. (But what about the part our nervous system plays? Chapters 9 and 10.)
   Mr. Miller *is* a Jew. (Beware of confusing levels of abstraction. Chapters 10 and 11.)
   Business *is* business. (This is a directive, not to be mistaken for a statement of fact. Chapter 7.)
   A thing *is* what it *is*. (Unless this is understood as a rule of language, there is danger of ignoring alternative ways of classifying, as well as of ignoring the fact that everything is in a process of change. (Chapters 9, 11, 12, and 18.)

5. Don't try to cross bridges that aren't built yet. Distinguish between directive and informative statements. (Chapter 7.)

6. Distinguish at least four senses of the word "true":

> Some mushrooms are poisonous. (If we call this "true," we mean that it is a *report that can be and has been verified*. Chapter 3.)
> Sally is the sweetest girl in the world. (If we call this "true," we mean that *we feel the same way* toward Sally. Chapters 5 and 8.)
> All men are created equal. (If we call this "true," we mean that this is *a directive which we believe should be obeyed*. Chapter 7.)
> $(x + y)^2 = x^2 + 2xy + y^2$. (If we call this "true," we mean that this statement is *consistent with the system of statements possible to be made in the language called algebra*. Chapter 13.)

7. When tempted to "fight fire with fire," remember that the fire department usually uses water. (Chapter 13.)

8. The two-valued orientation is the *starter, not the steering wheel.* (Chapter 13.)

9. Beware of definitions, which are words about words. Think with examples rather than definitions wherever possible. (Chapter 9.)

10. Use *index numbers* and *dates* as reminders that *no word ever has exactly the same meaning twice.*

> Cow$_1$ is *not* cow$_2$, cow$_2$ is *not* cow$_3$, . . .
> Smith$_{1983}$ is *not* Smith$_{1984}$, Smith$_{1985}$ is *not* Smith$_{1990}$. . . .

If these rules are too much to remember, the reader is asked to memorize *at least* this much:

> *Cow$_1$ is not cow$_2$, cow$_2$ is not cow$_3$. . . .*

This is the simplest and most general of the rules for extensional orientation. The word "cow" gives us the intensional meanings, informative and affective; it calls up in our minds the features that this "cow" has *in common* with other "cows." The index number, however, reminds us that this one is *different;* it reminds us that "cow" does *not* tell us "all about" the event; it reminds us of the *characteristics left out* in the process of abstracting; it prevents us from equating the word with the thing, that is, from confusing the abstraction "cow" with the extensional cow.

Symptoms of Disorder

Not to observe, consciously or unconsciously, such principles of interpretation is to think and react in primitive and infantile ways. There are a number of ways in which we can detect unhealthy reactions in ourselves. One of the most obvious symptoms is sudden displays of temper. When blood pressure rises, when quarrels become excited and feverish, and when arguments end up in snarling and name-calling, there is often a misevaluation somewhere in the background.

Another obvious symptom is worry—when we keep going round and round in circles. "I love her. . . . I love her. . . . If I could only forget that she is a *waitress*!" But waitress$_1$ is not waitress$_2$. "Gosh, what a terrible governor we've got! . . . We thought he was a businessman, but he proves to be only a *politician*." But politician$_1$ is not politician$_2$. As soon as we break these circles and think about *facts* instead of *labels*, new light is thrown on our problems.

Still another symptom of unhealthy reaction is a tendency to be oversensitive, easily hurt, and quick to resent insults. The immature mind, equating words with things, regards unkind words as unkind acts. Attributing to harmless sets of noises a power of injuring, such a person is "insulted" when those noises are uttered at him. So-called "gentlemen" in semisavage and infantile societies used to elevate reactions of this kind into "codes of honor." By "honor," they meant extreme readiness to pull out swords or pistols whenever they imagined that they had been "insulted." Naturally, they killed each other off much faster than was necessary, illustrating again a principle often implied in this book: the lower the boiling point, the higher the mortality rate.

It has already been pointed out that the tendency to talk too much and too readily is an unhealthy sign. We should also be wary of "thinking too much." It is a mistake to believe that productive thinkers necessarily "think harder" than people who never get anywhere. They only think more efficiently. "Thinking too much" often means that somewhere in the back of our minds there is a "certainty"—an "incontrovertible fact," an "unalterable law," an "eternal principle"—some statement which we believe "says all" about something. Life, however, is constantly throwing into the face of our "incontrovertible certainties" facts that do not fit our preconceptions: "politicians" who *aren't* corrupt, "friends" who *aren't* faithful, "benevolent societies" that *aren't* benevolent. Refusing to give up our sense of "certainty" and yet unable to deny the facts that do not fit, we are forced to "think and think and think." And, as we have seen before, there are only two ways out of such dilemmas: first, to deny the facts altogether, and secondly, to reverse the principle altogether, so that we go from "*All* insurance companies are reliable" to "*No* insurace companies are reliable." Hence, such infantile reactions as, "I'll *never* trust another woman!" "Don't *ever* say politics to me again!" "I'm through with lawyers for good!" "Men are *all* alike, the jerks!"

The mature mind, on the other hand, knows that words never say all about anything, and such a mind is therefore *adjusted to uncertainty*. In driving a car, for example, we never know what is going to happen next;

no matter how often we have gone over the same road, we never find *exactly* the same traffic conditions. Nevertheless, a competent driver travels over all kinds of roads, even at high speeds, without either fear or nervousness. Such a driver is *adjusted to uncertainty*—the unexpected blowout or the sudden hazard—and *does not feel insecure.*

Similarly, the intellectually mature person does not "know all about" anything. And this does not make him insecure, because he knows that the only kind of security life offers is the *dynamic security that comes from within: the security derived from infinite flexibility of mind—from an infinite-valued orientation.*

"Knowing all" about this, "knowing all" about that, we have only ourselves to blame when we find certain problems "insoluble." With some working knowledge of how language acts, in ourselves and others, we save both time and effort; we prevent ourselves from running around in verbal squirrel cages. With an extensional orientation, we are adjusted to the inevitable uncertainties of all our science and wisdom. And whatever other problems the world thrusts upon us, we at least escape those of our own making.

The Lost Children

Then there are the unhappy people who *don't* know "all about this" or "all about that," and *wish they did.* Being in a more or less chronic state of anxiety about not knowing all the answers, they are always looking for "the answer" that will forever still their anxieties. They drift from one church, political party, or "new thought" movement to another; they may drift from one psychiatrist to another if they are educated, or from one fortune-teller or astrologer to another if they are not. We find examples in such recent phenomena as TM (Transcendental Meditation), est (Erhard seminars training), the "flower children" movement of the sixties, followers of any number of Indian mysteries, the Reverend Moon (Unification Church), Scientology, and so on. Occasionally such people happen upon fortune-tellers, political leaders, or systems of thought that hit them just right. Thereupon they are suddenly overwhelmed with relief and joy. Feeling that they have found *the* answer to all their problems, they become passionately devoted to spreading the news to everyone they know.

A major source both of the excessive anxiety that such people feel and of their excessive enthusiasm when they do find their problems "solved" has been described by psychiatrists. An adult—an emotionally mature person—is independent, able to work out answers to problems, and able to realize that there is no one answer to everything. If, however, we have not been brought up to be independent—if, for example, we were deprived of love and care at an age when we needed love and care, or if we had parents who did too much for us through excessive and misdirected love—we may grow up physically mature but emotionally immature. No matter what our age, we continue to need a *parent symbol:* some figure of comforting authority to whom we can turn for "all the answers." If we are so troubled, we will successively seek one parent-symbol after another once we can no longer depend on our own parents—sometimes a kindly teacher, sometimes an authoritative and impressive clergyman, sometimes a fatherly or motherly employer, sometimes a political leader.

From our point of view as students of human linguistic behavior, the verbal aspects of this search for a parent-symbol deserve attention. Those who, for one reason or another, are unable to accept a priest, teacher, or political leader as a parent-symbol, may find a parent-symbol in a *big, systematic collection of words*—for example, a huge and difficult-to-understand philosophical work, a politico-economic philosophy, a system of "new thought," or the One Hundred Great Books. "Here! Here," they cry, "are all the answers in one place!" Finding "all the answers" in such collections of words is a sophisticated and, in our culture, a respectable form of both emotional immaturity and what we have earlier called naiveté regarding the symbolic process. It is emotional immaturity because it involves giving up independent thought in favor of dependence on a (verbal) parent symbol. It is nevertheless respectable, because those who manifest their immaturity in this way acquire, in doing so, an impressively complicated and abstract vocabulary that they exhibit on all possible occasions—and our culture respects the fluent talker, especially one who talks at high levels of abstraction. This dependence on verbal parent-symbols is also naive, because it assumes what we have already seen to be an impossible assumption, namely, that a verbal "map" can "say all" about the "territory" of experience.

This is not to say, of course, that an enthusiasm for a "great book," or for a hundred of them, is necessarily a symptom of immaturity. However, there is a world of difference between the enthusiasm of the emotionally immature and that of the mature. An immature person, discovering a new intellectual system or philosophy that somehow meets his or her needs, tends to adopt it uncritically, to repeat endlessly the verbal formulas provided, and *to resent any imputation that anything more needs to be discovered.*

The mature reader, on the other hand, pleased and excited by a newly found "great book," is nonetheless *eager to test it.* Are these new and exciting principles or human insights as general as they appear to be? Are they true in many different cultural or historical contexts? Do they need correction or revision or refinement? How do the principles or attitudes apply in specific cases and under different conditions? Through these and other questions, the mature reader may find that the newly discovered system is quite as important as it originally appeared to be, but, along with an increased sense of power, such a reader also gets a deep sense of *how much more there is to be learned.*

Indeed, the better and more widely useful a new philosophical or scientific synthesis is, the greater will be the number of fresh problems raised. The answers given to perplexing questions by Darwin in his *Origin of Species* did not stop biological inquiry; they gave biology the greatest spurt of fresh inquiry in modern times. The answers given by Freud to psychological questions did not stop psychology; they opened up whole new areas of investigation.

"Great books" are those which open great new questions. Great books are misread if their effect is to stop investigation. (For example, the communist use of the writings of Marx appears to me to be a misreading of books which were in their time important contributions to social science. The communists have treated all deviations from Marx—or at least deviations from their interpretations of Marx—as attacks upon "Truth," and they seem thereby to have rendered the progress of social science in the Soviet Union almost impossible.)[1]

In other words, the wiser people become, whether in science, religion, politics, or art, the less dogmatic they become. Apparently, the better we know the territory of human experience, the more aware we become of the limitations of the verbal maps we can make of our experience. We have earlier (Chapter 9) called this awareness of the limitations of maps "consciousness of abstracting." The mature person retains "consciousness of abstracting" even with respect to philosophies or systems of thought about which he or she feels the greatest enthusiasm.

"Know Thyself"

Another area in which "consciousness of abstracting" is necessary is in *what we say to ourselves about ourselves.* We are all a great deal more complex than Bessie the Cow, and even more than Bessie, we are constantly undergoing change. Furthermore, we all describe ourselves to ourselves in some kind of language (or other abstractions, like "mental pictures," "idealizations," or "images"). These descriptions of ourselves are more or less clearly formulated: "I am the home-loving type," "I am beautiful," "I am hopelessly unattractive," "I believe in efficiency," "I am kindhearted," "I can't understand mathematics," "I have a natural talent for music," "I'm not that kind of a girl," "I am not a snob," "I am a friend of the downtrodden," and so on. All such statements are *more or less* accurate "maps" of that "territory" which is ourselves. Some people make better maps of themselves than others. If a person makes a reasonably good map of himself, we say

[1] See Anatol Rapoport, "Dialectical Materialism and General Semantics," *ETC.*, V (1948), pp. 81–104.

that he "knows himself"—that he accurately assesses his strengths and limitations, his emotional powers and emotional needs.

The psychologist Carl R. Rogers refers to this "map" we make of ourselves as the "self-concept," which, according to his terminology, may be "realistic" or "unrealistic." What we do, how we dress, what manners or mannerisms we adopt, what tasks we undertake and what tasks we decline, what kind of society we seek, and so on, are determined not so much by our *actual* powers and limitations as by what we *believe to be* our powers and limitations—that is, by our "self-concepts."[2]

All that has previously been said in this book about maps and territories applies with special relevance to our "self-concepts." A map *is not* the territory: one's self-concept *is not* one's self. A map represents *not all* of the territory: one's self-concept *omits* an enormous amount of one's actual self—we never know ourselves *completely*. We can make maps of maps of maps, and so on: we can describe ourselves to ourselves, and then make about ourselves *any number of inferences and generalizations at higher levels of abstraction*.

The pitfalls of map–territory relationships therefore threaten the adequacy of our evaluations of ourselves just as much as they threaten the adequacy of our evaluations of other people and of external events. Indeed, as is suggested in the famous Socratic injunction, "Know thyself," it is more than probable that our wisdom in evaluating other people and external events rests largely upon our wisdom in evaluating ourselves. What kinds of "maps," then, do we make of ourselves?

Some people obviously have extremely unrealistic self-concepts. The person who says, "I have the ability to act as general manager" and accepts such a job, and then turns out not to have the ability, seriously disappoints himself and others. If another person says, "I'm not any good" and takes himself seriously when he says this, he may dissipate his talents, his opportunities, his entire life. The not uncommon sight of the middle-aged man or woman who dresses and acts like an eighteen-year-old is another instance of a person who lives in terms of an extremely *unrealistic* self-concept.

Students often defeat themselves by saying, "I'm not good at mathematics," "I can't sing," or "I just *can't* learn to spell." They will be poor at mathematics, singing, or spelling not because of lack of ability, but because their self-concepts prevent them from tackling mathematics and spelling with any hope of success.

Furthermore, there are those who do not seem to realize that their self-concepts do *not* include *all* the relevant facts about themselves. As psychia-

[2] See Carl H. Rogers, *Client-Centered Therapy* (1951) and *On Becoming a Person* (1961); also Prescott Lecky, *Self-Consistency: A Theory of Personality* (1948); Gardner Murphy, *Personality: A Biosocial Approach to Origins and Structure* (1947); Donald Snugg and Arthur Combs, *Individual Behavior* (1949); Raymond Rogers, *Coming into Existence* (1967).

trists have shown us time and again, we all have a way of concealing from others and from ourselves our deeper reasons for doing things; instead, we offer, in justification of our acts, more or less elaborate rationalizations.

Let us suppose, for example, that a critic has given as her reason for attacking a book its "shoddy argument and bad prose style." Let us suppose, furthermore, that the deeper reasons are entirely different, reasons such as professional jealousy, fear of the book's upsetting ideas, or a personal quarrel with the author ten years earlier. If the reviewer believes that her self-concept "says all" about herself, her picture of herself as "one who believes in rigorous logic and high standards of prose style" becomes to her a complete and adequate account of why she dislikes the book. In other words, the most common effect of not knowing that one's self-concept does not "say all" about one's self is *the tendency on the part of many people to believe their own rationalizations.* Some persons, indeed, believe their "self-concepts" so completely and sincerely—that is, they surround themselves with such airtight rationalizations—that they become incapable of any genuine self-knowledge.

Self-knowledge, of course, is often disturbing: statements of the kind, "My real reason for not liking this book is that I'm jealous of the author," "The reason I am not getting ahead is that I am less intelligent than my colleagues," and so on, are extremely difficult to face if we are emotionally insecure. Therefore, we often *need* to believe our rationalizations: "The book is shoddy in its arguments," "The reason I am not getting ahead is that my colleagues are conspiring against me." If the need to believe in these inaccurate maps is strong enough, we can shut our eyes to any amount of evidence that contradicts them.

How do we prevent ourselves from getting into this emotional predicament? Those who are already in it can probably be helped only by a professionally trained counselor or a psychiatrist. But for the rest of us, there remain the day-to-day problems of action and decision; the more realistic our self-concepts are, the more likelihood there is of fruitful action and sane decision. Can we do anything to achieve a greater realism about ourselves? It is important that we do, because those who cannot be realistic about themselves are, as a rule, also incapable of being realistic about their relations with other people.

Reports and Judgments

In at least one respect, people who are capable of some degree of self-insight can do for themselves what psychological counselors and many psychiatrists do. As we have seen, we manufacture false self-concepts because truer statements are unbearable. The reason they are unbearable is often that they involve the uncritical acceptance from our environment (from what our friends and neighbors say, or what we think they are saying) of *other people's judgments.* Using the word "judgment" here as we have used it in Chapter 3, notice the difference between "I am a service-station attendant" (which is a report) and "I am *only* a service-station attendant" (which involves a judgment, implying that I ought to be something different and that it is disgraceful that I am what I am).

One of the most important aspects of a psychiatrist's or counselor's assistance is the fact that the therapist does *not pass any judgments on us.* When the patient admits to being "only" a service-station attendant, or that ten years ago the patient lost a business through bankruptcy, the counselor indicates by word or by manner that, while the patient's feelings of shame or guilt or embarrassment are entirely understandable, the counselor does not condemn him for being what he is or for having done what he has done. In other words, the counselor helps the patient change the *judgment,* "I am *only* a service-station attendant and *therefore not much good,*" into the *report,* "I am a service-station attendant." The judgment, "I am a *bankrupt* and a *failure,*" is changed into "Ten years ago I lost my grocery store through bankruptcy." As a result of the accepting attitude of the psychiatrist or counselor, the patient is better able to accept himself.

The fact that we permit other people's judgments (and what we believe to be their judgments) to influence us unduly is one of the commonest reasons for feelings of inferiority, guilt, and insecurity. If a man, saying to himself, "I am black," simultaneously accepts the judgment of certain whites about blacks, he will find it very hard to be black, and may spend the rest of his life being angry, defensive, and miserable. If a woman makes two hundred dollars a week and accepts the real or imagined judgment of others that if she were any good she would be making five hundred, she will find it difficult to face the fact of making two hundred. The training suggested in Chapter 3 of *writing reports from which judgments are excluded* may be applied to thinking and writing *about ourselves.* Such self-descriptions are an especially helpful technique in arriving at more realistic self-concepts.

We should, in performing this exercise, put down facts about ourselves—especially the facts about which we feel some shame or embarrassment—and then ask with respect to each fact such questions as these: "Is it necessary to pass judgment at all on this fact?" "Who passes judgment on this fact anyway, and should I also do so?" "Are no other judgments possible?" "What does an unfavorable judgment on one of my actions *in the past* provide about what I am *today?*" Reports of the following kind may lead to such reevaluations as are indicated in the parentheses:

I am a service-station attendant. (Some people think it is somehow inferior to be a service-station attendant. Do *I* have to think so, too?)

I went through bankruptcy. (But that was ten years ago! I've had a lot more business experience since then. Who knows what will happen if I start again—in a different line of business? in a different location?)

I cracked up on the battlefield. (Who says I shouldn't have cracked up? Were they in South Vietnam? Did they have to go through what I did? I was psychologically wounded in battle; others were physically wounded. Why don't they give Purple Hearts to psychiatric casualties?)

Naturally, if one's rationalizations are deeply rooted, this technique is difficult to practice. For example:

My real reason for disliking this book is professional jealousy. (Oh, no! The author's arguments *are* shoddy and his style *is* awful!)

But, as we grow increasingly extensional about our own feelings—as we grow in our ability to accept ourselves, so that we are able to confront *without judgments of good or bad* such reports as, "I am below average in height," "I am not athletic," "I am the child of divorced parents," "My sister gets better grades than I do," "I never went to college," and so on— we progressively have less need to deceive ourselves. *In self-knowledge, as in science, the conquest of little areas leads progressively to the conquest of larger and more difficult areas.* As our self-concepts grow more realistic, our actions and decisions become progressively wiser, since they are based on a more accurate "mapping" of that complex territory of our own personalities.

Institutionalized Attitudes

Another way in which we can increase our extensional awareness of ourselves is by distinguishing between attitudes *institutionally* arrived at and attitudes *extensionally* arrived at. As we have seen in Chapter 17, we are all members of institutions, and as members of institutions we incorporate into ourselves certain institutionally demanded attitudes. If we are Democrats, we are expected to support Democratic candidates. If we belong to an employers' association, our fellow members may expect us to be hostile to labor unions. If we are Montagues, we are expected to be hostile to the Capulets.

A source of widespread misevaluation implicit in such institutionalized attitudes is that each of them involves a generalization at a high level of abstraction, while actual Democratic candidates, labor unions, and Capulets exist at the level of extensional fact. Many persons are, through emotional insecurity as well as through lack of an extensional orientation, unable to depart from institutionally expected attitudes. Seeking security by adopting the "official" point of view prevalent in the institutions of which they are members, they become excessively conventional and excessively given to commonplace ideas and emotions. They feel what they are expected to feel by their political party, their church, their social group, or their family; they think what they are expected to think. They find it both easier and safer not to examine too extensionally any *specific* Democratic candidate, any *specific* labor union, any *specific* Capulet, because extensional examination of any one of these *might* lead to an evaluation different from the institutionally accepted point of view.

The term often used to describe this process is "internalization." It refers to the process in which people take ideas, ideologies, beliefs, commands, and attitudes from the society in which they live and *make them part of themselves*, so that the ideas, ideologies, and so forth seem to come from within themselves and seem to be their own ideas and ideologies. The process of socialization involves getting young people (and older people, at times) to accept and internalize the belief system found in the society, so that they fit in and can relate to members of the society without difficulty. The values and beliefs and prohibitions found outside are incorporated into the personality and seem to come from inside.

But to have nothing but institutionalized attitudes is eventually to have no character of one's own, and therefore to have nothing original or creative to contribute to the institutions of which one is a member. Furthermore, there is the danger to one's personal adjustment implicit in continually living by high-level generalizations and repressing (or avoiding) extensional evaluations.

The rule already suggested for the avoidance of excessively intensional attitudes is helpful for the avoidance of excessively conventional, institutionalized attitudes, because intensional attitudes are often the result of the uncritical acceptance of institutional dogmas. With the application of the "cow$_1$ is not cow$_2$" rule, we begin to *look* in order to find out whether Democrat$_1$ differs in any important respects from Democrat$_2$, whether labor union$_1$ differs from labor union$_2$, whether Capulet$_1$ differs from Capulet$_2$. As the result of such extensional examination, we may find that the original institutional attitudes were the correct ones after all; or we may find it necessary, as Romeo and Juliet did, to depart from them. (Of course Romeo and Juliet were not always as extensional as they might have been. Had they not been prone to confusing inferences with facts, they might both have lived a little longer.) But whatever conclusions we may arrive at, the important thing is that they will be our own—the result of *our own* extensional examination of the events or objects to be evaluated.

People who are not accustomed to distinguishing between attitudes institutionally arrived at and those extensionally arrived at are capable of real self-deception. In a real sense, they don't know which of their opinions are simply parrotlike repetitions of institutional opinions and which are the result of their own experience and their own thinking. Lacking that self-insight, they are unable to arrive at realistic self-concepts; they are unable to map accurately the territory of their own feelings and attitudes.

Reading Toward Sanity

A few words, finally, need to be said on the subject of reading as an aid to extensional orientation. Studying books sometimes has the effect of producing excessive intensional orientation; this is especially true in literary study, for example, when the study of words—novels, plays, poems, essays—becomes an end in itself.

When the study of literature is undertaken, however, not as an end in itself, but as a guide to life, its effect is extensional in the best sense. Literature works by intensional means; that is, by the manipulation of the informative and affective connotations of words. By these means, it not only calls our attention to facts not previously noticed, but it also is capable of arousing feelings not previously experienced. These new feelings in turn call our attention to still more facts not previously noticed. Both the new feelings and the new facts, therefore, upset our intensional orientations, so that our blindness is removed little by little.

The extensionally oriented person, as has been repeatedly said, is governed not by words only, but by the facts to which the words refer. But supposing there were no words to guide us? Should we be able to guide ourselves to those facts? The answer is, in the vast majority of cases, no. To begin with, our nervous systems are extremely imperfect, and we see things only in terms of our training and interests. If our interests are limited, we see extremely little; a man looking for cigarette butts in the street sees little else of the world passing by. Furthermore, as everyone knows, when we travel, meet interesting people, or have adventures before we are old enough to appreciate such experiences, we often feel that we might just as well not have had them. Experience itself is an extremely imperfect teacher. Experience does not tell us *what* it is that we are experiencing. Things simply happen. And if we do not know *what to look for* in our experience, the happenings often have no significance to us whatever.

This is where *concepts* are particularly significant. The term "concept" is actually rather hard to define—dictionaries are almost useless here. Concepts are words that help us organize knowledge, that help us pull facts together in meaningful ways, that "explain" things. We all develop, knowingly or unknowingly, conceptual frameworks that help us understand the world—and much that you have learned in this book involves concepts, such as "verifiability," "denotation," "connotation," "intensional orientation," and so on. The conceptual framework of the psychologist involves such principles as "drives," "repression," "anxiety," and "sublimation." The conceptual framework of the sociologist involves such notions as "institution," "role," "class," and "mobility." A great deal of our education involves learning concepts and learning how to apply them to different aspects of life. It is through concepts that we are able to make sense of experience.

Many people put a great deal of stock in experience as such; they tend automatically to respect the person who has "done things." "I don't want to sit around reading books," they say; "I want to get out and do things! I want to travel! I want to have experiences!" But often the experiences they go out and get do them no good whatever. They go to London, and all they remember is their hotel and the American Express office; they go to Mexico and remember only their gastrointestinal difficulties. The result is that some people who have never traveled know more about the world than some people who have. We all tend to go around the world with our eyes shut unless someone opens them for us.

And this eyeopening, then, is the tremendous function that language, in both its scientific and its affective uses, performs. In the light of abstract scientific generalizations, "trivial" facts lose their triviality. When we have studied, for example, surface tension, the alighting of a dragonfly on a pool of water is a subject for thought and explanation. Those who have never read Wordsworth have missed something of the English lake country, even though they may have lived there all their lives; to those who have read Faulkner, a trip through Mississippi is a doubly meaningful experience. In the light of the subtleties of feeling aroused in us by literature and poetry and drama, every human experience is filled with rich relationships and significances.

The communications we receive from others, insofar as they do not simply retrace our old patterns of feeling and tell us things we already know, increase the efficiency of our nervous systems. Poets, as well as scientists, have aptly been called "the window-washers of the mind"; without their communications to widen our interests and increase the sensitivity of our perceptions, we could very well remain as blind as newborn kittens.

Language, as has been repeatedly emphasized in these pages, is social. Reading or listening, writing or talking, we are constantly involved in the processes of social interaction made possible by language. Sometimes, as we have seen, the result of that social interaction is the sharing of knowledge, the enrichment of sympathies and insight, and the establishing of human cooperation. But at other times, the social interaction does not come out so well: every exchange of remarks, as between two drunks at a bar or between two hostile delegates at the United Nations Security Council, leads progressively to the conviction on the part of each that it is impossible to cooperate with the other.

We come back, then, to the judgments explicitly announced at the beginning of this book—the ethical judgments on which the argument has been based throughout—that widespread intraspecific cooperation through the use of language is the fundamental mechanism of human survival, and that, when the use of language results, as it so often does, in the creation or aggravation of disagreements and conflicts, there is something wrong with the speaker, the listener, or both. Sometimes, as we have seen, this "something wrong" is the result of ignorance of the territory, which leads to the making of inaccurate maps; sometimes it is the result, through faulty evaluative habits, of refusing to look at the territory but insisting on talking anyway; sometimes it is the result of imperfections in language itself, imperfections which neither speaker nor listener has taken the trouble to examine; often it is the result of using language not as an instrument of social cohesion but as a weapon. The purpose of this book has been to lay before the reader some of the ways in which, whether as speakers or listeners, we may use or be used by the mechanisms of linguistic communication. What further use to make of these mechanisms is up to the reader.

Postscript

Although the principles that have been explained throughout this book have as their purpose the establishment of agreement and the avoidance of conflict, some people may be tempted to use them as weapons with which to stir up arguments, as clubs with which to beat people over the head: "The trouble with you, Joe, is that you've got a bad case of two-valued orientation," "For God's sake, Julia, stop being so intensional!" Those who use the formulations of this book in this way may be said to have understood it but dimly.

Appendix of Applications

Since one of the purposes of this book is to help the reader understand more clearly how language works and what language actually does in the course of our lives, a series of applications is offered for each chapter. These exercises offer a chance to apply the ideas just discussed and to test or to extend the reader's grasp of the material. Some invite the reader to challenge the author's ideas; many have no "right answer" or "wrong answer." They may be used for individual reflection, for group discussion, or as topics for written analysis. All should be used to explore the potential of language in action and thought.

Applications

Chapter 1

I. In order to test his reading comprehension after reading an essay, Benjamin Franklin would close the book and attempt to reproduce the essay in writing as accurately as he could in both form and content. Since most modern readers' stamina falls short of Franklin's, the following list is provided to gauge comprehension. Which of the following statements (a) are consistent with, (b) contradict, or (c) deal with concepts extraneous to those discussed in this chapter?

1. "Survival of the fittest" is the universal law governing the health or extinction of all species.

2. The Civil War is an example of an *intraspecific* struggle.

3. Rat poison is a weapon in an *interspecific* struggle.

4. The human ability to use language is irrelevant to any theory of human survival.

5. Many species of animals accumulate knowledge from one generation to the next.

6. Cultural and intellectual cooperation is the great principle of human life.

7. The coordination of effort necessary for the functioning of society is achieved through language, or it is not achieved at all.

8. Words are not really important; what is important is the ideas for which they stand.

9. Language, thought, and behavior are intimately related to each other.

10. When the use of language creates or aggravates disagreements and conflicts, there is something linguistically wrong with the speaker, the listener, or both.

II. Discuss the following quotations in relation to this chapter:

1. No more talk! Revolution now!   Political leaflet

2. It would be difficult to exaggerate the degree to which we are influenced by those we influence.   ERIC HOFFER, *The Passionate State of Mind*

III. Further topics for discussion:

    1. Are human beings by nature competitive or cooperative? What is the basic law of life, cooperation or competition?

    2. Competition is often regarded as the primary aspect of sports, since, in most cases, the goal is simply to win. Are there areas of cooperation in sports as well? As the number of participants increases, is more or less cooperation required? In terms of language, what is the value of having cheerleaders and a crowd of vocal supporters for a team? Can they actually affect actions in which they take no direct part?

    3. Do you adjust your listening to your surroundings? Do you listen, for example, to children and to adults in the same way? What about the way you listen to people of different nationalities, races, or political persuasions? Do you listen with a view toward *understanding* or *refuting* what the speaker is saying?

    4. Are words always necessary for communication?

    5. Ask yourself, "What constitutes my daily Niagara of words?" Try to estimate the number of words that come flooding in from radio, television, newspapers, books, magazines, correspondence, conversations, and other sources. Which of these do you absorb attentively, and to which do you expose yourself thoughtlessly, just to kill time? What important communications come to you from the past? To what advertisements do you pay special attention? How do you *select* what to listen to, what to read carefully? What do these selections reveal about the kind of person you are?

    The study of language has been one of humankind's most fascinating occupations. The following books are recommended for those who wish to investigate language more extensively:

    The relations between language and thought are discussed in Stuart Chase's *Power of Words* (1954), especially Chapter 10. Important source books in this area include Alfred Korzybski, *Science and Sanity: An Introduction to Non-Aristotelian Systems and General Semantics*, fourth edition (1958); and *Language, Thought, and Reality: Selected Writings of Benjamin Lee Whorf*, edited by John B. Carroll (1956).

    Language in Thought and Action argues that cooperation is more fundamental than conflict in human societies. Some books that deal with this subject are: Peter Kropotkin, *Mutual Aid: A Factor in Evolution* (1955); Lewis Coser, *The Functions of Social Conflict* (1956); Robert Ardrey, *The Territorial Imperative* (1966); and Konrad Lorenz, *On Aggression* (1966).

Chapter 2

The reader may wish to start keeping a scrapbook, or a file of clippings or observations that illustrate the ideas presented in this book. To shed light on this chapter, start a collection of quotations, newspaper articles, editorials, and so forth that illustrate in one way or another the confusion of symbols with things symbolized. Look for instances in which people seem to think that there are *necessary* connections between symbols and things symbolized—between words and what words stand for. The ensuing chapters will suggest other kinds of confusion to look for.

After a few such examples are collected and studied, the reader will be able to recognize similar patterns of thought in contemporaries and friends, and perhaps even in his or her own thinking.

I. In the following examples, the symbol plays an unusually strong, sometimes exaggerated role with respect to the thing symbolized. The reader should try to discern the assumptions, explicit or implicit, that govern the writer's use of symbols. Is the writer consciously distorting the "map," and if so, is the purpose to give a false impression of the territory, or to get the reader to "see" the territory in a new light?

1. That which we call a rose by any other name would smell as sweet.
WILLIAM SHAKESPEARE, *Romeo and Juliet*

2. No title of Nobility shall be granted by the United States: And no Person holding any Office of Profit or Trust under them, shall, without the Consent of the Congress, accept any . . . Title, of any kind whatever, from any King, Prince, or foreign State.
Constitution of the United States, Article 1

3. Much have I travelled in the realms of gold,
And many goodly states and kingdoms seen;
Round many western islands have I been
Which bards in fealty to Apollo hold.
Oft of one wide expanse have I been told
That deep-browed Homer ruled as his demesne
Yet did I never breathe its pure serene
Till I heard Chapman speak out loud and bold:
Then felt I like some watcher of the skies
When a new planet swims into his ken;
Or like stout Cortez when with eagle eyes
He stared at the Pacific—and with all his men
Looked at each other with a wild surmise—
Silent, upon a peak in Darien.
JOHN KEATS, "On First Looking into Chapman's Homer"

4.   "Looky here, Jim; does a cat talk like we do?"
"No, a cat don't."
"Well, does a cow?"
"No, a cow don't, nuther."
"Does a cat talk like a cow, or a cow talk like a cat?"

"No, dey don't."

"It's natural and right for 'em to talk different from each other, ain't it?"

"Course."

"And ain't it natural and right for a cat and a cow to talk different from *us*?"

"Why, mos' sholy it is."

"Well, then why ain't it natural for a *Frenchman* to talk different from us? You answer me that."

"Is a cat a man, Huck?"

"No."

"Well, den, dey ain't no sense in a cat talkin' like a man. Is a cow a man?—or is a cow a cat?"

"No, she ain't neither of them."

"Well, den, she ain' got no business to talk like either one er the yuther of 'em. Is a Frenchman a man?"

"Yes."

"*Well*, den! Dad blame it, why doan' he *talk* like a man? You answer me *dat!*"   SAMUEL CLEMENS (Mark Twain), *Huckleberry Finn*

5.   "There's glory for you!"

"I don't know what you mean by 'glory,'" Alice said.

Humpty Dumpty smiled contemptuously. "Of course you don't—till I tell you. I meant 'there's a nice knock-down argument for you!'"

"But 'glory' doesn't mean 'a nice knock-down argument,'" Alice objected.

"When *I* use a word," Humpty Dumpty said, "it means just what I choose it to mean—neither more nor less."

"The question is," said Alice, "whether you *can* make words mean so many different things."

"The question is," said Humpty Dumpty, "which is to be master—that's all."

LEWIS CARROLL, *Through the Looking-Glass*

Discrepancies between maps and territories have been the subject of comedy, satire, and general outbursts of moral indignation throughout most of human history. The following are a small sampling of books in this area:

Bergen Evans, *The Natural History of Nonsense* (1946). An amusing catalogue of errors, superstitions, and mistaken beliefs.

Daniel Boorstin, *The Image: A Guide to Pseudo-Events in America* (1964).

R. D. Laing, *The Divided Self* (1959). This remarkable investigation of schizophrenia deals, in a sense, with the same kind of phenomena described in the section on maps and territories.

Two excellent books on the nature and manipulation of symbols are Suzanne K. Langer, *Philosophy in a New Key* (1942) and I.A. Richards, *The Meaning of Meaning* (1989).

Chapter 3

I. The following statements represent the mix of reports, inferences, and judgments we encounter daily. The reader is asked to classify each one. Since some cannot be neatly classified in only one category, a single-word answer may not be sufficient. If any of the statements are inferences or judgments, what kinds of evidence would be needed to support them?

1. She goes to church only to show off her clothes.

   SAMPLE ANALYSIS: In usual circumstances under which such a statement would be made, this would be an inference, since people do not ordinarily admit that they go to church for that reason. A judgment is also strongly implied, since it is assumed that one ought to go to church for better reasons.

2. Stock prices were up slightly today in light trading.

3. Compared with the persecution of heresy in Europe from 1227 to 1492, the persecution of Christians by the Romans in the first three centuries after Christ was a mild and humane procedure. Making every allowance required of an historian and permitted to a Christian, we must rank the Inquisition, along with the wars and persecutions of our time, as among the darkest blots on the record of mankind, revealing a ferocity unknown in any beast.   WILL DURANT, *The Story of Civilization*, IV

4. Commuter—one who spends his life
   In riding to and from his wife;
   A man who shaves and takes a train
   And then rides back to shave again.   E. B. WHITE

5. The Nicaraguan people do not want war.

6. Many so-called religious people are hypocrites.

7. For rent: charming two-bedroom house in woods, easy walk to bus stop, $375 a month plus deposit.

8. An apple a day keeps the doctor away.

9. And Adam lived an hundred and thirty years, and begat a son in his likeness, after his image; and called his name Seth: And the days of Adam after he had begotten Seth were eight hundred years: and he begat sons and daughters: And all the days that Adam lived were nine hundred and thirty years: and he died.   Genesis 5:3–5

10. In his inaugural address, President Bush attempted to heal the wounds of the campaign by calling on Democrats to join in a new bipartisanship.

11. The committee was reviewing reports of the FBI investigations of former Senator Tower's life-style, including allegations of drinking and socializing with women other than his wife.

II. Once the verifiability of a statement has been ascertained, the task of verifying still remains. If any of the following are reports, how would you verify them?

1. $A^2 + B^2 = C^2$

2. Families of four with incomes of less than $9,000 a year live in poverty.

3. Hops can grow as much as eight inches in one day.

4. Water boils at 10° Celsius.

5. Cigarette smoking can be hazardous to your health.

III. Take a number of publications dealing with important issues in American society and try to discern the "slant" from which they are written. Compare, for example, your town's morning paper, *Commentary*, the *New Republic*, *Ebony*, the *New York Review of Books*, the *American Spectator*, *Mother Jones*, *Reader's Digest*, and *Rolling Stone*.

IV. To a surprising degree, we trust each other's reports. What kind of circumstances might have given rise to the kind of false reports that are the subject of the following news story? What kind of effect might such maps have had on the people and society that used them?
MOSCOW—The Soviet Union's chief cartographer acknowledged Friday that for the last 50 years the Soviet Union had deliberately falsified virtually all public maps of the country, misplacing rivers and streets, distorting boundaries and omitting geographical features, on orders of the secret police. . . . The apparent purpose is to thwart foreign military and intelligence operations.   *New York Times* News Service, September 2, 1988

V. In addition to the exercises in report writing and the exclusion of judgments and inferences as suggested in Chapter 3, the reader is asked to try writing reports heavily slanted *against* persons or organizations he or she *likes*, and reports heavily slanted *in favor* of persons or organizations the reader *dislikes*.

VI. "A youth and a man were killed and three teenagers seriously injured today in two auto accidents." Write:

1. A *report* of these accidents, inventing names and places.

2. A *slanted report* for a newspaper campaigning for stricter laws against drunken driving. (Be sure to use factual statements only, letting your readers make their own inferences and judgments.)

3. *A slanted report* for a newspaper highly critical of the local city government. (Again, use factual statements only.)

Chapter 4

I. Assuming the role of a dictionary editor and using only the following quotations, write a definition for the word "gyxpyx." Write a definition of ten to twenty words; a synonym is not acceptable.

1. His gyxpyx is twenty years old, but it still works.

2. Robin just bought a portable, electric gyxpyx.

3. The new clerk is as fast as blazes with the gyxpyx.

4. One of the keys on the gyxpyx is stuck.

5. I don't care what you say. I think a gyxpyx is better than an abacus.

From the following quotations, make up a definition of the word "wanky."

1. He seems to be perpetually wanky.

2. Some people feel most wanky in the early morning, but I get that way just before supper.

3. If you want to get over that wanky feeling, take Johnson's Homogenized Yeast Tablets.

4. . . . the wanky, wanky bluebell
   that droops upon its stem . . .

5. I'm not cross, just wanky.

II. In what contexts are the following questions likely to arise? Within those contexts, which questions are non-sense and which are not? Why? Can any of the non-sense questions be made verifiable by changing the wording?

1. Is democracy a failure?

   SAMPLE ANALYSIS: Unless there is reasonable agreement as to the extensional meaning of "democracy" and "failure," a discussion of this question is not likely to be fruitful. It might be broken up into smaller questions such as these: "Assuming that democracy is a success if 60 or more percent of those able to vote in presidential elections do vote, what was the percentage of voters in the elections of 1976, 1980, 1984, 1988 . . . ?" "Assuming that democracy may be said to be reasonably successful if intelligent but underprivileged children are given the opportunity to finish their schooling, what percentage of fourth-grade children with IQs of over 125 finish high school?" If, however, we talk chiefly in terms of intensional meanings of the terms "democracy" and "failure," disagreement and ill-feelings are likely to result. In many contexts where such a question is brought up for discussion, it would seem to be a non-sense question.

2. Is there a life after death?

3. Are women more conservative than men?

4. Is the universe expanding or contracting?

5. Is marijuana more harmful than alcohol?

III. Specify the conditions under which you would say "yes" to the following:

1. Jazz is dying out.

2. Do you love me?

3. Blacks are better athletes than whites.

4. All wars are immoral.

5. Dear Dorothy Dix: How can a wife tell when her husband loves her? I have been married ten years and my husband and I quarrel constantly. He beats me and swears at me, and then tells how much he loves me and cries over it all. Now I would like to leave him and go back to my folks, but he won't let me go. Says he can't bear to be separated from me. Please tell me what to do. Do you think he really loves me?

UNHAPPY WIFE, Chicago *Sun-Times*

IV. Listen closely to the arguments you hear or overhear in the next few days and ask yourself these questions:

1. What is the question at issue?

2. Is it a non-sense question, or could it be answered by observation of the disputed facts? What would we have to do to tell whether or not it is true?

3. To what extent do the participants reach an agreement? If the argument ends in disagreement, can we think of any procedure that might have helped to bring agreement?

4. Are there "key words" around which the dispute seems to resolve?

5. Do the disputants ever take each other's statements out of context, either consciously or unwittingly?

V. Here is a famous problem related to the "one word, one meaning" fallacy. How would you use the semantic principles discussed in this chapter to resolve the argument? What are the essential points of difficulty?

Some years ago, being with a camping party in the mountains, I returned from a solitary ramble to find everyone engaged in a ferocious metaphysical dispute. The corpus of the dispute was a squirrel—a live squirrel supposed to be clinging to one side of a tree-trunk; while over against the tree's opposite side a human being was imagined to stand. The human witness tries to get sight of the squirrel by moving rapidly around the tree, but no matter how fast he goes, the squirrel moves as fast in the opposite direction and always keeps the tree between himself and the man, so that never a glimpse of him is caught. The resultant metaphysical problem now is this: *Does the man go around the squirrel, or not?* He goes round the tree, sure enough, and the squirrel is on the tree; but does he go round the squirrel? In the unlimited leisure of the wilderness discussion had been worn threadbare. Everyone had taken sides, and was obstinate; and the numbers on both sides were even. Each side, when I appeared, therefore appealed to me to make it a majority. Mindful of the scholastic adage that whenever you meet a contradiction you must make a distinction, I immediately sought and found one, as follows . . .

WILLIAM JAMES

VI. Many meanings and contexts may affect, sometimes radically, the definitions of words. Take the following words (and any others you may wish to work with) and provide contexts, in sentence form, to clarify their different meanings.

Example: *pass*
I hope I pass the exam.
He was about to pass on to his eternal reward.
I was given a pass to the movies.
He caught the pass on the goal line and scored.
It's time to pass the hat.

freedom	love	habit	run
peace	society	right	set

Chapter 5

I. Bertrand Russell, on a British Broadcasting Company radio program called "The Brains Trust," gave the following "conjugation" of an "irregular verb."

I am firm.
You are obstinate.
He is a pig-headed fool.

The *New Statesman* and *Nation* offered prizes to readers who sent in the best "irregular verbs" of this kind. Here are some of the published entries.

I am sparkling. You are unusually talkative. He is drunk.

I am righteously indignant. You are annoyed. He is making a fuss about nothing.

I am fastidious. You are fussy. He is an old woman.

I am a creative writer. You have a journalistic flair. He is a prosperous hack.

I am beautiful. You have quite good features. She isn't bad-looking, if you like that type.

I daydream. You are an escapist. He ought to see a psychiatrist.

I have about me something of the subtle, mysterious fragrance of the Orient. You rather overdo it, dear. She stinks.

"Conjugate," in a similar way, the following statements:

1. I am willowy.

2. I am pleasingly plump.

3. I don't dance very well.

4. Naturally, I use a little makeup.

5. I collect rare old objects of art.

6. I have a sense of humor.

7. I have a cocktail or two before dinner.

8. I love my country.

9. I am cautious.

10. I believe in being frank.

II. In naming children, parents often take great care to select a name that they think will bring to the child good fortune rather than ill. If there is no necessary connection between the symbol and the thing symbolized, between the name and the newborn child, on what might parents' concept of "good" or "lucky" names be said to rest? Make a list of boys' and girls' names that have strong negative or positive connotations for you, and try to describe the reasons for your reactions. Would having a different name have made any difference in your own life?

III. Find an example of a slanted piece of reporting, perhaps an "interpretive" account of the kind favored by *Time* or *Newsweek*, that not only communicates facts but an attitude toward the persons or events. Can you distinguish the underlying facts being reported from the attitudes suggested? Rewrite the article, using the same facts but suggesting a different set of attitudes, a different slant.

IV. "Political language," said George Orwell in an essay entitled "Politics and the English Language," "is designed to make lies sound truthful and murder respectable." In the novel *1984*, he called the language of the totalitarian government "Newspeak." In a similar spirit, the National Council of Teachers of English issues an annual Doublespeak Award for public statements that are "grossly deceptive, evasive, euphemistic, confusing or self-contradictory." According to Editorial Research Reports, award-winning examples include the National Aeronautics and Space Administration's use of the term "recovered components" to refer to the bodies of the seven dead *Challenger* astronauts and the term "crew-transfer containers" for their coffins. Start a list of candidates for the Doublespeak Award. Are such word substitutions harmful? Are they beneficial? What effects do they have on the way people think and talk?

Chapter 6

I. For a few days, pay attention to the number of conversations that include remarks about the weather. Why does the weather make such an easy opening topic? What other topics have similar presymbolic value? What do phrases like "How do you do" really mean?

II. Try the following game with a group of people. Set aside a period of time during which the rule is that no one is permitted to say anything except the word "urglu" (to be uttered with any variations of pitch or tone necessary to convey different meanings) and that anyone using ordinary language during the period is to be fined. Observe what *can* and *cannot* be communicated by the use of a single non-sense word, by tone of voice, and by facial expressions and gestures.

III. Notice the different forms of presymbolic uses of language used in different classes and subcultures of society. A reader familiar with more than one class, region, or ethnic or religious group might be able to compare and contrast common usages. Do people use certain words or phrases to identify themselves to other members of the group? What happens when a person, on entering one group, uses presymbolic language associated with a different group?

IV. Try to live a whole day without any presymbolic uses of language, restricting yourself to (a) specific statements of fact that contribute to the hearer's information; (b) specific requests for needed information or services. This exercise is recommended only for those whose devotion to science and the experimental method is greater than their desire to keep their friends.

Chapter 7

I. The following statements, in the contexts in which they are usually found, are directives. Which of these directives have collective sanction, and which do not? What rewards (if any) are promised to those who follow the directives, and with what punishments (if any) are those who do not threatened? What is the likelihood in each case of the consequences following as promised?

1. If your key priority is excellence in every way automotive excellence can be measured, call or visit your Mercedes-Benz dealer today. They will be pleased to arrange an S-Class test drive.

    SAMPLE ANALYSIS: This is directive language, as it clearly attempts to influence the future behavior of the reader. We are free to ignore the directive, since it comes from a business and therefore does not have collective sanction. The reward offered is not only "automotive excellence" but recognition as someone whose "key priority is excellence in every way." But the promised test drive may not actually be available to every hopeful joyrider who walks through the dealership door; one must appear willing and able to consider spending upwards of $50,000 for an automobile.

2. We hold these truths to be self-evident, that all men are created equal, that they are endowed by their Creator with certain inalienable rights, that among these are life, liberty, and the pursuit of happiness.

    The Declaration of Independence

3. Thou shalt not make thee any graven image, or any likeness of any thing that is in heaven above, or that is in the earth beneath, or that is in the water beneath the earth.

    Thou shalt not bow down thyself unto them: for I the Lord thy God am a jealous God, visiting the iniquity of the fathers upon the children unto the third and fourth generation of them that hate me.

    And shewing mercy unto thousands of them that love me and keep my commandments.   Deuteronomy 5:8–10

4. You're in good hands with Allstate.

5. You can be sure, if it's Westinghouse.

6. *"The New Colossus"* (Inscription for the Statue of Liberty)

    Not like the brazen giant of Greek fame,
    With conquering limbs astride from land to land
    Here at our sea-washed sunset gates shall stand
    A mighty woman with a torch, whose fame
    Is the imprisoned lightning, and her name
    Mother of Exiles. From her beacon hand
    Glows world-wide welcome; her mild eyes command
    The air-bridged harbour that twin cities frame.
    "Keep, ancient lands, your storied pomp," cries she
    With silent lips. "Give me your tired, your poor,
    Your huddled masses yearning to breathe free.
    The wretched refuse of your teeming shore,

Send these, the homeless, tempest-tost to me,
I lift my lamp beside the golden door!"   EMMA LAZARUS

7. Private property. No trespassing.

8. Let us eat and drink; for tomorrow we shall die.   Isaiah 22:13

9. Gather ye rose-buds while ye may,
    Old time is still a-flying:
And this same flower that smiles today,
    Tomorrow will be dying.

The glorious lamp of heaven, the Sun,
    The higher he's a-getting
The sooner will his race be run,
    And nearer he's to setting.

That age is best which is the first,
    When youth and blood are warmer;
But being spent, the worse, and worst
    Times, still succeed the former.

Then be not coy, but use your time;
    And while ye may, go marry:
For having lost but once your prime,
    You may for ever tarry.   ROBERT HERRICK

II. "Ownership" is defined in this chapter as a set of directive agreements, recognized by society, as to who may enjoy the use of what things. But the freedom to use and enjoy what is "mine" is limited according to the kind of property. For example, I may drive "my" car only if it is duly registered with the state and if I have a valid driver's license. Explain the different meanings of the word "my" in these phrases:

my boyfriend	*my* country	*my* head
my mortgage	*my* hotel room	my past

III. The meaning of "rights" varies from "property rights" to "civil rights" to "parental rights" to "moral rights" to "human rights." Can one exercise "human rights" in the same way that one can exercise a "civil right" such as voting? Can you discern differences in the degree and type of collective sanction attached to various kinds of rights?

IV. Collect examples of political promises (this is easiest during an election campaign). The literature of third-party candidates may contain especially stunning examples. How many of these promises can be "kept"? By asking a series of carefully formulated questions, can you find out *exactly* where a candidate stands on a given issue?

Books dealing with the areas discussed in this chapter include:

The Folklore of Capitalism (1938) by Thurman Arnold. This famous and amusing book is a classic in analyzing how certain political and economic directives, rigidly followed, can prevent societies from understanding and solving their problems.

The Informed Heart (1960), by Bruno Bettelheim. An eminent psychologist derives a pattern for survival from his experiences at Dachau and Buchenwald. After examining Nazi methods in these concentration camps, the author explains the conditions that made living possible and applies the techniques of resistance to survival in today's mass society.

Law and the Modern Mind (1930), by Jerome Frank. A pioneering study of the semantics of law.

Survival Through Design (1954), by Richard Neutra. An architect describes design as both the coordinating factor in architecture and humanity's only defense against the hostile environment to be faced in the future.

The Silent Language (1959), by Edward T. Hall. An analysis of the various ways we have of communicating, and of the complications that arise when people from different cultures try to communicate with one another.

Man and His Symbols (1968) by Carl G. Jung.

Chapter 8

I. Classify each of the following as examples of metaphor, simile, allusion, or irony.

1. He's a regular Don Juan.

2. George finally met his Waterloo.

3. A meal without wine is like a day without sunshine.

4. My love is like a red, red rose.

5. He stole to the throne like a fox, ruled like a tiger, and died like a dog.

6. We're a mushroom committee: kept in the dark and covered with manure.
   —Congressman complaining about administrative secrecy

7. Every civilization is a fruit from the sturdy tree of barbarism, and falls at the greatest distance from the trunk.   WILL DURANT

8. Damn it!

II. All literary criticism that tries to discover exactly what an author is saying presupposes knowledge of principles such as those discussed in this chapter. The real application of these principles can only be made in abundant and careful reading and in the development of taste, through consciousness of what is going on in every piece of literature one reads, whether it be a magazine article, a Eudora Welty short story, or an Elizabethan play.

A useful practice, even for an experienced reader, is to take short passages of prose and verse—especially passages with which the reader is familiar—and to find out by careful analysis (a) what the author is trying to communicate; (b) what affective elements help him to convey that meaning; (c) what elements, if any, obscure communication; and (d) how successful, on the whole, the author is in conveying ideas and feelings to the reader. The following passages may serve as material for this kind of analysis:

1. It was a crisp and spicy morning in early October. The lilacs and laburnums, lit with the glory fires of autumn, hung burning and flashing in the upper air, a fairy bridge provided by kind Nature for the wingless wild things that have their home in the tree tops and would visit together; the larch and the pomegranate flung their purple and yellow flames in brilliant broad splashes along the slanting sweep of the woodland; the sensuous fragrance of innumerable deciduous flowers rose upon the swooning atmosphere; far in the empty sky a solitary oesophagus slept upon motionless wing; everywhere brooded stillness, serenity, and the peace of God.
   SAMUEL L. CLEMENS, "A Double-Barreled Detective Story"

2. O say, can you see, by the dawn's early light
   What so proudly we hailed at the twilight's last gleaming?
   Whose broad stripes and bright stars, through the perilous fight,
   O'er the ramparts we watched, were so gallantly streaming!
   And the rockets' red glare, the bombs bursting in air,
   Gave proof through the night that our flag was still there:
   O say, does that star-spangled banner yet wave
   O'er the land of the free and the home of the brave?
   FRANCIS SCOTT KEY

3. There is no history of mankind, there is only an indefinite number of histories of all kinds of aspects of human life. And one of these is the history of political power. This is elevated into the history of the world. But this, I hold, is an offense against every decent conception of mankind. It is hardly better than to treat the history of embezzlement or of robbery or of poisoning as the history of mankind. *For the history of power politics is nothing but the history of international crime and mass murder* (including, it is true, some of the attempts to suppress them). This history is taught in schools, and some of the greatest criminals are extolled as its heroes.
   KARL POPPER, *The Open Society and its Enemies*

4. *The Guitarist Tunes Up*

   With what attentive courtesy he bent
   Over his instrument;
   Not as a lordly conqueror who could

Command both wire and wood,
But as a man with a loved woman might,
Inquiring with delight
What slight essential things she had to say
Before they started, he and she, to play.

FRANCES CORNFORD

5. If there were dreams to sell
What would you buy?
Some cost a passing bell;
Some a light sigh
That shakes from Life's fresh crown
Only a rose-leaf down.
If there were dreams to sell,
Merry and sad to tell,
And the crier rung the bell,
What would you buy?

A cottage lone and still,
With bowers nigh,
Shadowy, my woes to still,
Until I die.
Such a pearl from Life's fresh crown
Fain would I shake me down.
Were dreams to have at will,
This best would heal my ill,
This I would buy.

THOMAS LOVELL BEDDOES, "Dream Pedlary"

III. The opening of a story, poem, essay, or book has special significance in setting the point of view, establishing the mood, gaining the reader's attention and interest. What can be inferred about the author's purpose from these beginnings?

1. I got another barber that comes over from Carterville and helps me out Saturdays, but the rest of the time I can get along all right alone. You can see for yourself that this ain't no New York City and besides that, most of the boys works all day and don't have no leisure to drop in here and get themselves prettied up.

You're a newcomer, ain't you? I thought I hadn't seen you round before. I hope you like it good enough to stay. As I say, we ain't no New York City or Chicago, but we have pretty good times. Not as good, though, since Jim Kendall got killed. When he was alive, him and Hod Meyers used to keep this town in an uproar. I bet they was more laughin' done here than in any town its size in America. . . .

RING LARDNER, "Haircut"

2. St. Agnes' Eve—Ah, bitter chill it was!
The owl, for all his feathers, was a-cold;

The hare limped trembling through the frozen grass,
And silent was the flock in woolly fold;
Numb were the Beadsman's fingers while he told
His rosary, and while his frosted breath,
Like pious incense from a censer old,
Seemed taking flight for heaven, without a death,
Past the sweet Virgin's picture, while his prayer he saith.

JOHN KEATS, "The Eve of St Agnes"

3. The Chevalier Tannhauser, having lighted off his horse, stood doubtfully for a moment beneath the ombre gateway of the mysterious hill, troubled with an exquisite fear lest a day's travel should have too cruelly undone the labored niceness of his dress. His hand, slim and gracious as La Marquise du Deffand's in the drawing by Carmontelle, played nervously about the gold hair that fell upon his shoulders like a finely curled peruke, and from point to point of a precise toilet the fingers wandered, quelling the little mutinies of cravat and ruffle.

AUBREY BEARDSLEY, "Under the Hill"

IV. A reader may make two kinds of identification with characters in a story. First, the reader may see in the story character a more or less realistic representation of himself or herself. (For example, the story character is shown as misunderstood by his parents, while the reader, because of the vividness of the narrative, recognizes personal experiences in those of the story character.) Secondly, the reader may find, by identifying with the story character, the fulfillment of the reader's own desires. (For example, the reader may be poor, and unattractive to the opposite sex, but may find symbolic satisfaction in identifying with a story character who is represented as rich, attractive, and romantically and sexually successful.) It is not easy to draw hard-and-fast lines between these two kinds of identification, but basically the former kind (which we may call "identification by self-recognition") rests upon the *similarity* of the reader's experiences with those of the story character, while the latter kind ("identification for wish-fulfillment") rests upon the *dissimilarity* between the reader's dull life and the story character's interesting life. Many (perhaps most) stories engage (or seek to engage) the reader's identification by *both* means.

Study carefully a story from a television drama, a "women's" magazine, or a "men's" magazine, analyzing plot and characterization to see in what ways and to what degree "identification by self-recognition" and "identification for wish-fulfillment" are produced in the reader by the author. Do not begin this analysis with literature of greater sophistication or higher quality, since these mechanisms are most clearly and simply revealed in fiction addressed to the general audience.

V. Read, watch, or listen carefully to a number of stories from popular magazines, from movies, television, or popular songs. What kind of elements do works in each group seem to have in common? Are there themes that seem to be forbidden in each group, as if by unspoken agreement? What role does wish-fulfillment play?

Chapter 9

I. Arrange the following statements in order of increasing abstraction, starting with the one at the lowest level of abstraction.

   A. 1. People these days don't have to work the way they used to.

      2. Olivia can edit her compositions in half the time if she uses a computer.

      3. Computers save a lot of work.

      4. A computer can be used for writing, editing, and printing letters and compositions.

      5. Electronic devices have made our lives easier.

   B. 1. James Watt is a great American.

      2. James Watt favored oil and gas exploration in the national parks.

      3. James Watt is a leading conservative.

      4. James Watt believed the government should make its resources available to private businesses.

      5. James Watt was President Reagan's first secretary of the interior.

II. Try to apply the following terms to the extensional world by going down the abstraction ladder. Use operational definitions for guidance—tell "what to do and what to observe in order to bring the thing defined, or its effects, within the range of one's experience." Try to translate the illustrative quotations into operational definitions; if you cannot, explain why. Do any of these quotations employ circularity or dead-level abstracting?

   1. *Beauty:* "Beauty is in the eye of the beholder."

   2. *Philosophy:* "There are more things in Heaven and earth, Horatio,/ Than are dreamt of in your philosophy."

      Hamlet, Act I, Sc.5, 11. 166–177

   3. *National security:* The administration claimed release of the documents could endanger national security.

   4. *Wealth:* The United States is a nation of great wealth.

   5. *Art:* Art is a spiritual necessity for all people.

   6. *Power:* The legislative and executive branches are engaged in a continuing struggle, each seeking to expand its power at the expense of the other.

III. Analyze the following passages in terms of levels of abstraction:

1. A *phobia* is a recurrent and persistent fear of a particular object or situation which in "objective" reality presents no actual danger to the subject—although (cf. Case 1) in his unconsciously equated experience, the patient may conceive the symbolized danger to be overwhelming. Phobias, indeed, are originally derived from situation-related fears, and differ from the latter only in their "rationality," symbolic spread, and generalization to remote aspects of the situation. For instance, fear of a rampant tiger is directly understandable, but it is justifiable to consider abnormal the reactions of a severely ailurophobic patient who exhibits fear within a mile of a well-protected zoo, cannot bear the approach of a kitten, and experiences anxiety when any animal of the genus *Felis* is shown on a motion picture screen. In neither the "normal" or "abnormal" instance, be it noted, need the fear be based on a direct experience with the "object" feared, although in both the tiger is, of course, symbolically equated with physical danger. The difference lies in this: that the phobia, unlike the fear, is based on no rational conscious reasons whatever, but springs from experiences deeply repressed and not necessarily related to a direct attack by a big or little cat at any time in the patient's life. To illustrate:

   Case 7: Anne A———, an eighteen-year-old girl, was brought to the psychiatric outpatient clinic by her . . .

   JULES MASSERMAN, *Principles of Dynamic Psychiatry*

   SAMPLE ANALYSIS: The author starts with a definition of phobia that names the general conditions under which a fear may be called a phobia. The second sentence is also general and adds information about the origin of a phobia and shows how it differs from "situation-related fears." So far, the author seems to be writing at a high level of abstraction without much progress up or down the abstraction ladder. However, the third sentence goes down the abstraction ladder to a specific example capable of being visualized by the reader ("rampant tiger"), and also gives examples of specific situations (zoo, kitten, moving pictures) where fear may be termed a phobia. After more general explanations, there is a case history of a specific patient, Anne A———, reporting facts at still lower (descriptive) levels of abstraction. Whether or not other scientists agree with Dr.Masserman in calling this case a phobia, we at least know that, when *he* uses the word, this is the kind of case *he* is talking about. So far as relationships between higher and lower levels of abstraction are concerned, this passage is a good extensionally directed definition of phobia.

2. A function . . . is a table giving the relation between two variable quantities, where a change in one implies some change in the other. The cost of a quantity of meat is a function of its weight; the speed of a train is a function of the quantity of coal consumed; the amount of perspiration given off, a function of the temperature. In each of these illustrations, a change in the second variable: weight, quantity of coal consumed, and temperature, is correlated with a change in the first variable: cost, speed,

and volume of perspiration. The symbolism of mathematics permits functional relationships to be simply and concisely expressed. Thus $y=x$, $y=x^2$, $y=\sin x$, $y=\operatorname{csch} x$, $y=e^x$ are examples of functions.

EDWARD KASNER AND J. R. NEWMAN,
Mathematics and the Imagination

3. A producer of educational films once remarked to me that it is impossible to shoot footage of "work." You can shoot Joe hoeing potatoes, Susan polishing her car, Bill spraying paint on a barn, but never just "work." "Work," too, is a shorthand term, standing, at a higher level of abstraction, for a characteristic that a multitude of activities, from dishwashing to navigation to running an advertising agency to governing a nation, have in common.

S. I. HAYAKAWA, *Language in Thought and Action*

4. The mode of production of material life determines the general character of the social, political and spiritual processes of life. It is not the consciousness of men that determines their being, but, on the contrary, their social being determines their consciousness.

KARL MARX, Preface to *A Contribution to the Critique of Political Economy*

IV. Find written examples of particularly good or poor uses of abstraction—newspaper editorials, art and music criticism, and philosophy may be fertile areas to explore—and analyze the uses of abstraction employed. Watch for dead-level abstracting and describe its effects on the reader.

V. Alfred Korzybski, in *Science and Sanity* (1933), points out that consciousness of abstracting enables us, among other things, to become aware of what happens when we go from lower to higher levels of abstraction with a single term. For example, to worry about worry or to fear fear may lead to morbid responses, but, with another group of words, the higher level of abstraction reverses or annuls the lower-level effects, as in "hatred of hatred." Consider the responses that are likely to be the outcome when you

1. are curious about curiosity;

2. doubt your doubts;

3. are nervous about your nervousness;

4. reason about reasoning;

5. try to know about knowing;

6. are impatient with your impatience;

7. are intolerant of intolerance;

8. are in love with love.

VI. "We know that every word is an abstraction, but we forget. We know that every word is a class word that abstracts (takes away from the whole object named) only the similarities of the class to which the object is ascribed and leaves out all the differences. But we forget."

BESS SONDEL, *The Humanity of Words*

Examine instances of such forgetting in your own experience. What were the consequences of this forgetting?

Chapter 10

I. For the scrapbook or card index begun after Chapter 2, find some clippings and quotations that illustrate the basic principles dealing with the relationship between language and behavior. Here are some sample headings:

Straight reports.
Stories featuring inferences, with full awareness that they are inferences.
Reacting to judgments as if they were reports.
Shifts of meaning resulting from changes in context.
Snarl-words and purr-words mistaken for reports.
Slanting.
Quarrels over non-sense questions.
Social conversation.
Overreacting to affective connotations of words.
Directives mistaken for reports.
Disillusionment caused by directives imperfectly understood.
Dead-level abstracting.
Meaningless use of high-level abstractions.
Higher- and lower-level abstractions properly related.
Seeing and believing.
The little man who wasn't there.

Other headings will suggest themselves in the chapters to follow. The study of the relationships between language and behavior can be pursued at any time, anywhere—at work, at school, at church, in a department store, at parties, at meetings, in all one's reading, and in the course of intimate family or personal relationships. Even a desultory collection of examples of language in action, if carefully noted and pondered over, will help the reader understand what the writer of this book is saying and *why he wants to say it*. Collectors of such examples will no doubt find reasons for wishing to refine, expand, or correct some of the statements made in this book. Further progress in the scientific study of the relationships between language and behavior depends upon such corrections and improvements of the present generalizations. The reader's cooperation is earnestly invited.

II. Define each of the following terms:

radioactivity   criminal
vampire   political pressure

flying saucer	folk music
obscenity	Thursday
semantics	money

For each word, try each of the following kinds of definitions.

1. Definition by synonym: "*Attain* means to achieve."

2. Definition by classification and differentiation (Aristotelian definition): "*Autocracy* is a form of government in which power is held by one person."

3. Definition by enumerating words to which the defined word refers collectively: "*Spices* are cinnamon, cloves, ginger, and such."

4. Extensional definition: definition by pointing to, or exhibiting, that which is defined (see Chapter 4).

Indicate which of the foregoing terms are *not* capable of being defined operationally.

III. The confusion of abstractions with reality is one of the most apparent errors of human thought. Often this confusion results from our apparent inability or unwillingness to understand the processes of reality. Oliver Wendell Holmes recognized this failing when he noted, "Men heap together all the mistakes of their lives and create a monster called Destiny." The following sentences contain words especially likely to become separated from that which they represent. Take each sentence and try to relate the key abstraction to the real world, following the kind of analysis used in this chapter with the word "Jew." Do you find some of the words are too general or abstract to contain substantial meaning?

1. *Kids* are great.

2. The *people* are infinitely wise.

3. *Religion* has enslaved humanity for centuries.

4. Something has to be done about all the *crazies* floating around now.

5. *Crime* has become a way of life for too many people.

6. *Winning* isn't everything; it's the only thing.

IV. One way to avoid the dangers of confusing levels of abstraction would be to follow the method of the Academy of Lagado, as described in Jonathan Swift's *Gulliver's Travels:*

An expedient was therefore offered, that since words are only names for things, it would be more convenient for all men to carry about them such things as were necessary to express the particular business they are to discourse on. . . . I have often beheld two of those sages almost sinking under the weight of their packs, like pedlars among us; who when they met in the streets would lay down their loads, open their sacks, and hold conversation. . . . Another great advantage proposed by this invention was that it would serve as an universal language to be understood in all civilized nations.

Before dismissing the scheme of the Lagadoan philosophers with a laugh, try to think of situations in which it is advantageous to communicate with objects instead of talking. Using the ideas about abstraction in this and the previous chapter, can you describe the shortcomings of the philosophers' scheme? If such a scheme were in use, how could a modification of it be discussed?

V. Racial and religious prejudice survive within American society. Anti-Semitic literature, which has been abundant for centuries, is still published, though usually not by reputable publishing houses. Those who have never done so should, at least once in their lives, expose themselves to the furious anti-Semitic writings of Adolf Hitler (Norman H. Baynes, ed., *The Speeches of Adolf Hitler*, 2 vols., 1942) and his colleagues of the Third Reich. Hitler's attempt to destroy the Jews must never be forgotten as an example of how far racial madness can be carried. See William Shirer, *The Rise and Fall of the Third Reich* (1960); Gerald Reitlinger, *The Final Solution: The Attempt to Exterminate the Jews of Europe, 1939–1945* (1953); and Jacques Barzun, *Race, a Study in Superstition* (revised edition, 1965). If you find contemporary examples of antiblack, anti-Semitic, or other "hate" literature, analyze its premises and its authors' methods with the tools of this book.

Other works on racial and religious prejudice include:

Ashley Montagu, *Man's Most Dangerous Myths: The Fallacy of Race* (fifth edition, 1974). First published in 1942, this influential book by an anthropologist distinguishes between scientific and false notions of race.

C. Vann Woodward, *The Strange Career of Jim Crow* (1966), a history of segregation.

Alex Haley, *Roots* (1976). The coauthor of *The Autobiography of Malcolm X* traces his own family tree to its roots in Africa.

Robert F. Heizer and Alan Jan Almquist, *The Other Californians: Prejudice and Discrimination under Spain, Mexico and the United States to 1920* (1972). The treatment of Indians, Mexicans, Chinese, Japanese, and blacks is vividly presented by examples of the laws, official reports, and contemporary correspondence.

Kenneth B. Clark, *Dark Ghetto: Dilemmas of Social Power* (1965), a leading black sociologist on the problems of the inner city.

Arnold Forster and Benjamin R. Epstein, *The New Anti-Semitism* (1974). Based on studies by the Anti-Defamation League of B'nai B'rith, this book outlines anti-Semitic attacks in the United States, Western Europe, Soviet Union, and Latin America.

Reinhold Niebuhr, *Pious and Secular America* (1958), an analysis of some of the theological forces behind racism and anti-Semitism.

Thomas Sowell, *The Economics of Politics and Race* (1983). A distinguished black economist examines issues of racial groups in more than a dozen countries. See also Sowell's *Ethnic America,* which surveys the major American ethnic groups and reexamines many widely held beliefs about interracial matters.

Chapter 11

I. Much humor depends on unexpected shifts of classification. Analyze some magazine jokes, a comedian's dialogue, or the script of a comedy and note how many depend on classification changes. Also look for allusions, exaggeration, facetiousness, and insults. Here are some examples, starting with some real chestnuts:

1. Taxi driver: It's not just the work I enjoy. It's the people I run into.

    Breck's Gold Box

2. Prison librarian: And what would you like to read today?
   Prisoner: Got any escape literature?

3. "The difference between bop and Dixieland? In bop, they flat their fifths; in Dixieland, we drink them."   — attributed to Eddie Condon

4. He looked out of the window and called to his wife, "There goes that woman Bill Jones is in love with."
   She dropped the cup she was drying, hurtled through the door, craned her neck to look. "Where? she panted.
   "There," he pointed, "that woman at the corner in the tweed coat."
   "You idiot," she said. "That's his wife."
   "Of course," he replied.   *Wall Street Journal*

5. Soviet leader (shown in a cartoon handing a rocket to a Russian general): Remember, ours are called *factors of peace* and theirs, *instruments of aggression*.   *Settimana* (Rome)

6. Two Romanians are on a bus. One is sitting down, and the other is standing inadvertently on the first man's foot. The man sitting down asks, "Are you a member of the Communist Party?" "No," says the standing man. "Are you in the military?" asks the sitting man. "No, I'm not," says the standing man. "Do you work for the government in any capacity?" asks the sitting man. "No," says the standing man. "Then get the hell off my foot," says the sitting man.

II. Classification schemes are arbitrary and tied to our interests, not eternal and unchanging. As a demonstration, collect several dozen different objects (such as you might find in various rooms in a house) and ask someone to divide the objects into two piles. Ask him or her to repeat this operation four or five times, using different systems of classification each time. Do not give any suggestions or hints as to what classifications to use. Record the systems and the nature of classifications. What problems arose with what objects? If a classification is made that you do not understand, ask the reason for it. If some persons need more than two categories and want to make more than two piles of objects, find out why. After repeating this experiment with several people, record your findings and see what conclusions you can reach. (This exercise is based on "Semantic Play Therapy," as described by Salvatore Russo and Howard Jaques in an article of that title that appears in *Our Language and Our World*, S. I. Hayakawa, ed., [1959].)

III. As you follow current events over the next few weeks, make note of social and political disputes that revolve around problems of classification. Can you suggest ways in which any of these disputes could be approached by changing the classifications used? By methods that rely less on classification than other techniques? What stands in the way of such solutions?

IV. "In either case society will get the decision it collectively wants, even if it has to wait until the present members of the Supreme Court are dead and an entirely new court is appointed."

To what might the word "society" refer to in this sentence? Do you agree with the assertion that legal institutions reflect the collective will of citizens? If you do not agree, what do you believe is reflected by laws and court rulings? Could a similar statement be made about the responsiveness of institutions in other countries? What kinds of qualifications would you have to make in order to make such a statement about this or another society?

Chapter 12

I. Fervid belief in a cause is one of the strongest and most uncompromising promoters of the two-valued orientation. The Ku Klux Klan, People for the Ethical Treatment of Animals, National Rifle Association, ardent pacifists, smitten lovers, and so on may find it difficult to avoid the two-valued orientation. Discuss the pros and cons of the two-valued orientation in a particular situation or issue on which you hold strong convictions.

II. The two-valued orientation appears in each of the following passages at higher levels of feeling as well as in crude form, qualified as well as unqualified. Analyze each statement carefully, especially in the light of the questions: "How much confidence can I safely repose in the judgment of the author of this passage? A great deal? None at all? Or is there not enough evidence to be able to say?"

1. It's time we hit the sawdust trail. It's time we revived the idea that there
is such a thing as sin. . . . It's time we brought self-discipline back into
style. . . . So I suggest:

 Let's look at our educational institutions at the local level, and if
Johnny can't read by the time he's ready to get married, let's find out
why.

 Let's look at the distribution of public largess, and if, far from allevi-
ating human misery, it is producing the sloth and irresponsibility that in-
tensifies it, let's get it fixed.

 Let's quit being bulldozed and bedazzled by self-appointed longhairs.
Let's have the guts to say that a book is dirt if that's what we think of
it. . . . And if some beatnik welds together a collection of rusty cogwheels
and old corset-stays and claims it's a greater sculpture than Michelangelo's
"David," let's have the courage to say that it looks like junk and may well
be. . . .

 I am fed up to here with the medicine men who try to pass off pretense
for art and prurience for literature. . . .

 In this hour of misbehavior, self-indulgence and self-doubt . . . let
there be a fresh breeze of new pride, new idealism, new integrity.

JENKIN LLOYD JONES,
address to the American Society of Newspaper Editors

2. If you're not part of the solution, you're part of the problem.

3. War is the product of imperialism and the system of exploitation of man
by man. Lenin said that "war is always and everywhere begun by the
exploiters themselves, by the ruling and oppressing classes." So long as
imperialism and the system of exploitation of man by man exist, the imperialists and reactionaries will invariably rely on armed force to maintain
their reactionary rule and impose war on the oppressed nations and
peoples. This is an objective law independent of man's will. . . .

 In the last analysis, whether one dares to wage a tit-for-tat struggle
against armed aggression and suppression by the imperialists and their
lackeys, whether one dares to fight a people's war against them, means
whether one dares to embark on revolution. This is the most effective
touchstone for distinguishing genuine from fake revolutionaries and
Marxist-Leninists.

LIN PIAO, "Long Live the Victory of the People's War"

4. We meet in the midst of a nation brought to the verge of moral, political,
and material ruin. Corruption dominates the ballot box, the Legislatures,
the Congress, and touches even the ermine on the bench. The people are
demoralized; most of the states have been compelled to isolate the voters
at the polling place to prevent universal intimidation or bribery. The
newspapers are largely subsidized or muzzled, public opinion silenced,
business prostrated, our homes covered with mortgages, labor impover-
ished, and the land concentrated in the hands of capitalists. . . . The
fruits of the toil of millions are boldly stolen to build up colossal fortunes

for a few, unprecedented in the history of mankind, and the possessors of these in turn despise the Republic and endanger liberty. From the same prolific womb of governmental injustice we breed the two greatest classes—tramps and millionaires.

IGNATIUS DONNELLY, Preamble to the platform of the first national convention of the People's Party, Omaha, Nebraska, July 4, 1892

5. The history of all hitherto existing society is the history of class struggles. Free man and slave, patrician and plebeian, lord and serf, guild master and journeyman, in a word, oppressor and oppressed, stood in constant opposition to one another, carried on an uninterrupted, now hidden, now open fight, a fight that each time ended either in a revolutionary reconstitution of society at large or in the common ruin of the contending classes.

MARX AND ENGELS, *Communist Manifesto*

III. Read, ponder, and digest:

A husband and wife have a quarrel which they cannot resolve, so they go to the local wise man, who resides down the street from them. The husband speaks first, and tells the wise man about all the terrible things his wife has done to him. He argues that the wife is the cause of all the trouble.

"You're right," said the wise man.

"What do you mean?" said the wife, who then proceeded to tell her side of the story. She listed all the terrible things her husband had done and claimed he was to blame.

"Yes," said the wise man, nodding his head, "you are right."

"Wait a minute," said the wise man's wife, who happened to hear the conversation. "How can the husband be right and the wife be right when they contradict each other?"

"You are right, too," said the wise man.

IV. For those interested in exploring the subject of logic in greater detail, there are a number of excellent books on the subjects of logic and logical thinking.

Morris Cohen and Ernest Nagel, *An Introduction to Logic and Scientific Method* (1934), contains a fine discussion of Aristotle's laws of thought in Chapter 9, "Some Problems in Logic."

John Passmore, *A Hundred Years of Philosophy* (1957). Chapter 17 is particularly relevant to the matters discussed in this chapter. The discussion of John Stuart Mill and British Empiricism is also useful.

Stuart Chase, *Guides to Straight Thinking* (1956), has many amusing examples of errors in the thinking process.

Robert H. Thouless, *How to Think Straight* (1950), is especially good on the subject of *enthymeme*, a syllogism with one of its propositions missing.

Monroe C. Beardsley, *Thinking Straight* (1975), is a popular primer on the elements of logic.

Chapter 13

I. What are the relative advantages and disadvantages of two-valued and multi-valued orientations in dealing with the following problems and situations. State the reasons for your conclusions.

1. Arguing for a preference for abstract rather than representational art.

2. Agreeing with the Soviet Union on nuclear-arms control.

3. Dealing with a proposal to build low-income public housing in your neighborhood.

4. Deciding whether to allow representatives of the American Nazi Party or the American Communist Party to speak on campus.

5. Writing a script to be broadcast to the people of an *enemy* nation during time of war.

6. Leading an infantry unit into battle.

7. Taking drugs.

8. Normalizing relations with Iran.

9. Teaching children table manners.

II. The essential feature of the multi-valued orientation is its inherent capacity to enable us to see more deeply into reality, or to appreciate finer shadings and subtle nuances of its possibilities. However, as with the levels of abstraction discussed in Chapters 10 and 11, the multi-valued orientation contains certain dangers as well as advantages. Discuss the following passage in the light of this and the preceding chapter. Does this passage imply we would be better off with a simpler method of evaluation? Is it easier to act with a two-valued orientation?

He who sees different ways to the same end will, unless he watches carefully over his own conduct, lay out too much of his attention upon the comparison of probabilities, and the adjustment of expedients, and pause in the choice of his road, till some accident intercepts his journey. He whose penetration extends to remote consequences, and who, whenever he applies his attention to any design, discovers new prospects of advantage, and possibilities of improvement, will not easily be persuaded that his project is ripe for execution; but will superadd one contrivance to another, endeavor to unite various purposes in one operation, multiply complications, and refine niceties, till he is entangled in his own scheme, and bewildered in the perplexity of various intentions.

SAMUEL JOHNSON, *The Rambler*

III. One of the most effective ways of understanding and applying some of the central ideas in this chapter is to experiment, along with other people who have read it, with seeing how these ideas work.

For example, in a group of people who are familiar with the distinctions made in this book, choose some controversial subject of genuine interest to the group, such as the right to abortion, gun control, the conflict between the rights of crime victims and of criminal suspects, the morality of wearing fur coats, or nuclear-arms control. Ask two members of the group to present a discussion of the chosen subject with one person persistently maintaining a two-valued orientation on the subject ("All censorship is bad," "The closed shop is undemocratic") and with the other person taking an opposing two-valued orientation.

Then ask two other members of the group to discuss the same subject, again with one of them maintaining a two-valued orientation but this time with the second person using the approach suggested in this chapter ("Tell me more," "Let's see").

The role-playing suggested here need not be lengthy—a three- to five-minute demonstration will usually suffice. A discussion of the demonstration, followed perhaps by another demonstration, will help to get the "feel" of "verbal jousting" as compared with the "systematic application of multi-valued orientation." In general discussion following such a demonstration, let the role-taker who has been most "on the spot" have the first chance to criticize what has been done, then his or her collaborator, and then those who were present as spectators.

Chapter 14

I. Compare (or contrast) the ideas in the following excerpts with the point of view presented in this chapter. What other ways of explaining art do you find in these passages? How useful are they? This material may provide the basis for your own short essay, "What Is Art For?"

1. The end of writing is to instruct; the end of poetry is to instruct by pleasing.   SAMUEL JOHNSON, *Preface to Shakespeare*

2. Rhythm is a matter dependent upon emotion. What is strongly felt will express itself naturally in a rhythmical and varied form.
                                    BERTRAND RUSSELL, "History as an Art"

3. The office of ourselves [poets] . . . has been,
   For the worst of us, to say they so have seen;
   For the better, what it was they saw; the best
   Impart the gift of seeing to the rest.
                                    ROBERT BROWNING, "Sordello"

4. Art is anything you can get away with.
                                    MARSHALL MCLUHAN, The Medium Is the Massage

5. All Nature is but art, unknown to thee
All chance, direction, which thou canst not see
All discord, harmony not understood;
All partial evil, universal good
And, spite of pride, in erring reason's spite,
One truth is clear: Whatever IS, is right.

ALEXANDER POPE, Essay on Man

6. Give heed, my brethren, to every hour when your spirit would speak in similes: there is the origin of your virtue.

FRIEDRICH NIETZSCHE, Thus Spake Zarathustra

7. Nobody at all is quite in a position to choose with certainty among modern works. To sift the wheat from the chaff is a process that takes an exceedingly long time. Modern works have to pass before the bar of the taste of successive generations; whereas, with classics, which have been through the ordeal, almost the reverse is the case. *Your taste has to pass before the bar of the classics.* That is the point. If you differ with a classic, it is you who are wrong, and not the book. If you differ with a modern work, you may be wrong or you may be right, but no judge is authoritative to decide. Your taste is unformed. It needs guidance and it needs authoritative guidance.   ARNOLD BENNETT, *Literary Taste: How to Form It*

8. The business of art is to reveal the relation between man and his circumambient universe, at the living moment. As mankind is always struggling in the toils of old relationships, art is always ahead of the "times," which themselves are always far in the rear of the living moment.

When van Gogh paints sunflowers, he reveals, or achieves, the vivid relation between himself, as man, and the sunflower, as sunflower, at that quick moment of time. His painting does not represent the sunflower itself. We shall never know what the sunflower is. And the camera will *visualize* the sunflower far more perfectly than van Gogh can.

The vision on the canvas is a third thing, utterly intangible and inexplicable, the offspring of the sunflower itself and van Gogh himself. The vision on the canvas is for ever incommensurable with the canvas, or the paint, or van Gogh as a human organism, or the sunflower as a botanical organism. You cannot weigh nor measure nor even describe the vision on the canvas. . . .

It is a revelation of the perfected relation, at a certain moment, between a man and a sunflower. . . . And this perfected relation between man and his circumambient universe is life itself, for mankind. . . . Man and the sunflower both pass away from the moment, in the process of forming a new relationship. The relation between all things changes from day to day, in a subtle stealth of change. Hence art, which reveals or attains to another perfect relationship, will be for ever new.

If we think about it, we find that our life *consists in* this achieving of a pure relationship between ourselves and the living universe about us. This is how I "save my soul" by accomplishing a pure relationship between me and another person, me and other people, me and a nation, me and a race of men, me and animals, me and the trees or flowers, me and the earth, me and the skies and sun and stars, me and the moon: an infinity of pure relations, big and little. . . . This, if we knew it, is our life and our eternity: the subtle, perfected relation between me and my whole circumambient universe. . . .

D. H. LAWRENCE, "Morality and the Novel," Phoenix

II. Discuss the impact of violence in comics, movies, or television upon the individual "psyche" and upon society at large. If the mass media are part of our "equipment for living," what kind of a job do they do in this respect? The following passages offer some different opinions on this topic.

1. The first comic books appeared in 1935. Not having anything connected or literary about them, and being as difficult to decipher as the *Book of Kells*, they caught on with the young. The elders of the tribe, who had never noticed that the ordinary newspaper was as frantic as a surrealist art exhibition, could hardly be expected to notice that the comic books were as exotic as eighth century illuminations. So, having noticed nothing about the *form*, they could discern nothing of the *contents*, either. The mayhem and violence were all they noted. Therefore, with naive literary logic, they waited for violence to flood the world. Or, alternatively, they attributed existing crime to the comics. The dimmest-witted convict learned to moan, "It wuz comic books done this to me."

MARSHALL MCLUHAN, Understanding Media

2. Whether crime and violence programs arouse a lust for violence, reinforce it when it is present, show a way to carry it out, teach the best method to get away with it, or merely blunt a child's (and adult's) awareness of its wrongness, television has become a school for violence.

In this school young people are never, literally never, taught that violence is, in itself, reprehensible. The lesson they do get is that violence is the great adventure and the sure solution, and he who is best at it wins. We are training not only a peace corps but also a violence corps. I do not advocate that violence should be entirely eliminated from TV. But it should be presented as a fact of life, not as life itself.

FREDERIC WERTHAM, "School for Violence," The New York Times,
July 5, 1964

III. Select several poems for analysis in the light of what has been said in this chapter. Try to determine:

—What personal tensions the author seems to be trying to remove;
—What symbolic strategies are employed;
—Whether these strategies might be applicable to other people and other situations;
—To what extent the author has succeeded in ordering personal experiences into a coherent, meaningful whole;
—In what particular ways, if any, each of these poems is likely to serve as "equipment for living."

Chapter 15

I. "Whatever the object for sale is, the copywriter, like the poet, must invest it with significance so that it becomes symbolic of something beyond itself." The reliance of advertising upon affective connotations, coupled with a relative absence of information, is well known. But it is useful to examine specific advertisements, separating verifiable information about the product from affective and symbolic meanings, to see exactly how each advertisement "works." What do the products symbolize? Place the two kinds of assertions, the informational, and the affective and symbolic, side by side and see what you come up with.

1. You'll enjoy *different* tomato juice made from *aristocrat* tomatoes.

Advertisement

SAMPLE ANALYSIS:

Information About Product	*Affective and Symbolic Meanings*
Tomato juice is made from tomatoes.	Because you have cultivated and discriminating tastes, you will prefer tomato juice made from superior, exclusive tomatoes to that made from common, ordinary tomatoes. An average person may not notice the difference, but you will. To drink our tomato juice is to symbolize your own aristocratic taste and aristocratic way of life.

2. For men of Distinction . . . LORD CALVERT. It is only natural that Lord Calvert is the whiskey preferred by so many of America's most distinguished men. For this "custom" blended whiskey . . . so *rare* . . . so *smooth* . . . so *mellow* . . . is produced expressly for those who appreciate the finest. (For an interesting analysis of this advertisement, see Marshall McLuhan's *The Mechanical Bride*. McLuhan's *Culture Is Our Business* also deals with advertising.)

3. Relationships with BMW coupes last twice as long as other love affairs.

4. If he wants things to heat up, tell him to try a little ice.
   A little ice has been known to cause temperatures to rise morning, noon and night. If superb diamond jewelry is something you can warm up to, ask the man in your life to see the Ice on Ice Collection. Diamond jewelry that's cool, calm and definitely collectable. The exquisite Ice on Ice jewelry starts at $1,490. And is a surefire way to turn up the heat.

5. You deserve a break today—at McDonald's.

6. (A woman peers through her window to see a striking young man in an open topcoat, a long scarf around his neck, looking back at her as he stands next to an exotic black roadster.)

He stood motionless by the car door.

There was a lovely vision of her in the window and he didn't want to break the spell.

He had cancelled a meeting in Brussels and flown halfway across a continent to be with her for one evening. It was the kind of thing he said he would never do.

But now, as he saw her face bathed in the soft light, it all seemed worth it.

Gucci Nobile. For men.

7. What good is color *unless* it can last longer than . . . a passionate kiss, . . . a romantic dinner, . . . a double feature?

Coty '24' Lipstick lasts—in 48 non-feathering shades as vivid as your imagination. To make the beauty of your lips absolutely enduring. Creme, for the feel of velvet, and Luminescent, for a soft shimmer. Coty '24'—a lipstick you can have a lasting relationship with.

Coty makes it *last*.

8. New Virginia Slims. What is this new extra-long cigarette for women? Is it just a normal ordinary cigarette we call "a woman's cigarette?" No. We tailor it for women. We tailor it for the feminine hand. Virginia Slims are slimmer than the fat cigarettes men smoke. They have the kind of flavor women like—rich, mild, Virginia flavor. YOU'VE COME A LONG WAY.

II. Read and discuss the following passage:

Consider the advertisement for *Pango Peach*, a new color introduced by Revlon in 1960. A young woman leans against the upper rungs of a ladder leading to a palm-thatched bamboo tree-house. *Pango Peach* are her *sari*, her blouse, her toe and finger nails, and the cape she holds. A sky of South Pacific blue is behind her, and the cape, as it flutters in the wind, stains the heavens *Pango Peach*. "From east of the sun—west of the moon where each tomorrow dawns . . ." The idea of the ad is to make a woman think she is reading real poetry when she is not, and at the same time to evoke in her the specific fantasy that will sell the product. Millions will respond to poetry as a value and feel good when they think they are responding to it. . . .

In the ad Pango Peach is called "A many splendoured coral . . . pink with pleasure . . . a volcano of color!" It goes on to say that "It's a full ripe peach with a world of difference . . . born to be worn in big juicy slices. Succulent on your lips. Sizzling on your fingertips . . . Go Pango Peach . . . your adventure in paradise." Each word in the advertisement is carefully chosen to tap a particular yearning and hunger in the American woman. . . . The mouthful of oral stimuli—"ripe," "succulent," "juicy,"—puts sales resistance in double jeopardy because mouths are even more for kissing than for eating.   JULES HENRY, *Culture Against Man*

Notice that Henry, while he does not use the terms used in this book, is concerned with many of the same problems. If such advertisements aim to tap yearnings and hungers of the American woman, what picture of women do we get from advertising? Select some interesting advertisements from magazines and discuss the role advertising has played in giving people images of "femininity" and "masculinity" and of the "proper" relation between the sexes.

III. Examine some ads for their nonverbal messages. What is going on among the several naked people in the ads for "Obsession" by Calvin Klein? In the photographs in various kinds of liquor ads? In the series of photographs used by several makers of blue jeans?

IV. In his book *Mythologies*, the distinguished French critic Roland Barthes deals with the "ideological" content of advertisements and other aspects of daily life. Take some advertisements and examine them in terms of the ideology (social and political messages) hidden in them.

Chapter 16

I. Find some examples of intensional orientation from pulp fiction magazines, advertising, political statements, or articles about education. Which of the semantic errors listed on page 173 can be found in your examples? Could you "re-orient" your examples by rewriting them? Do you suspect that the writer is using intensionally oriented words accidentally or on purpose? Why?

II. Try your hand at writing jargon. Take any (or all) of the following roles (or poses) and write a jargon-filled letter to an imaginary person on some relevant problem:

1. Government bureaucrat

2. Military officer

3. Educational administrator

4. Psychologist

5. Sports columnist

Try writing *only* cliches, so you will become aware of them (and can avoid them) in your regular writing.

III. Examine the following passages and distinguish between those that are essentially "intensional" (based on words rather than facts to which words should guide us) and those that are essentially "extensional" (based upon the things for which words stand). Explain how you reached your conclusions.

1. My Great Books class recently spent two hours in trying to come to an agreement on what "peace" really is. At the beginning of the class, all the

members were confident that they knew what the word meant—at the end, nobody was quite sure. Is peace merely the absence of armed conflict? If so, slavery would be peace. Is it the absence of "physical" conflict? Then what about psychological warfare, which subjugates a people without firing a shot?

Is it possible to have peace without justice? Without government? Without love? Without religion? Can nations which respect no common authority really have peace between them, or simply an uneasy truce? Is the jungle in a state of peace when the animals are not fighting, or is it always in a state of potential warfare?

SIDNEY J. HARRIS, Chicago Daily News

2. I asked professors who teach the meaning of life to tell me what is happiness.

And I went to famous executives who boss the work of thousands of men.

They all shook their heads and gave me a smile as though I was trying to fool with them.

And then one Sunday afternoon I wandered out along the Desplaines River

And I saw a crowd of Hungarians under the trees with their women and children and a keg of beer and an accordion.   CARL SANDBURG

3. The rebellion in Detroit, during the "violent summer" of 1967 (by August there had been riots in over 30 cities, climaxed by Detroit in which 1300 buildings were razed and 2700 businesses looted), showed how hard it was—by sensible economic and political reasoning—to explain entirely the reasons for revolt in terms of injustice, or to explain the course it took. Some of the curious features of the Detroit rebellion were that it was not a "race" riot but an aggressive outburst in which whites and Negroes joined in "integrated" looting, that it expressed the alienated spirit of a mass of have-nots sharing a subculture of poverty; that there was an emotional satisfaction in burning and destruction for its own sake (mood of nihilism, carnival spirit, "burn, baby, burn!") which made it clear that psychological rather than mere economic explanations were needed; and, finally, that this peak outburst had occurred in a city where progress in racial reconciliation had been perhaps greatest in the nation.

ORRIN E. KLAPP, The Collective Search for Identity

IV. Read and consider the following:

1. Our disputes are purely verbal. I ask what is nature, pleasure, circle, and substitution. The question is one of words, and is answered in the same way. "A stone is a body." But if you insisted: "And what is a body?"— "Substance."—"And what is substance?" and so on, you would finally drive the respondent to the end of his lexicon. We exchange one word for another, often more unknown. I know better what is man than I know what is animal, or mortal, or rational. To satisfy one doubt, they give me three; it is the Hydra's head.   MONTAIGNE, "Of Experience"

2. *The Father.* But don't you see that the whole trouble lies here. In words, words. Each one of us has within him a whole world of things, each man of us his own special world. And how can we ever come to an understanding if I put in the words I utter the sense and value of things as I see them; while you who listen to me must inevitably translate them according to the conception of things each one of you has within himself. We think we understand each other, but we never really do.

LUIGI PIRANDELLO, *Six Characters in Search of an Author*

Chapter 17

I. Watch television with the sound off; include some programs that you are not already familiar with. What are they about? Can you follow without the words? What things seem to have been important to the people who assembled the pictures and directed the action? If you have a videocassette recorder, play the same programs back with the sound on and compare your impressions with the ones you get from the words. What kind of programs depend most on words? What impressions did you get from watching the news with no sound?

II. Using the same method, study the techniques used in commercials and music videos. The camera angle establishes the viewer's "point of view"—often in the figurative as well as the literal sense. What effects can camera angle alone create? What is the effect of the rhythm of the editing, from fast cuts to shots of long duration? On looking at a complicated commercial over and over again, can you discern visual elements and story lines that you weren't conscious of on first viewing?

III. Compare an edition of a local newspaper, a national newspaper, a local news broadcast, and a network television news program from the same day. List the stories included in each; these lists are called news "budgets." Do the stories that were most important in the newspaper appear with the same prominence on television, and vice versa? Can you discern why a particular story got more prominent "play" in one medium than another?

IV. Examine the same set of print and broadcast stories and try to determine the kind of events on which each was based. How many are "pseudoevents," such as press conferences and ribbon-cuttings staged primarily for reporters and cameras, and how many are "real" events, either earthquakes, crimes, rescues, or government actions? Can you always tell the difference between events and pseudoevents?

V. Produce an illustrated essay using slides, still photographs, or video pictures to accompany a spoken text. Add tape-recorded music if it seems appropriate. Richard Breyer and Peter Moller of Syracuse University, who suggest this project as a basic exercise in "television literacy," note that it contains all the basic elements of production—shot selection, composition, sound-picture juxtaposition, and editing—that go into making a television program.

VI. For further reading on television and American society, the following books are suggested:

Charles Montgomery Hammond, *The Image Decade: Television Documentary 1965-1975* (1981)

Carl Lowe, ed., *Television and American Culture* (1981)

J. Fred MacDonald, *Television and the Red Menace: The Video Road to Vietnam* (1985)

William C. Adams, ed., *Television Coverage of the 1980 Presidential Campaign* (1983)

Martin Schram, *The Great American Video Game: Presidential Politics in the Television Age* (1987)

Marshal McLuhan, *Understanding Media: The Extensions of Man* (1964)

John P. Robinson, Mark R. Levy et al., *The Main Source: Learning from Television News* (1986)

Chapter 18

I. List the most serious examples of cultural lag to be found in your community, or in another community with which you are familiar. How would an extensionally oriented person ask questions that would be useful in helping to solve some of the problems created by cultural lag? Where can you get information and assistance in answering these questions?

(The term "cultural lag" was popularized by William Fielding Ogburn, a sociologist, who wrote, "The thesis is that the various parts of modern culture are not changing at the same rate, some parts are changing much more rapidly than others; and that since there is a correlation and interdependence of parts, a rapid change in one part of our culture requires readjustments through other changes in the various correlated parts of culture." *Social Change*, 1922.)

II. Discuss the following passage with reference to this question—what similarities do you find between general semantics and pragmatism?

A conviction that consequences in human welfare are a test of the worth of beliefs and thoughts has some obvious beneficial aspects. It makes for a fusion of the two superlatively important qualities, love of truth and love of neighbor. It discourages dogmatism and its child, intolerance. It arouses and heartens an experimental spirit which wants to know how systems and theories work before giving complete adhesion. It militates against too sweeping and easy generalizations, even against those which would indict a nation. Compelling attention to details, to particulars, it safeguards one from seclusion in universals; one is obliged, as William James was always saying, to get down from noble aloofness into the muddy stream of concrete things. It fosters a sense of the worth of communication of what is known. This takes effect not only in education, but in a belief that we do not fully know the meaning of anything till it has been imparted, shared, made common property.   JOHN DEWEY, *The New Republic*

III. Two friends of yours, both strongly opinionated but not at all well-informed, one vigorously in favor of and the other vigorously opposed to "socialized medicine" (whatever either of them might mean by the term), are coming to your house tonight to spend the evening in conversation. Prepare some remarks you can throw into the discussion and some questions you can ask that might help make them see the problem of medical-care distribution as a problem of institutional adjustment (of course, you will avoid using such fancy terms) and that might therefore help them keep the discussion at more extensional levels than would otherwise be the case. Warning: Do not start out by making them define "socialized medicine" (see Chapter 9, On Definitions, and Chasing Oneself in Verbal Circles).

IV. Read, ponder, and digest:

Triolet

To an indolent student
in a class in general semantics

To a mouse, cheese is cheese; that's why mousetraps work.
                         WENDELL JOHNSON, *People in Quandaries*

To a rodent, cheese is cheese;
That's why mousetraps work.
No date or index, if you please,
To a rodent, cheese *is* cheese
Without semantic subtleties
(Listen, you mouse-brained jerk!).
To a rodent, cheese is cheese;
That's why mousetraps. (Work!)   S. I. HAYAKAWA

V. Organized religions are among the oldest of human institutions. Are they subject to cultural lag? List examples of ways in which various religious groups in your community or the world at large have adjusted—or failed to adjust—their beliefs, practices, and teachings to reflect the changing world around them.

VI. Discuss the following passage in relation to the ideas about fear of change. Do the Durants' ideas conflict with or supplement the belief in cooperation expressed in Chapter 1 of this book?

So the conservative who resists change is as valuable as the radical who proposes it—perhaps as much more valuable as roots are more vital than grafts. It is good that new ideas should be heard, for the sake of the few that can be used; but it is also good that new ideas should be compelled to go through the mill of objection, opposition, and contumely; this is the trial heat which innovations must survive before being allowed to enter the human race. It is good that the old should resist the young, and that the young should prod the old.

WILL AND ARIEL DURANT, *The Lessons of History*

Selected Bibliography

Adams, William C. (ed.). *Television Coverage of the 1980 Presidential Campaign.* Norwood, N.J.: Ablex Publishing, 1983.

Arnold, Thurman, W. *The Folklore of Capitalism.* New Haven, Conn.: Yale University Press, 1937.

———. *The Symbols of Government.* New Haven, Conn.: Yale University Press, 1935.

Ayer, A. J. *Language, Truth and Logic.* New York: Oxford University Press, 1936.

Barnlund, Dean C., and Franklyn S. Haiman. *The Dynamics of Discussion.* Boston: Houghton Mifflin, 1960.

Barthes, Roland. *Mythologies.* New York: Hill & Wang, 1972.

Bell, Eric Temple. *The Search for Truth.* New York: Reynal and Hitchcock, 1934.

Benedict, Ruth. *Patterns of Culture.* Boston: Houghton Mifflin, 1934.

Bentley, Arthur F. *Linguistic Analysis of Mathematics.* Bloomington, Ind.: The Prinicipia Press, 1932.

Berne, Eric. *Games People Play: The Psychology of Human Relationships.* New York: Grove Press, 1964.

Berrien, F. K., and Wendell H. Bash. *Human Relations: Comments and Cases.* New York: Harper, 1957.

Bloomfield, Leonard. *Language.* New York: Henry Holt, 1933.

Bois, J. Samuel. *The Art of Awareness.* Dubuque, Iowa: William C. Brown, 1978.

———. *Explorations in Awareness.* New York: Harper, 1957.

Breal, Michael. *Semantics: Studies in the Science of Meaning.* New York: Henry Holt, 1900. Republished New York: Dover Publications, 1964.

Bridgman, P. W. *The Logic of Modern Physics.* New York: Macmillan, 1927.

Brown, Norman O. *Life Against Death.* New York: Vintage, 1959.

Bruner, Jerome, Jacqueline J. Goodnow and George A. Austin. *A Study of Thinking.* New York: John Wiley, 1956.

Burke, Kenneth. *A Grammar of Motives.* Englewood Cliffs, N.J.: Prentice-Hall, 1945.

———. *The Philosophy of Literary Form.* Baton Rouge: Louisiana State University Press, 1941.

Burrow, Trigant. *The Social Basis of Consciousness.* New York: Harcourt Brace Jovanovich, 1927.

Carnap, Rudolf. *Philosophy and Logical Syntax.* London: Psyche Miniatures, 1935.

Carpenter, Edmund, and Marshall McLuhan (eds.). *Exploration in Communication*, Boston: Beacon Press, 1960.

Cassirer, Ernst. *An Essay on Man*. New Haven, Conn.: Yale University Press, 1944.

Chase, Stuart. *Danger—Men Talking*. New York: Parents' Magazine Press, 1969.

——. *Roads to Agreement*. New York: Harper, 1951.

——. *Power of Words*. New York: Harcourt Brace Jovanovich, 1954.

——. *Guides to Straight Thinking*. New York: Harper, 1956.

Cherry, Colin. *On Human Communication*. New York: Science Editions, 1957.

Chisholm, Francis P. *Introductory Lectures on General Semantics*. Lakeville, Conn.: Institute of General Semantics, 1945.

Dantzig. Tobias. *Number: The Language of Science*. New York: Macmillan, 1933.

Deutsch, Karl W. *Nationalism and Social Communication*. New York: John Wiley, 1953.

Doob, Leonard W. *Public Opinion and Propaganda*. New York: Henry Holt, 1948.

Efron, Edith. *The News Twisters*. Los Angeles: Nash Publications, 1971.

Embler, Weller. *Metaphor and Meaning*. DeLand, Fla.: Everett/Edwards, 1966.

Empson, William. *Seven Types of Ambiguity*. London: Chatto and Windus, 1930.

Epstein, Edward Jay. *News from Nowhere*. New York: Random House, 1973.

ETC. A Review of General Semantics (quarterly); published since 1943 by the International Society for General Semantics, San Francisco, California.

Frank, Jerome. *Law and the Modern Mind*. New York: Brentano, 1930.

Fromm, Erich. *Escape From Freedom*. New York: Rinehart, 1941.

Garey, Doris. *Putting Words in Their Places*. Chicago: Scott, Foresman, 1957.

Gorman, Margaret. *General Semantics and Contemporary Thomism*. Lincoln: University of Nebraska Press, 1962.

Grotiahn, Martin. *The Voice of the Symbol*. New York: Delta, 1971.

Hammond, Charles Montgomery. *The Image Decade*. New York: Hastings House, 1981.

Haney, William V. *Communication and Organizational Behavior: Text and Cases*. Homewood, Ill.: Richard D. Irwin, 1967 revised edition.

Hardy, William G. *Language, Thought, and Experience*. Baltimore: University Park Press, 1978.

Hayakawa, S. I. (ed.). *Language, Meaning and Maturity: Selections from ETC.*, 1943–1953. New York: Harper, 1954.

—— (ed.). *Our Language and Our World: Selections from ETC.*, 1953–1958. New York: Harper, 1959.

—— (ed.). *The Use and Misuse of Language*. New York: Fawcett, 1962. Selections from *Language, Meaning and Maturity* and *Our Language and Our World*.

Hockett, C. F. *A Course in Modern Linguistics*. New York: Macmillan, 1958.

Horney, Karen. *The Neurotic Personality of Our Time*. New York: W. W. Norton, 1937.

Howard, Philip. *Weasel Words*. New York: Oxford University Press, 1979.

——. *Words Fail Me*. New York: Oxford University Press, 1981.

Popper, Karl R. *The Open Society and Its Enemies*. London: Hutchinson, 1950.

Postman, Neil. *Language and Reality*. New York: Holt, Rinehart and Winston, 1966.

Rapoport, Anatol. *Fights, Games, and Debates*. New York: Harper, 1960.

———. *Operational Philosophy*. New York: Harper, 1969.

———. *Science and the Goals of Man*, New York: Harper, 1971.

Real, Michael R. *Mass-Mediated Culture*. Englewood Cliffs, N.J.: Prentice-Hall, 1977.

Richards, I. A. *Interpretation in Teaching*. New York: Harcourt Brace Jovanovich, 1938.

———. *The Philosophy of Rhetoric*. New York: Oxford University Press, 1936.

———. *Practical Criticism, A Study of Literary Judgment*. New York: Harcourt Brace Jovanovich, 1929.

———. *Science and Poetry*. New York: W. W. Norton, 1926.

Robinson, John P. *The Main Source*. Beverly Hills, CA: Sage Publications, 1986.

Rogers, Carl R. *Counseling and Psychotherapy*. Boston: Houghton Mifflin, 1942.

———. *Client-Centered Therapy*. Boston: Houghton Mifflin, 1951.

———. *On Becoming a Person*. Boston: Houghton Mifflin, 1961.

Rogers, Raymond. *Coming Into Existence*. New York: Delta, 1967.

Rokeach, Milton. *The Open and Closed Mind*. New York: Basic Books, 1960.

Rothwell, J. Dan. *Telling It Like It Isn't*. Englewood Cliffs, N.J.: Prentice Hall, 1982.

Ruesch, Jurgen. *Disturbed Communication*. New York: W. W. Norton, 1957.

———. *Therapeutic Communication*. New York: W. W. Norton, 1961.

Ruesch, Jurgen, and Gregory Bateson. *Communication: The Social Matrix of Psychiatry*. New York: W. W. Norton, 1951.

Ruesch, Jurgen, and Weldon Kees, *Nonverbal Communication*. Berkeley: University of California Press, 1956.

Salomon, Louis B. *Semantics and Common Sense*. New York: Holt, Rinehart and Winston, 1966.

Sapir, Edward. *Language: An Introduction to the Study of Speech*. New York: Harcourt Brace Jovanovich, 1921.

Schaff, Adam. *Introduction to Semantics*. New York: Pergamon Press, 1962.

Schram, Martin. *The Great American Video Game: Presidential Politics in the Television Age*. New York: Morrow, 1987.

Skinner, B. F. *Verbal Behavior*. New York: Appleton-Century-Crofts, 1957.

Slater, Philip. *The Pursuit of Loneliness*. Boston: Beacon Press, 1971.

Smith, Bruce L., Harold D. Lasswell and Ralph D. Casey. *Propaganda, Communication, and Public Opinion: A Comprehensive Reference Guide*. Princeton, N.J.: Princeton University Press, 1946.

Snygg, Donald, and Arthur Combs. *Individual Behavior*. New York: Harper, 1949.

Stefansson, Vilhjalmur. *The Standardization of Error*. New York: W. W. Norton, 1927.

Szasz, Thomos S. *The Myth of Mental Illness*. New York: Harper, 1961.

Taylor, Edmond. *The Strategy of Terror*. Boston: Houghton Mifflin, 1940.

Thayer, Lee (ed.). *Communication: General Semantics Perspectives*. New York: Spartan Books, 1970.

Thurman, Kelly. *Semantics*. Boston: Houghton, Mifflin, 1960.

Ullmann, Stephen. *Semantics: An Introduction to the Science of Meaning*. Oxford: Basil Blackwell & Mott, Ltd., 1962.

Vaihinger, Hans. *The Philosophy of "As If."* New York: Harcourt Brace Jovanovich, 1924.

Veblen, Thorstein. *The Theory of the Leisure Class*. New York: Modern Library, 1934.

Victor, George. *Invisible Men*. Englewood Cliffs, N.J.: Prentice-Hall, 1973.

Vygotsky, L. S. *Thought and Language*. New York: John Wiley, 1962.

Wagner, Geoffrey. *On The Wisdom of Words*. Princeton, N.J.: Van Nostrand, 1968.

Walpole, Hugh R. *Semantics*. New York: W. W. Norton, 1941.

Weinberg, Harry L. *Levels of Knowing and Existence*. New York: Harper, 1959.

Weiss, Thomas S., and Kenneth H. Hoover, *Scientific Foundations of Education*. Dubuque, Iowa: Wm. C. Brown, 1964.

Welby, V. *What Is Meaning?* New York: Macmillan, 1903.

Whorf, Benjamin Lee. *Language, Thought and Reality: Selected Writings of B. L. Whorf*; edited by John B. Carroll. New York: John Wiley, 1956.

Wiener, Norbert. *Human Use of Human Beings: Cybernetics and Society*. Bostoon: Houghton Mifflin, 1950.

Wilson, John. *Language and the Pursuit of Truth*. New York: Cambridge University Press, 1956.

Windes, Russel R., and Arthur Hastings. *Argumentation and Advocacy*. New York: Random House, 1965.

Wright, Will. *Six Guns and Society*. Berkeley: University of California Press, 1975.

Yerkes, Robert M. *Chimpanzees: A Laboratory Colony*. New Haven, Conn.: Yale University Press, 1943.

Young, J. Z. *Doubt and Certainty in Science: A Biologist's Reflections on the Brain*. New York: Oxford University Press, 1951.

Copyrights
and Acknowledgements

Index

I

J